ues

PARENT'S GUIDE TO

THE BEST BOOKS FOR CHILDREN

REVISED AND UPDATED

The New York Times
PARENT'S GUIDE TO
THE BEST BOOKS
FOR CHILDREN

REVISED AND UPDATED

EDEN ROSS LIPSON

TIMES T BOOKS

RANDOM HOUSE

Originally published in different form in 1988 by Times Books, a division of
Random House, Inc.

LIBRARY OF CONGRESS CATALOGING-IN-PUBLICATION DATA
Lipson, Eden Ross.
  The New York Times parent's guide to the best books for
children/Eden Ross Lipson.—Rev. ed.
    p.   cm.
  Includes bibliographical references and indexes.
  ISBN 0-812-91889-4
  1. Bibliography—Best books—Children's literature. 2. Children's
literature—Bibliography. 3. Reading—Parent participation. 4. Children—
Books and reading. I. New York Times. II. Title.
III. Title: Parent's guide to the best books for children.
Z1037.L724   1991
[PN1009.A1]
011.62—dc20   91-2675

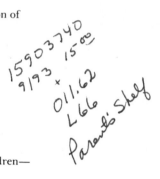

Because the copyright page cannot legibly accommodate all the necessary
permissions, they begin on page 501.

Special thanks to Peter Smith for moving mountains of permissions.

Art direction by Naomi Osnos

Text design and picture editing by Beth Tondreau Design
Project coordinator Mary A. Wirth

Manufactured in the United States of America

9 8 7 6 5 4 3

This book is for
Delari, Tara, Margo, and Garth Johnston
and for Neal, who made it possible.

PREFACE TO THE REVISED EDITION

Children's books are everywhere today, brightly displayed, enthusiastically sold. In the fall of 1991 there are more bookstores in the United States carrying children's books than ever before, but at the same time we are in the midst of a national educational crisis and our school and public library budgets are being cut. Choosing and finding books to share with the children we know and love, is harder than ever.

This revised edition of *The New York Times Parent's Guide to the Best Books for Children* is larger, better illustrated and better indexed, and, I hope, easier to use. The guide is meant to be an enticing introduction to children's books, not a restrictive or limiting menu. Not all prizewinning books are here because it is a selective guide. Some beloved books are out of print.

The most important way we teach children the value of books is by reading ourselves. The communications revolution has brought videocassette recorders and home computers into our living rooms so that sophisticated amusements are perpetually available in many American homes.

Reading picture and story books with very young children establishes a wonderful ritual that too often dissipates when youngsters learn to read. It is particularly difficult to persuade school-age children that they should use their precious leisure time reading to themselves if they see the adults who tell them to "go read" parked in front of the television or computer screen.

Continue to read with children as they grow. If you can, read ahead of them, even if just a chapter a night. Their books are generally short and interesting. You will honor the children with your attention to their concerns, and will be happily surprised by the writers you meet.

[603]

ACKNOWLEDGMENTS

This would have been an impossible book to write alone, never mind revise just three years later.

Again, my thanks go first to the children's publishing industry. Scholars interested in the implications of gender might do well to observe the courtesy and collegiality that continue to characterize it even as commercial pressures mount. I have received the same kind of generous support in revising this book as I had in initially preparing it. I appreciate the courtesy and kindness of the individual editors, with their encyclopedic knowledge of their backlists, and also the diligence and goodwill of the young assistants and associates who checked bibliographic information and cleared permissions for the wonderful illustrations that appear on these pages.

Within the large and fascinating institution that is *The New York Times*, the *Book Review* remains a tiny, rather protected enclave, a rare catbird seat from which we denizens watch the changing currents and themes in American life. I owe thanks to the four editors I have worked with: my friend John Leonard, who hired me; Harvey Shapiro, who twice feared I would have a baby in the office; Mike Levitas, who thought, correctly, that I would have fun handling children's books; and Rebecca Sinkler, who, as a mother and grandmother, has brought special supervisory insight to the children's coverage.

If "friendship is a sheltering tree," as a little sampler says, then I am blessed to live in a lush and verdant grove. I feel the strength and support of many friends whom I hardly see in the rush of daily life. Fleeting phone calls, postcards, letters, pictures of growing children. Life is rushing by and we are all overscheduled and overworked. But because the supporting bonds of friendship carry energy back and forth, they endure. We have helped each other over time, made life not just bearable but fun.

Moving closer to home, I am so lucky for knowing, watching, loving four growing, blooming children. I salute my father, Judge Milton Lipson, for his splendid taste in life's companions. Paul and Iris Brest gave us Notebook II, their nifty software system, before there was a book to think about; it continues to be a wonderfully flexible program for this kind of project. I am grateful to the dedicated women behind the scenes at Random House and Times Books who labored so skillfully on the details of manuscript and production. Amy Kellman, the distinguished children's librarian at the Carnegie Library of Pittsburgh, spontaneously offered corrections to the first edition of this book, an unselfish gesture I continue to find worthy of awe as well as gratitude. She has vetted more lists in the preparation of this edition than either of us ever imagined. The mistakes remaining are all mine.

I can't thank Neal Johnston properly. He understood me, the project, and the technology. He gave enormous amounts of his time, even when he realized I still wasn't going to list Tarzan and the Hardy Boys. He says he only made my vision possible, but I know this book is as much his as mine.

[138]

CONTENTS

INTRODUCTION

This book is for the converted. It is for people who know and love particular children and want to help them to grow up loving to read. It is for adults who understand absolutely that reading is the key to the future, and also to the preservation of civilization, but who read for their own interests and entertainment as well, and fervently hope their children will, too.

One of the pleasures of being a parent, grandparent, godparent, or just an attentive adult to a child is helping to choose books. They make such wonderful gifts. Books cost more or less the same as toys, last much longer, and give endless pleasure. It is also true that "children can possess a book in a way they can never possess a video game, a TV show, or a Darth Vader doll," as the artist-writer Chris Van Allsburg said in his 1982 Caldecott Medal speech. "A book comes alive when they read it. They give it life themselves by understanding it." And bring it back to life by remembering it. Just think of your own favorites. How many chills and terrors, tears and joys remain fresh? How many passages can you remember without hesitation?

[145]

Of course, as Katherine Paterson, a Newbery Medal winner and the author of *The Bridge to Teribithia* and *The Great Gilly Hopkins* among other novels, has noted, "If we prescribe books as medicine, our children have a perfect right to refuse the nasty-tasting spoon."

So, do choose books for birthdays, books for holidays, books for spring, books for school, books for Saturday, books for laughter, books for tears, books to find out what happened next, or what if. . . . But in choosing or giving books, remember to try to find titles that children can embrace, not suffer; seize, not shove away for the deferred or postponed gratification of something to "grow into," like a winter coat. Beverly Cleary, the author of the beloved Ramona series, remembers, "When I was a child, a relative gave me *Ivanhoe* to grow into. I was so disappointed that I still have not grown into it."

This selective guide to more than a thousand of the best books for children published in the United States is organized to help you fend off such disappointments and find books that will intrigue and delight now. It is a mixture of classic, standard, and distinguished new titles. There are lots of books for lap-listening babies and toddlers, books to read aloud with preschoolers, books for beginning readers to read to themselves, books for middle-school children to devour or dabble in as they begin to sort out their lives, and, finally, a few books for teenagers struggling toward maturity. Some are noble classics, some are just fun; others may be helpful directly or indirectly as they address real issues children face.

The purpose of the guide is to help you look for the next book to give to your favorite child. But there are truths and tricks to choosing, and as the sign in Manhattan's Gotham Book Store says, "So many books, so little time." If we met, say, on a street corner, and you asked me to help you find a book for your child, just the way people really do ask me, I would quickly, like a teacher or librarian or a clerk in a good bookstore, turn to question back to you: How old a child? A boy or a girl? Where does he or she live? Siblings? Intact family? Special interests? A book to read aloud, or a book for a child to read to herself? I would go on asking questions until I could make an educated guess of an appropriate title.

In the same way, I have organized the guide with its dozens of special indexes so that you can tailor your choices in many different ways to suit the tastes and interests of your child, and yours as well. The same title may appear in many indexes because the ways we see and understand books change as we ourselves grow. Karla Kuskin, the artist-illustrator, said about a picture in one of her books showing a large number of sleeping animals, "Over there on the right, one cat with one eye open . . . looking at a mouse. A two-and-a-half- or three-year-old will spot that cat immediately, a six-year-old will take longer, a twelve-year-old may miss it." And, she added, "At thirty-seven you hardly have a chance."

[7]

As you browse through the listings and the indexes, or as illustrations catch your eye, I hope you will find many books you know, or vaguely remember, especially if you are a "baby boomer" and came of age after World War II, because more than 150 of them were published before 1966. Once, on a summer holiday in Greece, my family took a day trip by boat from Crete to the island of Santorini. Settled on deck at sunset on the return trip, tired and relaxed, the youngest children were "reading" their well-loved copy of *D'Aulaires' Book of Greek Myths*. A man passed by and saw the book. He returned a few minutes later with one of his friends and pointed excitedly, saying, "There, that's the book I was telling you about, that's the one I had," and then turned to me, saying with real urgency, "Where did you get it?"

For the purpose of this guide I have included only a few young adult titles. Teenagers have many independent paths to finding their own books. Young children are much more dependent on adult assistance. Similarly, I have not included books published for adults that are now considered children's titles and found on standard reading lists. It's sometimes a very fine judgment, and today it is often a marketing, or business, decision whether a book is published for adults or children. But *Catcher in the Rye* and *To Kill a Mockingbird* were originally adult titles and have become identified as children's books. (Indeed, the only adults who read them today, it seems, are parents.) I have also confined the guide to titles issued by children's trade book publishers because I wanted them to be accessible to ordinary readers like your family and mine, who browse in ordinary bookstores and libraries.

THE GUIDE

Main titles are numbered consecutively and divided into groups according to text level from wordless through picture books, story books, early readers, middle and advanced readers. Remember that wordless books are not necessarily for babies, and children can pleasurably listen to stories that are much too hard for them to read independently.

Within each section, books are listed alphabetically by title. Each main title carries important bibliographic information—the author, illustrator, publisher in hardcover and paperback, date of original publication, and a notation of certain important prizes.

The John Newbery and Randolph Caldecott medals, endowed by Frederic G. Melcher and his family and administered by the Association for Library Service to Children, are the best-known children's book prizes in the United States. Each year a changing committee of children's librarians gives a medal to the author of "the most distinguished contribution to American literature" (Newbery) and to the artist of the "most distinguished American picture book for children" (Caldecott) as well as a variable number of Honor Books. In bookstores and libraries you can recognize the winners because they usually have gold and silver stickers on their jackets.

Since 1952, *The New York Times* has annually asked a changing panel of judges to choose what they consider to be the best illustrated books of the year. They usually pick around ten, but the number varies. In recent years the *Times* has given each of the artists a certificate, and made sticker labels available to the publishers. Cheering for the home team, I have included mention of the New York Times Best Illustrated winners where appropriate.

I have tried to describe each book as succinctly as possible, in one paragraph that also refers to other books in the series or related titles. The voice in the entries is mine. While there are no negative reviews, my tone, of course, reflects my own taste and enthusiasms. Since you need to establish a baseline of familiarity with any critic, and that is what I am here, why don't you begin by looking up a half-dozen of your own favorite children's book titles. If you find the descriptions jibe with your memory and affection, then this is a book you can use to find other books, and I'll explain how. If the descriptions don't seem appropriate to you for any reason, this may not be the guide for you.

AVAILABILITY

Publishing in the United States, including the children's publishing industry, is in a state of flux, with titles going in and out of print at a great and unpredictable rate. Publishing houses are constantly being bought, sold, combined, and recombined. In selecting the main titles in the guide, I had the help of members of the Children's Book Council, the nonprofit trade organization of the children's publishing industry. I wrote and asked the editors at each house to annotate their catalogues to show me which titles on their back list—i.e., previously published books—sold steadily and best and which favorite titles I might have otherwise overlooked. I also talked to editors, writers, teachers, librarians, journalists. The selections reflect my judgment and opinions.

As I worked on the book, the titles I describe were all in print, which means available for bookstores and libraries to order for you if they don't have them in stock. But it took me more than a year and a half to put the guide together, and I knew, just watching paperback editions cross my desk, that there were substantial changes in who published what even in that short period of time. So, just before press time, we sent the final lists of titles (not the comments) back to the publishers and asked them to help make sure the bibliographic information was as accurate as possible.

Paperback publishers change with some frequency licenses to reprint hardcover books. Some hardcover titles have technically gone out of print, but they still should be available in libraries. The list is as sound as we could make it. Errors of omission, of course, are entirely my fault, and I would hope to correct them in subsequent editions.

[30]

THE INDEXES

The key to the indexes lies in the fact that each main title book (each title with its own entry) has a permanent record. Every reference to the book carries the record number, and you can use it to go back into the guide and get bibliographic information for ordering, or refresh your memory of the book's description.

The first index includes every book mentioned in the guide, main titles, series titles, and related titles, using the record number of the main title as the reference number. The related titles are in italic. Then follow indexes by author and illustrator, which will help you find another book by someone whose work you have enjoyed. The books in the guide are listed by reading level, but a special set of indexes suggests listening levels and suitability of books for younger children. Some books almost ask to be read aloud, so there is also an index of those pleasurable titles.

The subject indexes cover a wide range of special interests. But a word of warning. Bibliotherapy—looking to a book to solve a problem —is a little like over-the-counter cold remedies: It may help, but it isn't likely to solve the problem alone. I have included some fine books about sibling rivalry, death, divorce, health issues; loving families working with children to address those problems integrate such books into their lives. The books just help. It's the family attention that really counts.

These are indexes of familiar categories—fairy tales, folktales, bedtime tales—and some more specialized ones as well: books about minorities, science, music. In truth I don't think the indexes of boys' and girls' books are particularly controversial or troublesome in this day and age; if I did, I wouldn't have included them. Children are different. There are many books directed specifically to boy readers or girl readers, and my simple purpose is to encourage reading by appealing to children's enthusiasms. Those two categories are suggestions, not rules or orders. In the same spirit of pursuing or following up on expressed interests, I have included an index of titles featured on *Reading Rainbow,* the popular public television program about children's books.

Please take some time to play with the guide and the indexes. A reference book can be full of serendipitous surprises if you let it fall open to random pages. If you are working your way, book by book, through a special index, flip occasionally to another, or scout around for a new book by a writer you admire.

DESIGN AND ILLUSTRATIONS

The illustrations scattered throughout the guide are from the books I review in it. Each one carries the record number of the book it is from. The record numbers run consecutively through the book and will lead you back to the entry in the main text, where you will find the full bibliographic information.

The guide has unusually wide margins. We always tell children not to write in books, and generally speaking, that's right. But if you are really using this guide and you buy and borrow books for more than one child, take a pencil and make notes in the margin about which books you give to those children, at what age and for what occasion and how they were received. That way the guide goes forward with your family, and also becomes a meaningful reading record.

I end where I began, hoping for our future that your children will learn to enjoy reading books as much as you and I do. Have fun.

Wordless Books

The reader supplies the language
to accompany these all-picture books.
But please do not assume that because there are
no words, the titles in this section are for
very young children. Some are extremely
sophisticated and are meant
for older readers.

THE ANGEL AND THE SOLDIER BOY   [1]

Written and illustrated by Peter Collington
Cloth: Knopf
Paper: Knopf
Published: 1987

After a pirate story, a little girl falls asleep with some little toys on her pillow. The soldier boy comes alive and tries to defend the child's piggy bank from the pirate. The angel rescues him. The whole exciting adventure is set out in finely drawn panels.

ANIMAL ALPHABET   [2]

Written and illustrated by Bert Kitchen
Cloth: Dial
Paper: Pied Piper
Published: 1984   Prizes: New York Times Best Illustrated Book

This large format alphabet book features stern roman letters adorned with exotic animals meticulously painted in somber colors. Younger children may peer at it, but older children are more likely to be intrigued by the intensity of the art and the power of the illustrations. There is a companion volume, *Animal Numbers*, in which animals are shown with their offspring illustrating numerals.

[1]

ANNO'S COUNTING BOOK   [3]

Written and illustrated by Mitsumasa Anno
Cloth: T. Y. Crowell/HarperCollins
Paper: Harper Trophy
Published: 1977

The great Japanese artist sets his rich and complex counting book in a countryside that looks like New England. Each full-color picture represents a succeeding month, as well as time of day, and the growth and development of a small town, with houses, roads, plantings, all sorts of things to count in number sequence. While preschoolers can look at and talk about it, this is a picture book to return to with children in the early grades for more discussion.

ANNO'S FLEA MARKET [4]

Written and illustrated by Mitsumasa Anno
Cloth: Philomel
Published: 1984

One of the remarkable wordless narratives by the distinguished Japanese artist, this book could easily be a scroll, it unrolls so fluidly. The eye moves across a landscape into a town where an amazingly rich flea market takes place. The market combines objects and people from many times and cultures, and proceeds with a kind of majestic serenity, and then ends. Older children and adults will find numerous detailed items to ponder.

ANNO'S JOURNEY [5]

Written and illustrated by Mitsumasa Anno
Cloth: Philomel
Paper: Philomel
Published: 1978

One man in a small boat arrives at an unknown shore. The reader has a kind of bird's-eye view of the wordless pages as the traveler sets off and the shore gives way to meadows, forest, farmlands, and a European city. This is a good book to begin with if you are not familiar with the remarkably complex picture books by the great Japanese children's book artist. With their extraordinary detail and complex construction yet simple narrative movement, they are for all ages. Indeed, children tend to accept a richness of detail and cross-cultural complexity in his work that adults often find awesome. If this book intrigues you, then look for the brilliant "guidebooks" *Anno's Britain*, *Anno's Italy*, and *Anno's Medieval World*.

[5]

THE BEAR AND THE FLY [6]

Written and illustrated by Paula Winter
Paper: Crown
Published: 1976   Prizes: New York Times Best Illustrated Book

Three bears at dinner. Enter one fly. Chaos ensues. Hilarious, ridiculous, undignified, amusing chaos. No need for words in this three-color caper.

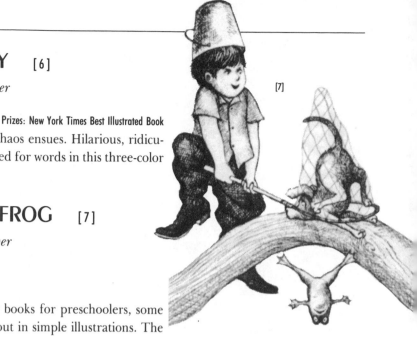

A BOY, A DOG AND A FROG [7]

Written and illustrated by Mercer Mayer
Cloth: Dial
Paper: Pied Piper
Published: 1967

In the first of four droll and appealing books for preschoolers, some discoveries and adventures are spelled out in simple illustrations. The other titles include *A Boy, A Dog, A Frog; A Friend; One Frog Too Many; Frog on His Own;* and *Frog, Where Are You?*

CHANGES, CHANGES [8]

Written and illustrated by Pat Hutchins
Cloth: Macmillan
Paper: Aladdin
Published: 1971   Prizes: New York Times Best Illustrated Book

A delightful wordless adventure involves the transformation and reconfiguration of two wooden figures, a man and a woman, and brightly colored blocks that turn into a boat, a wagon, eventually even into a home.

THE GREY LADY AND THE STRAWBERRY SNATCHER [9]

Written and illustrated by Molly Bang
Cloth: Four Winds
Paper: Scholastic
Published: 1980   Prizes: Caldecott Honor

This eerie adventure involves a basket of strawberries, a skateboard, and more. The full-color illustrations of the grey lady and the green creature with a purple hat who follows her through swamp and wood are lush and startling.

HAPPY BIRTHDAY, MAX!   [10]

Written and illustrated by Hanne Turk

Cloth: Picture Book Studio

Published: 1984

One of a number of stories about Max, a dapper and imaginative mouse. Here he stages an elaborate birthday picnic for himself alone on a hill. Some of the other titles include *Good Night Max, Max the Artlover,* and *Rainy Day Max.*

IS IT RED? IS IT YELLOW? IS IT BLUE?   [11]

Written and illustrated by Tana Hoban

Cloth: Greenwillow

Paper: Mulberry

Published: 1978

This handsome book illustrates the primary colors with clarity and wit, using simple, attractively reproduced photographs of everyday objects. Tana Hoban sets a standard for photojournalism and concept books for the very young. Her work is remarkably engaging to look at, and each new idea is demonstrated so clearly that even the youngest child can understand. Some of the other titles for preschoolers are *I Read Signs; I Walk and Read; Shapes, Shapes, Shapes; Children's Zoo; Is It Rough? Is it Smooth? Is it Shiny?;* and *26 Letters and 99 Cents.* There are also chunky board books for toddlers, including *What Is It?; Red, Blue, Yellow Shoe; 1, 2, 3;* and *Panda, Panda.*

[8]

MOONLIGHT   [12]

Written and illustrated by Jan Ormerod

Cloth: Lothrop, Lee & Shepard

Paper: Puffin

Published: 1982

The bedtime rituals in one little girl's family on an evening when, in fact, her parents fall asleep before she does are described in this quiet and appealing book. Closely observed and illustrated with delicacy and intimate detail in soft colors. The companion book is *Sunshine,* about morning rituals in the same family. These are delightful to read with toddlers and preschoolers.

ON CHRISTMAS EVE   [13]

Written and illustrated by Peter Collington
Cloth: Knopf
Published. 1990

How does Santa deal with houses without chimneys? After the little
child in this story writes her note and goes to sleep, a tiny fairy appears.
The Christmas sprite lights the tree downstairs, then opens the door to
a troop of tiny fairies, who all take candles from her tree and go out to
light the way for Santa in the snowy street. The sleeping girl almost
wakes up, just for suspense. Fine, realistic pencil drawings, in varying
sizes, on each double-page spread give a narrative rhythm to the tale.

PADDY'S EVENING OUT   [14]

Written and illustrated by John S. Goodall
Cloth: McElderry
Published: 1973

Paddy Pork is the pig-hero of a series of adventure books told in lavish
full-color, full-page, and half-page illustrations. The ingeniously conceived half pages speed the action. Paddy, who appeals to grown-ups

almost as much as to children of school age and under, lives in a bucolic world earlier in this century. He is lovable and accident-prone, and also appears in *Paddy Goes Traveling, Paddy Pork—Odd Jobs, Paddy Pork's Holiday, Paddy's Evening Out,* and *Paddy Under Water.* There are also several books about the charming mice Grips and Naughty Nancy that use the same format and are equally appealing.

PETER SPIER'S RAIN [15]

Written and illustrated by Peter Spier
Cloth: Doubleday
Paper: Zephyr
Published: 1981

It is a clear, fair summer's day as a young girl and her younger brother go out to play in the yard. Soon the sky darkens and it begins to rain. The storm lasts all day and the children and their dog are in and out of the house. They explore in the garden, splash out to the park, and study their neighborhood. A delightful book of closely observed details of daily life and the magic of rain. The full-color illustrations are affectionately drawn and appeal to preschoolers as well as to their older siblings.

PICNIC [16]

Written and illustrated by Emily Arnold McCully
Cloth: Harper & Row/HarperCollins
Paper: Harper Trophy
Published: 1984

It's a perfect summer day, so the mouse family sets off in a red pickup truck to have a picnic by a lake. One child falls out and the family doesn't notice that she's missing till late afternoon. No real damage is done and there is a happy ending. A wordless charmer. The companion books are *First Snow, School,* and *New Baby.*

[16]

THE SNOWMAN [17]

Written and illustrated by Raymond Briggs
Cloth: Random House
Paper: Random House
Published: 1978

A boy builds a snowman that comes to life in his dreams. This book has unusual, almost haunting power. Perhaps it comes from the snowman's wise expression throughout the full-color cartoon format. *Building a Snowman* is a book version of the story.

WILL'S MAMMOTH   [18]

Written by Rafe Martin
Illustrated by Stephen Gammel
Cloth: Putnam
Published: 1989

Sometimes grown-ups just don't know anything. Will's parents told him that "all the mammoths had disappeared ten thousand years ago." But out in his own backyard, in the snow, Will finds a glorious, seething mass of mammoths. It's an essentially wordless book of joyful adventure.

THE YELLOW UMBRELLA   [19]

Written and illustrated by Henrik Drescher
Cloth: Bradbury
Published: 1987   Prizes: New York Times Best Illustrated Book

In this giddy little book, two monkeys, a parent and child, open one yellow umbrella and simply take off. The umbrella carries them high into the sky away from the city and over mountains, then turns into a boat to cross seas. It is a wonderful trip. Perfect for reading with a toddler, but older children will pore over it for the pleasures of the quirky details.

[18]

Picture Books

These books have simple texts, and for the most part, a very young child can read and understand what they are about. Some picture books can be grasped at a glance, others will continue to reveal detail and nuance as a child studies them, and perhaps take on personal meaning as treasured favorites. Picture books are principally for pre-school children, but school-age children often continue to enjoy them.

A APPLE PIE   [20]

Written and illustrated by Tracey Campbell Pearson
Cloth: Dial
Published: 1986

An alphabet book based on the nursery rhyme. In this version that folds out to become an eighteen-foot poster, twenty-six children sit at a very long table and attack that tasty baked dish. The full-color illustrations look delicious.

AARDVARKS, DISEMBARK!   [21]

Written and illustrated by Ann Jonas
Cloth: Greenwillow
Published: 1990

Everyone knows how the animals got onto Noah's Ark, but how did they get off? He ordered them out, alphabetically, calling the names of those he knew from A to Z, then calling to the others who remained, "Disembark, everyone." Turn the book in your hand ninety degrees and follow the 132 species, all accurately painted and in proportion to one another, as they climb down Mt. Ararat. It's a perfect companion to Peter Spier's *Noah's Ark*.

ABIYOYO   [22]

Written by Pete Seeger
Illustrated by Michael Hays
Cloth: Macmillan
Paper: Aladdin
Published: 1986

The full-color illustrations capture the exuberant words of Pete Seeger's beloved song story about the magician and his son who played the ukelele and vanquished the monster Abiyoyo. The music is included at the end.

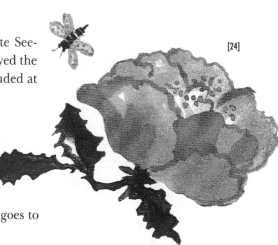

[24]

ALL BY MYSELF   [23]

Written and illustrated by Anna Grossnickle Hines
Cloth: Clarion
Published: 1984

Here is gentle bibliotherapy for preschoolers—one night Josie goes to the bathroom in the dark all by herself. Hooray!

Picture

Books

ALL GOD'S CRITTERS GOT A PLACE IN THE CHOIR [24]

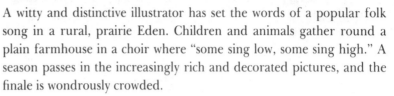

[24]

Written and illustrated by Margot Zemach
Cloth: Dutton
Published: 1989

A witty and distinctive illustrator has set the words of a popular folk song in a rural, prairie Eden. Children and animals gather round a plain farmhouse in a choir where "some sing low, some sing high." A season passes in the increasingly rich and decorated pictures, and the finale is wondrously crowded.

ALL SMALL [25]

Written by David McCord
Illustrated by Madelaine Gill Linden
Cloth: Little, Brown
Paper: Little, Brown
Published: 1986

A fine collection of twenty-five short poems by a modern master.

ALPHABATICS [26]

Written and illustrated by Suse MacDonald
Cloth: Bradbury
Published: 1986

Prizes: Caldecott Honor

The letters of the brilliantly colored alphabet roll over and turn into appropriate things—*a* becomes an ark, *f* becomes a fish, *g* a giraffe, and the single word appears on the page with the illustration. *Numblers* is a jolly companion book.

[24]

[28]

ALPHABEARS: AN ABC BOOK   [27]

Written by Kathleen Hague
Illustrated by Michael Hague
Cloth: Henry Holt
Published: 1985
This alphabet book stars cute bears, with a 1920s quality to the illustrations. There is a companion volume called *Numbers: A Counting Book.*

AMOS & BORIS   [28]

Written and illustrated by William Steig
Cloth: Farrar, Straus & Giroux
Paper: Penguin
Published: 1971   **Prizes: New York Times Best Illustrated Book**
This splendid and affecting story of the true friendship between a whale and a mouse shows, rather than announces, the merits of cooperation and helpfulness. It is also, of course, funny, and the illustrations are playful.

AND MY MEAN OLD MOTHER WILL BE SORRY, BLACKBOARD BEAR   [29]

Written and illustrated by Martha Alexander
Cloth: Dial
Paper: Pied Piper
Published: 1972

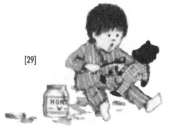

[29]

A little boy has an argument with his mother and runs away to live in the woods with his friend Blackboard Bear. *Blackboard Bear* and *I Sure*

Am Glad to See You, Blackboard Bear are other stories about Anthony and his imaginary friend (who is always pictured in black and white, as if he'd just stepped off a blackboard).

ANGELINA BALLERINA   [30]

Written by Katharine Holabird
Illustrated by Helen Craig
Cloth: Clarkson N. Potter
Published: 1983

The first in a series of books about a little mouse who wants to be a ballerina and gets her heart's desire. The rather English full-color illustrations are particularly whimsical and appealing, and include wonderful bits of backstage detail. Other titles in the series feature Angelina's cousin Henry and include *Angelina on Stage*, *Angelina's Christmas*, and *Angelina at the Fair*.

ANGRY ARTHUR   [31]

Written by Hiawyn Oram
Illustrated by Satoshi Kitamura
Cloth: Dutton
Paper: Unicorn
Published: 1989

Arthur wants to stay up and watch television, and when his mother says no, he has a tantrum. What a tantrum! It ends up being a universe quake. The brilliant illustrations are jagged and tense and explosive, like Arthur's temper. And when it's over . . . he can't remember what upset him so.

ANIMALS SHOULD DEFINITELY *NOT* WEAR CLOTHING   [32]

Written by Judi Barrett
Illustrated by Ron Barrett
Cloth: Atheneum
Paper: Aladdin
Published: 1970

Some things are just silly to think about—a walrus in a tie and jacket, and many other possibilities are included in this book. The illustrations are, well, suitable. *Animals Should Definitely NOT Act Like People* is the funny companion volume.

[30]

ANNO'S ALPHABET: AN ADVENTURE IN IMAGINATION [33]

Written and illustrated by Mitsumasa Anno
Cloth: T. Y. Crowell/HarperCollins
Paper: Harper Trophy
Published: 1975
Prizes: New York Times Best Illustrated Book

An alphabet book by the great Japanese artist relatively early in his career indicates the richness of his imagination. Look carefully at the wooden letters and tools as they are shaped and transformed. The *j* yields a juggler.

ANTARCTICA [34]

Written and illustrated by Helen Cowcher
Cloth: Farrar, Straus & Giroux
Paper: Sunburst
Published: 1990

The colors of Antarctica, at least as seen here, are intense, based, it seems, on the colors of the emperor penguin—yellow, black, and orange—and seen against a snowy sky. The book is mostly about the life cycle of the penguins but incorporates environmental lessons and warnings. The text is simple and the pictures might intrigue even lap listeners. It has considerable appeal to older children, who can place the information and images in some context. *Rain Forest,* about another environment, is also visually interesting.

[31]

APE IN A CAPE: AN ALPHABET OF ODD ANIMALS [35]

Written and illustrated by Fritz Eichenberg
Cloth: HBJ
Paper: Voyager
Published: 1952
Prizes: Caldecott Honor

An alphabet book of unusual animals and original rhymes—dove in love, goat in a boat. The illustrations may seem old-fashioned to adult eyes, but their large size and simplicity remain appealing to the very young.

APPLEBET [36]

Written by Clyde Watson
Illustrated by Wendy Watson
Cloth: Farrar, Straus & Giroux
Paper: Sunburst
Published: 1982

The organizing principle of this cheerful, rhyming alphabet book is that a farmer and her daughter are taking apples to a country fair.

AN ARTIST [37]

Written and illustrated by M. B. Goffstein
Cloth: Harper & Row/HarperCollins
Published: 1980   Prizes: New York Times Best Illustrated Book

A small book with tiny, precise pen-and-ink illustrations with dabs of color shows, in a way young children can absorb, what it means to be an artist. The artist pictured here has a beard and a hat. There are also books about *A Writer* and *An Actor*.

AS I WAS GOING UP AND DOWN [38]

Written and illustrated by Nicola Bayley
Cloth: Macmillan
Published: 1986

A happy little book of nonsense rhymes illustrated in intricate, delicate pictures.

THE BABY'S BEDTIME BOOK [39]

Written and illustrated by Kay Chorao
Cloth: Dutton
Published: 1984

A collection of classic poems and songs, with gentle, pretty illustrations of curly-haired toddlers and babies. The two companion volumes are *The Baby's Lap Book* and *The Baby's Story Book*.

A BEAR'S BICYCLE   [40]

Written by Emilie Warren McLeod
Illustrated by David McPhail
Cloth: Joy Street/Little, Brown
Paper: Joy Street/Little, Brown
Published: 1975

A book about bicycle safety couched in comic terms—the little boy rider follows all the rules; it is his gigantic teddy bear who's the terror on the road. The full-color bears are a special attraction.

THE BERENSTAIN BEARS AND THE SPOOKY OLD TREE   [41]

Written and illustrated by Jan and Stan Berenstain
Cloth: Random House (Beginner Books)
Published: 1978

By thoroughly exploring an old tree, inside and out, three little bears work through spatial concepts—into, up, through, etc. This is for infant to toddler readers and different from the Berenstains' other popular books for slightly older children, which deal with issues and behavior.

BIG SISTER AND LITTLE SISTER   [42]

Written by Charlotte Zolotow
Illustrated by Martha Alexander
Cloth: Harper & Row/HarperCollins
Paper: Harper Trophy
Published: 1966

Sometimes you just have to run away from your bossy big sister to find out how she really feels about you.

[30]

BLUEBERRIES FOR SAL   [43]

Written and illustrated by Robert McCloskey
Cloth: Viking
Paper: Puffin
Published: 1948   Prizes: Caldecott Honor

The parallel adventures of a little girl and a baby bear, both of whom go hunting blueberries with their mothers one summer morning in Maine. They each lose track of time and follow the wrong mothers. Suffice it to say they end up with the right ones. The story is appealing to contemporary blueberry pickers, as it was to their parents.

BONES, BONES, DINOSAUR BONES   [44]

Written and illustrated by Byron Barton
Cloth: Harper & Row/HarperCollins
Published: 1990

The remarkable achievement here is explaining to toddlers and preschoolers, who know so much about dinosaurs, what paleontologists do. Because the brilliantly colored illustrations are almost childlike in their simplicity, the narrative works. *Dinosaurs, Dinosaurs* is a delightful introductory book about the long-gone giants.

BRINGING THE RAIN TO KAPITI PLAIN: A NANDI TALE   [45]

Written by Verna Aardema
Illustrated by Beatriz Vidal
Cloth: Dial
Paper: Pied Piper
Published: 1981

A cumulative story (like *The House That Jack Built*) from East Africa about how Ki-pat brought the rain to the "dry, oh so dry, Kapiti Plain." The rhythms and repetitions in the text are so engaging the story almost asks to be read out loud, and the full-color pictures evoke the widest and driest of plains.

BUNCHES AND BUNCHES
OF BUNNIES [46]

Written by Louise Matthews
Illustrated by Jeni Bassett
Cloth: Dodd, Mead
Paper: Scholastic
Published: 1978

The bunches of bunnies, lots and lots of them, are arranged across these pages to help teach the principles of multiplication.

CAN I KEEP HIM? [47]

Written and illustrated by Steven Kellogg
Cloth: Dial
Paper: Pied Piper
Published: 1971

The narrator, a little boy, is so desperate for a pet that he tries to persuade his mother to let him keep a succession of creatures—a dog, bear cub, tiger, and even another little boy. The full-color cartoon-style illustrations capture his longing perfectly.

CAPS FOR SALE [48]

Written and illustrated by Esphyr Slobodkina
Cloth: Harper & Row/HarperCollins
Paper: Harper Trophy
Published: 1947

A peddler dozes under a tree and the naughty monkeys snatch his wares, the pile of caps, right off his head. A wonderful, classic picture book, endlessly entertaining, for generation upon generation. Acting out the story, or just playing monkey, is a very satisfying preschool game.

A CARIBOU ALPHABET [49]

Written and illustrated by Mary Beth Owens
Cloth: Dog Ear Press
Paper: Sunburst
Published: 1988

This unusual alphabet was inspired by the Maine Caribou Transplant Project and celebrates those denizens of the northern woods as the

[48]

illustration on each page tells more about them and their habitat. The letters themselves are part of the story—two bulls spar in the circles that make the letter *b*.

CAT GOES FIDDLE-I-FEE [50]

Written and illustrated by Paul Galdone
Cloth: Clarion
Paper: Clarion
Published: 1985
A bright resetting of the English folk song that is a barnyard of rhyme introducing favorite farm animals and their sounds.

CATCH ME & KISS ME & SAY IT AGAIN [51]

Written by Clyde Watson
Illustrated by Wendy Watson
Cloth: Philomel
Paper: Philomel
Published: 1978
This bubbling collection of short rhymes and verses has cheerful three-color illustrations of sturdy children and a winsome cat.

[51]

A CHILD'S PRAYER   [52]

Written and illustrated by Jeanne Titherington
Cloth: Greenwillow
Published: 1989

In this setting of a traditional evening prayer, "Now I lay me down to sleep," a little boy and his father are alone in the child's room. The soft pencil illustrations are filled with rich Christian symbolism but in an understated, familiar, comforting way, to be noticed or discussed only if it fits in your family's ritual and routine.

CLOUDY WITH A CHANCE
OF MEATBALLS   [53]

Written by Judith Barrett
Illustrated by Ron Barrett
Cloth: Atheneum
Paper: Aladdin
Published: 1978   Prizes: New York Times Best Illustrated Book

It's a wild story Grandpa makes up. He says that in the magical land of Chewandswallow meals come from the sky. But what happens when the weather changes? Silly to even think about. The illustrations are both sophisticated and outrageously funny, and appeal to most school-age children.

COLOR ZOO   [54]

Written and illustrated by Lois Ehlert
Cloth: Harper & Row/HarperCollins
Published: 1989   Prizes: Caldecott Honor

There are exotic animals hiding in the shapes and cutouts that pile up and rearrange on each succeeding page, so, for example, a tiger becomes a mouse. The companion book to this one is *Color Farm,* but all the artist's work is brilliant-hued and distinctive.

[53]

Picture Books

CORDUROY   [55]

Written and illustrated by Don Freeman
Cloth: Viking
Paper: Puffin
Published: 1968

Corduroy is a small stuffed bear, waiting in a department store, who eventually goes home with a little black girl named Lisa. His adventures continue in *A Pocket for Corduroy*. Although the story is complete and understood by young children, there are some appealing abridgments of *Corduroy* available for even younger children in a thick board format.

CRANBERRY THANKSGIVING   [56]

Written and illustrated by Wende and Harry Devlin
Cloth: Four Winds
Published: 1971

This is the first in a series of funny, cartoonish books about life in a town called Cranberry. Its real significance—and it is genuine—is that the last page gives a very simple, and by now time-honored, recipe for cranberry bread that is used in schools and homes around the United States. Other holiday-related titles include *Cranberry Christmas, Cranberry Halloween,* and *Cranberry Valentine.*

CRASH! BANG! BOOM!   [57]

Written and illustrated by Peter Spier
Cloth: Doubleday
Paper: Zephyr
Published: 1972

A book of inspired imagination, filled with detailed illustrations of all manner of things, from soldiers in a marching band with their instruments to zoo animals and birds. The text, such as it is, consists of approximations of the sounds each and every creature and thing makes.

CURIOUS GEORGE [58]

Written and illustrated by H. A. Rey
Cloth: Houghton Mifflin
Paper: Houghton Mifflin
Published: 1942

The first of a series of books about a small monkey, captured in Africa by a man wearing a yellow hat and brought back to live in a city. George's curiosity leads him to wreak havoc everywhere he goes. But he is always well-meaning, rather like many of his most devoted preschool admirers. Other original titles include *Curious George Gets a Medal* and *Curious George Rides a Bike*. There are also sixteen titles with illustrations taken from the animated television series in which the color and drawings are not as vibrant as in the original books.

DANCING IN THE MOON: COUNTING RHYMES [59]

Written and illustrated by Fritz Eichenberg
Cloth: HBJ
Paper: Voyager
Published: 1955

Verses with ridiculous premises for counting from 1 to 20, accompanied by large, distinctive, eccentric illustrations.

DANIEL O'ROURKE [60]

Written and illustrated by Gerald McDermott
Cloth: Viking
Paper: Puffin
Published: 1986

A bright, and very green, version of a classic Irish folktale. Perfect for St. Patrick's Day, and top o' the day to you. For more in the same spirit, try *Tim O'Toole and the Wee Folk: an Irish Tale*.

Picture Books

A DARK DARK TALE [61]

Written and illustrated by Ruth Brown
Cloth: Dial
Paper: Pied Piper
Published: 1981

A mysterious night, a moor, a cat, a search, a very simple vocabulary, heightened suspense, and a surprise comic ending to a mysterious, colorful adventure. Very young children get the joke.

DAWN [62]

Written and illustrated by Uri Shulevitz
Cloth: Farrar, Straus & Giroux
Paper: Sunburst
Published: 1974

The text of this lovely picture book comes from a Chinese poem about an old man and his grandson. They are asleep by the shore of a mountain lake and dawn approaches. The full-color illustrations capture the subtle changes of light in the early morning.

THE DAY JIMMY'S BOA ATE THE WASH [63]

Written by Trinka Hakes Noble
Illustrated by Steven Kellogg
Cloth: Dial
Paper: Pied Piper
Published: 1980

The day Jimmy's pet snake goes along on the class trip to the farm makes a memorable story. The full extent of the mayhem is revealed

in the dizzy, funny illustrations. *Jimmy's Boa Bounces Back* tells about what happens when the boa goes to a proper tea party. Just try and guess what happens in *Jimmy's Boa and the Big Splash Birthday Bash*.

[66]

DON'T TOUCH MY ROOM [64]

Written by Patricia Larkin
Illustrated by Patience Brewster
Cloth: Little, Brown
Paper: Joy Street/Little, Brown
Published: 1985

Aaron is determined not to share his very special bedroom with anyone, especially not his baby brother. Time passes, however, and predictably, things get better. A sequel of sorts, set years later, is *Oh Brother*.

DRUMMER HOFF [65]

Written by Barbara Emberley
Illustrated by Ed Emberley
Cloth: Prentice Hall
Paper: Simon & Schuster Books for Young Readers
Published: 1967   Prizes: Caldecott Medal

The simplest cumulative rhyme and precise funny illustrations describe the firing of a cannon by a gaggle of soldiers dressed in the style of the American Revolution.

EACH PEACH PEAR PLUM, AN "I SPY" STORY [66]

Written and illustrated by Janet and Allan Ahlberg
Cloth: Viking
Paper: Puffin
Published: 1979

[66]

An enchanting picture book set on a summery afternoon in the countryside in which nursery rhyme characters, like Goldilocks, the Three Bears, Bo Peep, and Jack and Jill, can be spotted by sharp-eyed readers before they can be fully seen.

Picture Books

THE ELEPHANT AND
THE BAD BABY [67]

Written by Elfrida Vipont
Illustrated by Raymond Briggs
Cloth: Coward
Paper: Coward
Published: 1987

It's never clear just why the baby is "bad" (because babies never are), but in this jolly add-along tale, the elephant and the infant go "rumpeta, rumpeta, rumpeta" down the road and are followed by half the town before it's time for pancakes. The illustrations are amusing and somehow plausible.

THE EMERGENCY ROOM [68]

Written and illustrated by Harlow Rockwell
Cloth: Macmillan
Published: 1985

An elementary and straightforward introduction to that place most families somehow end up visiting at least once. This is for very young children, and the author has done *My Dentist* and *My Doctor* for them as well.

THE EMPEROR'S NEW CLOTHES [69]

Written by Hans Christian Andersen
Illustrated by Anne Rockwell
Cloth: Harper & Row/HarperCollins
Paper: Harper Trophy
Published: 1982

In this version of the story of the vain, silly emperor and the wicked and clever thieves, the illustrations are particularly airy and light. The amusing emperor is very pink and silly in only his crown and curly, pointed beard.

[66]

ERNEST AND CELESTINE [70]

Written and illustrated by Gabrielle Vincent

Paper: Mulberry

Published: 1982

The first in a series of books from a Belgian author about Ernest the bear and Celestine the little mouse. The affection between them, the delicacy of the illustrations, and the plausibility of their adventures are all endearing. In this story, Celestine loses her duck-doll in the snow and Ernest tries to solve the problem. Other titles include *Bravo, Ernest and Celestine,* the wordless *Breakfast Time, Ernest and Celestine,* and *Ernest and Celestine's Patchwork Quilt.* There are more, all charming and evocative.

[70]

EYES OF THE DRAGON [71]

Written by Margaret Leaf
Illustrated by Ed Young

Cloth: Lothrop, Lee & Shepard

Published: 1987

Here is a deftly written and dramatically illustrated cautionary tale based on the wise Chinese principle that one should not paint the eyes of the dragon. A great artist paints a dragon on the wall of little Li's village, but his grandfather the magistrate won't pay till the artist puts in the dragon's eyes. Foolish magistrate.

A FARMER'S ALPHABET [72]

Written and illustrated by Mary Azarian

Cloth: Four Winds

Paper: Godine

Published: 1981

This rugged, rural alphabet book has handsome woodcuts depicting traditional farm life.

Picture Books

FATHER FOX'S PENNYRHYMES   [73]

Written by Clyde Watson
Illustrated by Wendy Watson
Cloth: T. Y. Crowell/HarperCollins
Paper: HarperCollins
Published: 1971

A cheerful collection of fine nonsense verses, with delicate cartoon panels of illustrations that include details and conversational commentary on the verses. *Father Fox's Feast of Songs* is by the same author and illustrator.

FEELINGS   [74]

Written and illustrated by Aliki
Cloth: Greenwillow
Paper: Mulberry
Published: 1984

A catalog of emotions—witty illustrations of faces showing sorrow, joy, love, hate, pride, fear, frustration, and more. Since some children have difficulty explaining their emotions—often because they don't have the words for them—this is useful as well as entertaining, and excellent for shared reading. *Manners* is a companion book.

FINDERS KEEPERS   [75]

Written and illustrated by Will and Nicholas Mordvinoff
Cloth: HBJ
Paper: Voyager
Published: 1951   Prizes: Caldecott Medal

Who owns the bone two dogs have found? A funny story with funny pictures just right for lap listeners and small children, although adults will see the illustrations as old-fashioned.

[79]

FINGER RHYMES   [76]

Written and illustrated by Marc Brown
Cloth: Dutton
Published: 1980

Finger rhymes are those rhymes and games you do with babies and very young children in which everyone ends up laughing. The animal-filled illustrations in this pleasing collection are encouraging for older readers, who may have to follow the instructions. The companion volumes are *Hand Rhymes* and *Party Rhymes*.

FIRST FLIGHT [77]

Written and illustrated by David McPhail
Cloth: Little, Brown
Paper: Joy Street
Published: 1987

A little boy goes on his first airplane trip to visit his grandmother. His teddy bear turns into the traveling companion who acts out every behavioral fantasy and neurosis. Stylishly done, with both humor and sympathy.

[79]

FIRST THERE WAS FRANCES [78]

Written and illustrated by Bob Graham
Cloth: Bradbury
Published: 1986

An ebullient book about the growth of a household, starting with Frances, adding Graham, then more and more people and animals. The full-color illustrations have a giddy quality that adds to the general merriment.

FISH EYES: A BOOK YOU CAN COUNT ON [79]

Written and illustrated by Lois Ehlert
Cloth: HBJ
Published: 1990   Prizes: New York Times Best Illustrated Book

Deep in the cobalt-blue sea of these pages there are amazing, brilliant flip-flopping fish. Their shapes and colors and numbers increase imaginatively. The simple rhymed text and the cutout holes for little fingers on each page invite the very young reader or listener to chant aloud and help turn the page. The distinctive collage style can be found aboveground in *Growing Vegetable Soup*, *Planting a Rainbow*, and *Feathers for Lunch*.

FIVE LITTLE FOXES AND
THE SNOW   [80]

Written by Tony Johnston
Illustrated by Cyndy Szekeres
Paper: HarperCollins
Published: 1987

It starts to snow the week before Christmas, and in the cozy den, Gramma Fox has her hands full trying to manage the five little foxes as well as her knitting project. All is revealed on Christmas morning. A delightful story of anticipation with funny full-color illustrations. The text has a nice cadence for reading aloud.

FIVE MINUTES' PEACE   [81]

Written and illustrated by Jill Murphy
Cloth: Putnam
Published: 1986

In this slice-of-life for-mommies book, Mrs. Large's elephant children follow her everywhere. She finally retreats to the bathtub. They come in to surprise her. Then guess who get to play in the tub while their mother catches a cup of coffee in peace in the kitchen? The Larges reappear in *All in One Piece.*

[86]

FIX-IT   [82]

Written and illustrated by David McPhail
Cloth: Dutton
Paper: Unicorn
Published: 1984

The television won't work and Emma Bear is in despair. Her parents try to distract her, even read to her, and then, when the infernal machine is finally back in order, she is busy reading to her doll. Her adventures continue in *Emma's Pet* and *Emma's Vacation.*

FOOLISH RABBIT'S BIG MISTAKE [83]

Written by Rafe Martin
Illustrated by Ed Young
Cloth: Putnam
Paper: Sandcastle
Published: 1985

In this retelling of an African version of a story adults might recognize as Chicken Little and Henny Penny, a foolish rabbit dreams under an apple tree. The illustrations take on a gleaming intensity as the chaos builds. Good for reading aloud.

FORGET-ME-NOT [84]

Written by Paul Rogers
Illustrated by Celia Berridge
Paper: Puffin
Published: 1984

Sidney is a very absentminded lion, and on the way to a day at the seaside, he manages to lose something on every page. Sharp young eyes love finding missing objects in these whimsical illustrations.

FOUR BRAVE SAILORS [85]

Written by Mirra Ginsburg
Illustrated by Nancy Tafuri
Cloth: Greenwillow
Published: 1987

The four sailors are fearless mice, brave and true, and their white ship sails over waves of wondrous blues. The pictures fill the page and very little children are caught up in the exciting voyage.

FOX'S DREAM [86]

Written and illustrated by Tejima
Cloth: Philomel
Paper: Philomel
Published: 1987   Prizes: New York Times Best Illustrated Book

This large-format book follows a solitary fox on a snowy winter's night, capturing his dreams and an exciting chase of a snow rabbit in thrilling, and technically dazzling, woodcuts by a contemporary Japanese master.

[86]

Picture Books

FREDERICK [87]

Written and illustrated by Leo Lionni
Cloth: Pantheon
Paper: Random House   **Prizes: Caldecott Honor**
Published: 1967   **New York Times Best Illustrated Book**

The first of the wonderful books about Frederick the mouse, a day-dreamer and poet who, when winter comes, is also an entertainer. The artist works in a distinctive full-color collage style. (There is a one-volume collection of six Frederick books, *Frederick's Fables: A Leo Lionni Treasury of Favorite Stories*, as well as other individual picture books.)

FREIGHT TRAIN [88]

Written and illustrated by Donald Crews
Cloth: Greenwillow
Paper: Puffin
Published: 1978   **Prizes: Caldecott Honor**

A freight train hurtles across the pages through day and night from the city into the countryside, with a sense of speed that is quite magical as the train becomes almost an abstraction of color. A wonderful book to read with young children. *Trucks* and *Flying* are also exciting.

FRIENDS [89]

Written and illustrated by Helme Heine
Cloth: McElderry
Paper: Aladdin
Published: 1982

[89]

A rooster, a mouse, and a pig are best friends and have a fine time together. The witty and lighthearted full-color illustrations are ebullient. The companions also appear in the small-size, charming "Three Friends" series—*The Alarm Clock, The Visitor,* and *The Racing Cart.*

[88]

FROG WENT A-COURTIN' [90]

Written by John Langstaff
Illustrated by Feodor Rojankovsky
Cloth: HBJ
Paper: Voyager
Published: 1955   Prizes: Caldecott Medal

This is a charming, old-fashioned fancy-dress version of a familiar song. Miss Mouse is quite coy. The large format works very well with very young children.

GEORGE SHRINKS [91]

Written and illustrated by William Joyce
Cloth: Harper & Row/HarperCollins
Paper: Harper Trophy
Published: 1985

In this beautifully realized dream fantasy, George wakes up to find that his parents are out, he has shrunk to tiny size, and must nevertheless deal with a whole list of household chores. The illustrations capture the problems of scale perfectly—the toothbrush, the cat, the garbage, and a tiny George.

GERALDINE'S BLANKET [92]

Written and illustrated by Holly Keller
Cloth: Greenwillow
Paper: Mulberry
Published: 1984

Geraldine's pink blanket was a baby present from Aunt Bessie. It's worn now and patched, and when Aunt Bessie sends her a doll, Geraldine preserves and transfers her affections simultaneously by using the scraps for a doll dress. Gentle story, gentle illustrations.

[87]

GILA MONSTERS MEET YOU AT THE AIRPORT   [93]

Written by Marjorie Weinman Sharmat
Illustrated by Byron Barton
Cloth: Macmillan
Paper: Penguin
Published: 1980

Moving is bad enough, but what if you are from the big city and when the airplane lands, giant lizards meet you? The little boy meets a boy out west who has similarly outlandish fantasies about life in New York.

GOING TO THE POTTY   [94]

Written by Fred Rogers
Illustrated by Jim Judkis
Cloth: Putnam
Paper: Putnam
Published: 1986

Television's Mr. Rogers's series of "First Experience" books are as low-key and reassuring as his faithful audience might expect. This photo essay, with its familiar, plausible families, deals with one of life's great transitions. The text is direct and encouraging. Other titles in the series include *Going to Day Care, Going to the Doctor,* and *The New Baby. I Have To Go! A Sesame Street Toddler Book* deals with the same urgent subject as this one cheerfully.

GONE FISHING   [95]

Written by Earlene Long
Illustrated by Richard Brown
Cloth: Houghton Mifflin
Paper: Sandpiper
Published: 1983

In this laconic little story of a boy and his father, they get up before dawn, see all sorts of creatures on their expedition, catch two fish, and experience both delight and genuine satisfaction. Nicely illustrated, and underscores the concept of large and small.

GOOD MORNING, CHICK   [96]

Written by Mirra Ginsburg
Illustrated by Byron Barton
Paper: Mulberry
Published: 1980

Young children like this barnyard story with bright, simple full-color illustrations. A baby chick comes out of its little white house and goes exploring the new world it has entered.

GOODBYE HOUSE   [97]

Written and illustrated by Frank Asch
Cloth: Prentice Hall
Published: 1986

A father helps his child bid farewell to the house after the moving van has emptied it. A problematic and upsetting situation, handled in a thoughtful and soothing way.

GOODNIGHT MOON   [98]

Written by Margaret Wise Brown
Illustrated by Clement Hurd
Cloth: Harper & Row/HarperCollins
Paper: Harper Trophy
Published: 1947

One of the most popular of all American books for the bedtime rituals of very young children. A small rabbit settles down for the night in that familiar but fantastic place "the great green room" and says good night to all the things and creatures there. The illustrations, subtle and complex as well as droll, are perhaps even more soothing than the text.

GRANDFATHER TWILIGHT   [99]

Written and illustrated by Barbara Helen Berger
Cloth: Philomel
Paper: Philomel
Published: 1984

A peaceful bedtime book with some gentle magic. Grandfather Twilight spreads dusk and mysterious shadow with his magic pearl, which,

[90]

as darkness comes and he reaches the shore, is transformed into the rising moon. The full-color illustrations have a luminous quality that is captivating.

GRANPA [100]

Written and illustrated by John Burningham
Cloth: Crown
Published: 1985

Captured in an airy, light style of illustration that suggests memory rather than immediate experience, this series of vignettes about the relationship between a little girl and her grandfather is winsome and appealing.

THE GROWING-UP FEET [101]

Written by Beverly Cleary
Illustrated by DyAnne DiSalvo Ryan
Cloth: Morrow Junior Books
Paper: Dell Yearling
Published: 1987

Jimmy and Janet are four-year-old twins whose adventures are recounted in an appealing series of books, including *Janet's Thingamajigs* and *Two Dog Biscuits*. This story is about red boots that stretch to fit growing feet.

Prickly

[102]

THE GUINEA PIG ABC [102]

Written and illustrated by Kate Duke
Cloth: Dutton
Paper: Unicorn
Published: 1983

The letters in this sunny ABC are made by a troupe of appealing guinea pigs with unusual acrobatic skills. *Guinea Pigs Far and Near* features the same cast illustrating concepts such as behind, beside, and between.

HAPPY BIRTHDAY, MOON   [103]

Written and illustrated by Frank Asch
Cloth: Prentice Hall
Paper: Simon & Schuster Books for Young Readers
Published: 1982

This is one of a series of simple stories illustrated in a particularly appealing and rather childlike fashion that young children find very pleasing. Other favorites include *Good-Night, Horsey, Bear's Bargain,* and *Bread & Honey.*

HAROLD AND THE PURPLE CRAYON   [104]

Written and illustrated by Crockett Johnson
Cloth: Harper & Row/HarperCollins
Paper: Harper Trophy
Published: 1955

One night when Harold can't sleep, he takes his purple crayon and draws himself a walk. He follows the moon, goes to a desert isle, climbs a stair, and ends up home and in bed. Simple and glorious, this book is especially loved by very young children. The related titles are *Harold's ABC, Harold's Circus,* and *Harold's Trip to the Sky.*

[104]

HARRY AND THE TERRIBLE WHATZIT   [105]

Written and illustrated by Dick Gackenbach
Cloth: Clarion
Paper: Clarion
Published: 1978

Harry follows his mother down into the dark cellar to save her from the terrible two-headed Whatzit that amazingly shrinks when confronted by Harry's courage. Emboldened, Harry even sends it away. Reassuring to youngsters passing through a monster phase.

[105]

Picture Books

THE HATING BOOK [106]

Written by Charlotte Zolotow
Illustrated by Ben Shecter
Cloth: Harper & Row/HarperCollins
Paper: Harper Trophy
Published: 1969

A small, classic story about the vicissitudes of being best friends.

HAVE YOU SEEN MY DUCKLING? [107]

Written and illustrated by Nancy Tafuri
Cloth: Greenwillow
Paper: Mulberry
Published: 1984   Prizes: Caldecott Honor

In a series of stunning double-page illustrations executed in a bold but vaguely Oriental style, the mother duck looks for her eighth duckling, whom the reader can see in some visible but cleverly camouflaged corner. Great fun for very young children. *Early Morning in the Barn* is about three chicks who sing with other barnyard animals.

HECTOR PROTECTOR AND AS I WENT OVER THE WATER: TWO NURSERY RHYMES [108]

Written and illustrated by Maurice Sendak
Cloth: Harper & Row/HarperCollins
Paper: Harper Trophy
Published: 1965

Knowing the text of these familiar nursery rhymes is no preparation for the exuberant interpretation in this witty edition. In particular, Hector's protestations about hating green are memorable.

[107]

A HOLE IS TO DIG: A FIRST BOOK OF DEFINITIONS   [109]

Written by Ruth Krauss
Illustrated by Maurice Sendak
Cloth: Harper & Row/HarperCollins
Paper: Harper Trophy
Published: 1952   Prizes: New York Times Best Illustrated Book

This little book fits perfectly into preschool- and kindergarten-size hands and is full of wonderful things to think about. The small line-drawing illustrations capture wistful, funny, ordinary children in motion. The text sets out fine child-evolved definitions—arms are to hug. A favorite for decades.

HOLES AND PEEKS   [110]

Written and illustrated by Ann Jonas
Cloth: Greenwillow
Published: 1984

Here is a reassuring book for toddlers who worry about holes (such as toilets) that are sometimes scary and find things they can peek at (say, through a buttonhole) less frightening. The illustrations have a bright, appealing simplicity.

HONEY, I LOVE AND OTHER LOVE POEMS   [111]

Written by Eloise Greenfield
Illustrated by Diane and Leo Dillon
Cloth: T. Y. Crowell/HarperCollins
Paper: Harper Trophy
Published: 1978

A collection of short poems about emotions and ordinary childhood experiences. The illustrations of black children are appealing.

Picture Books

HOORAY FOR SNAIL [112]

Written and illustrated by John Stadler
Cloth: T. Y. Crowell/HarperCollins
Paper: Harper Trophy
Published: 1984

The idea of Snail hitting a home run, which means that Snail must circle the bases, is a joke everyone, even the young sports fan, can see coming and enjoy all the way around. *Snail Saves the Day* shifts the action to the football field.

HOW DO I PUT IT ON? [113]

Written by Shigo Watanabe
Illustrated by Yasuo Ohtomo
Cloth: Philomel
Paper: Philomel
Published: 1979

One of a series of concept books for very young children that deal with the issues of "doing it all by myself." The illustrations show a cheerful little bear, but the reader understands who the series is really about. Other titles include *I Can Take a Walk, I Can Build a House!* and *I'm the King of the Castle.*

HUMPHREY'S BEAR [114]

Written by Jan Wahl
Illustrated by William Joyce
Cloth: Henry Holt
Published: 1987

His father thinks Humphrey is too old to sleep with his bear, so in his dream Humphrey goes off to sea with the stuffed animal. The illustrations are quite magical.

[112]

HURRY HOME, GRANDMA!   [115]

Written by Arielle North Olson
Illustrated by Lydia Dabcovich
Cloth: Dutton
Paper: Unicorn
Published: 1984

Grandma is an explorer and Timothy and Melinda are very anxious that she get home in time for Christmas. She makes a grand entrance.

I AM A BUNNY   [116]

Written by Ole Risom
Illustrated by Richard Scarry
Cloth: Golden/Western
Published: 1967

"I am a bunny. I live in a hollow tree." This tall, sturdy book with its very simple text and illustrations that capture the seasons in the life of a little rabbit wearing red overalls is a timeless favorite, especially with toddlers. There are companion stories: *I Am a Kitten, I Am a Puppy,* and, for those old enough to get the Sesame Street joke, *I Am a Monster.*

I GO WITH MY FAMILY
TO GRANDMA'S   [117]

Written by Riki Levinson
Illustrated by Diane Goode
Cloth: Dutton
Paper: Unicorn
Published: 1986

Five cousins and their families from the five boroughs of New York City assemble at their grandparents' home in Manhattan on a summer day around the turn of the century. The text is simple and straightforward, and the detailed illustrations showing the different families and different children are rich and intriguing, as well as fun to count. *Watch the Stars Come Out* tells of immigrants' arrival in America.

[112]

Picture Books

I KNOW AN OLD LADY WHO SWALLOWED A FLY   [118]

Written and illustrated by Nadine Bernard Wescott
Cloth: Joy Street/Little, Brown
Paper: Little, Brown
Published: 1981

A brightly illustrated setting of the folk song about that silly old woman who kept on swallowing larger and larger things until eventually she swallowed a horse. She died, of course. Glen Rounds has done a manic alternative version, almost scary for the very youngest, irresistible to school-age and older readers. It features a demonic and possibly demented fly that gets larger and loonier with each turning page.

I LOVE MY BABY SISTER (MOST OF THE TIME)   [119]

Written by Elaine Edelman
Illustrated by Wendy Watson
Paper: Penguin
Published: 1984

As this little girl describes life with her baby sister, she is very honest about the initial disadvantages of the situation. Nevertheless, she hopes that as the baby gets older, they will play together.

I WANT TO BE AN ASTRONAUT   [120]

Written and illustrated by Byron Barton
Cloth: T. Y. Crowell/HarperCollins
Paper: Harper Trophy
Published: 1988   Prizes: New York Times Best Illustrated Book

There are only five short sentences in this giddy, imaginative "travel" book for small dreamers. Space is brilliantly blue, the astronauts look a lot like Lego figures, and the earth looks comforting and not so far away. The simplicity of the illustrations, in which the figures are outlined with strong black lines, is persuasive. Let's go.

I WON'T GO TO BED! [121]

Written by Harriet Ziefert
Illustrated by Andrea Baruffi
Cloth: Little, Brown
Published: 1987

Harry won't. So his father leaves him downstairs. As the hours grow later, things seem larger and stranger than they do in the daytime, until the appealing little boy falls asleep on the floor. The illustrations are spare and colorful as well as witty.

[123]

IF YOU GIVE A MOUSE A COOKIE [122]

Written by Laura Joffe Numeroff
Illustrated by Felicia Bond
Cloth: Harper & Row/HarperCollins
Published: 1985

The logic to this wonderfully nonsensical book is perfectly sound, as it must be to lead the reader through such a caper about the consequences of greed. You see, if you give a mouse a cookie, well then, logically, he'll ask for a glass of milk. . . . Need one add that it's a chocolate chip cookie and the winsome mouse in overalls has a wonderfully pert nose?

IKTOMI AND THE BERRIES [123]

Written and illustrated by Paul Goble
Cloth: Orchard Books
Published: 1989

The Lakota Indians called their trickster character Iktomi, and in this [123] story the foolish fellow doesn't understand that the buffalo berries he sees in the water are really reflections. In this and several other Iktomi tales (*Iktomi and the Boulder* and *Iktomi and the Ducks*) the format—with stylized illustrations and participant clues in the text—is designed to be read aloud with young children.

Picture Books

THE INSIDE-OUTSIDE BOOK OF
NEW YORK CITY   [124]

Written and illustrated by Roxie Munro
Cloth: Dodd, Mead/Putnam
Published: 1985   Prizes: New York Times Best Illustrated Book

Views of famous sights and buildings in New York City, including the
Statue of Liberty, the spire of the Chrysler building, the front car of a
subway train, and many more, are seen from the outside and the inside
in witty colored drawings. A wonderful idea, handsomely executed and
full of details. Companion books of sorts are *Christmas in New York, The
Inside-Outside Book of Washington, D.C.,* and *The Inside-Outside Book of
London.*

IS THIS A HOUSE FOR
HERMIT CRAB?   [125]

Written by Megan McDonald
Illustrated by S. D. Schindler
Cloth: Orchard Books
Published: 1990

The hermit crab must find a new home, and he trudges across the sand
(even the pages are sandy-colored) trying out different domiciles just
lying there on the beach—a rock, driftwood, a plastic pail—till the right
place comes along. Text and illustrations are perfectly married, making
this a delightful story as well as fine natural science for the very young.

[125]

IT DOES NOT SAY MEOW AND OTHER
ANIMAL RIDDLE RHYMES   [126]

Written by Beatrice Schenk de Regniers
Illustrated by Paul Galdone
Cloth: Clarion
Paper: Clarion
Published: 1972

Rhymed riddles about nine familiar animals, from ant to elephant. The
verse is on the right side of the page, the illustrated answer follows on
the next double page. Preschoolers revel in such questions.

IT'S RAINING SAID JOHN TWAINING: DANISH NURSERY RHYMES   [127]

Written and illustrated by N. M. Bodecker, Translator
Cloth: McElderry
Paper: Aladdin
Published: 1973
The distinguished translator/illustrator offers a delightful collection of Danish nursery rhymes that American children find enchanting.

JAMBO MEANS HELLO: SWAHILI ALPHABET BOOK   [128]

Written by Muriel Feelings
Illustrated by Tom Feelings
Cloth: Dial
Paper: Pied Piper
Published: 1974

A fine anthropological alphabet book that conveys a vision of tribal life in East Africa. A companion volume, *Moja Means One,* is a counting book. This is really for school-age children and interested adults.

JAMES MARSHALL'S MOTHER GOOSE   [129]

Written and illustrated by James Marshall
Cloth: Farrar, Straus & Giroux
Paper: Sunburst
Published: 1979

This cheerful Mother Goose collection is illustrated in a distinctive style by the artist who created *George and Martha* and *The Stupids.* The pictures are broad and cartoonish, the selection of verses all bright and cheery as well as familiar.

[128]

Picture Books

JESSE BEAR, WHAT WILL YOU WEAR? [130]

Written by Nancy White Carlstrom
Illustrated by Bruce Degen
Cloth: Macmillan
Published: 1986

A lilting rhyme that begins as Jesse Bear wakes up and makes some decisions about his day. A happy book, with happy illustrations, for preschoolers who enjoy making the same kinds of decisions. The bears are wonderful, and they return in *It's About Time, Jesse Bear* and *Better Not Get Wet, Jesse Bear.*

JULIUS, THE BABY OF THE WORLD [131]

Written and illustrated by Kevin Henkes
Cloth: Greenwillow
Published: 1990

Lily, the anxious but charming mouse who first appeared in *Chester's Way,* is really furious and jealous and distraught when her baby brother arrives. The sharp, pointy illustrations fairly quiver till things resolve.

JUST PLAIN FANCY [132]

Written and illustrated by Patricia Polacco
Cloth: Bantam
Paper: Bantam
Published: 1990

There are many stories about Amish children, but few of them are picture books. Here, two little sisters find an abandoned egg that hatches into a chick who earns its name—Fancy. The illustrations are enchanting and largely respectful of Amish ways.

[132]

THE LADY AND THE SPIDER [133]

[130]

Written by Faith McNulty
Illustrated by Bob Marstall
Cloth: Harper & Row/HarperCollins
Paper: Harper Trophy
Published: 1986

Spider lives quietly in a vegetable garden. One day, the lady who tends the garden picks the head of lettuce in which he lives, but stops short of destroying him. This is fine science writing for very young children, accessible for preschoolers, and of interest to school-age children.

LATKES AND APPLESAUCE: A HANUKKAH STORY [134]

Written by Fran Manushkin
Illustrated by Robin Spowart
Cloth: Scholastic
Published: 1990

A blizzard has made it impossible to dig potatoes and gather apples for the traditional Hanukkah dinner of latkes and applesauce, and supplies are running low, nevertheless the poor family takes in a stray kitten and dog. At the end of the storm, on the eighth night, the new pets reveal a modest miracle. A most appealing holiday tale.

LET'S GO SWIMMING WITH MR. SILLYPANTS [135]

Written and illustrated by M. K. Brown
Cloth: Crown
Published: 1986

Mr. Sillypants, whose name doesn't nearly convey what a ridiculous-looking fellow he is, signs up for swimming lessons and immediately becomes terrified of water. He has an explicit dream about his fears and then goes to try to learn how to swim. The illustrations are witty, and, well, silly.

[135]

Picture Books

A LION FOR LEWIS [136]

Written and illustrated by Rosemary Wells
Cloth: Dial
Paper: Pied Piper
Published: 1982

Tagalong Lewis is always just a beat behind his older siblings, either too late for their games or the brunt of them. Then one day he finds a stuffed lion suit in the attic. The full-color illustrations are appealing, especially when Lewis gets into that lion. A special favorite of preschool younger siblings.

THE LITTLE DUCK [137]

Written by Judy Dunn
Illustrated by Phoebe Dunn
Paper: Random House
Published: 1976

A fine series of paperback photo-essays is all about small creatures. This simple story is about a year in the life of a duck, lovingly hatched and raised by a small boy. The photography, particularly of the hatching egg, is very clear and uncluttered. Other titles in the series include *The Little Goat, The Little Kitten, The Little Lamb, The Little Puppy,* and *The Little Rabbit.*

[141]

THE LITTLE ENGINE THAT COULD [138]

Written by Watty Piper
Illustrated by George and Doris Hauman
Cloth: Platt & Munk
Published: 1930

One of the basic books of American childhood, this is the saga of the little engine that thought it could help deliver toys and fruits to the children living over the mountain. Avoid the gussied-up editions. The little engine need not pop up or go fast; it is, after all, just a little engine, like the very young child who is listening to the chant . . . "I think I can, I think I can . . ."

[138]

THE LITTLE FIR TREE [139]

Written by Margaret Wise Brown
Illustrated by Barbara Cooney
Cloth: T. Y. Crowell/HarperCollins
Paper: Harper Trophy
Published: 1954; reissued 1979

A Christmas story about a lame boy and a little fir tree that is brought to him. The small, delicately illustrated format is appealing.

THE LITTLE FUR FAMILY [140]

Written by Margaret Wise Brown
Illustrated by Garth Williams
Cloth: Harper & Row/HarperCollins
Paper: Harper Trophy
Published: 1951

This is about a day in the life of a little fur child, ending with a bedtime song. The little fur family is "warm as toast, smaller than most." The cover is fuzzy fake fur.

LITTLE GORILLA [141]

Written and illustrated by Ruth Bornstein
Cloth: Clarion
Paper: Clarion
Published: 1976

A very simple and appealing story about wide-eyed Little Gorilla, who grows and grows and grows and is still loved, even when he is a big gorilla. Very young children find it a soothing tale, perhaps because the small gorilla is so easy to identify with. A toddler favorite.

Picture

Books

THE LITTLE ISLAND [142]

Written by Golden MacDonald
Illustrated by Leonard Weisgard
Cloth: Doubleday
Paper: Zephyr
Published: 1946   Prizes: Caldecott Medal

The little island is the hero of a low-key illustrated fantasy. It communes with visiting creatures, including lobsters, seals, and a kitten, and muses about life. If the quiet anthropomorphizing seems vaguely familiar, it is because the author of this old-fashioned charmer is Margaret Wise Brown using a pseudonym.

LOUANNE PIG IN THE TALENT SHOW [143]

Written and illustrated by Nancy Carlson
Cloth: Carolrhoda
Paper: Penguin
Published: 1986

One of a series of simple, believable adventures of a very nice little pig who might be just like someone in your neighborhood. Both the text and the illustrations are uncluttered and bright. Other titles include *The Mysterious Valentine, The Perfect Family, Making the Team,* and *Witch Lady.* The author also writes and illustrates comparable series about Loudmouth George, a rabbit, and Harriet, a charming golden retriever.

[145]

LUCY & TOM'S 1 2 3 [144]

Written and illustrated by Shirley Hughes
Cloth: Viking
Published: 1987

This story comes from a series of concept books for toddlers and preschoolers about two engaging little children, Lucy and Tom, who deal with the alphabet, a busy day, counting, and Christmas. Though the books were first published in Britain in the 1970s, they have only recently become widely available here. *Lucy & Tom's Day, Lucy & Tom's Christmas,* and *Lucy & Tom's a. b. c.* are available in paperback.

MADELINE [145]

Written and illustrated by Ludwig Bemelmans
Cloth: Viking
Paper: Puffin
Published: 1939   Prizes: Caldecott Honor

"In an old house in Paris that was covered with vines" begins the beloved story, and the singsong rhymed text carries the twelve little girls
and their headmistress, dear Miss Clavel, through a series of madcap
adventures. The brilliant, busy Gallic illustrations capture, and indeed
encapsulate, a sense of Paris as so many people, children and adults,
believe it once was. Other titles include *Madeline and the Bad Hat*, *Madeline and the Gypsies*, *Madeline in London*, and *Madeline's Rescue*.

[145]

THE MAGGIE B [146]

Written and illustrated by Irene Haas
Cloth: McElderry
Paper: Aladdin
Published: 1975

Margaret Barnstable has a very simple fantasy—she dreams of spending a perfect day aboard the sturdy little ship the *Maggie B*, with only
her baby brother, James, for company. But because it is a fantasy, the
enchanting vessel comes equipped with a top-deck farm and a peach
tree, among other unusual amenities. It is very easy to substitute names
of real siblings when reading the nicely cadenced text aloud.

[146]

Picture Books

MAKE WAY FOR DUCKLINGS [147]

Written and illustrated by Robert McCloskey
Cloth: Viking
Paper: Puffin
Published: 1941   Prizes: Caldecott Medal

In Boston, where there is a higher order to things, a family of ducklings on their way to the Public Gardens can stop traffic. It doesn't matter a whit if these illustrations seem old-fashioned—they are endearing and firmly establish the park as an estimable place to raise a family.

MAMA DON'T ALLOW [148]

Written and illustrated by Thacher Hurd
Cloth: Harper & Row/HarperCollins
Paper: Harper Trophy
Published: 1984

Noise, noise, noise! The Swamp Band plays loudly all night for the Alligator Ball. Lush, funny illustrations and a new setting for a familiar folk song.

THE MAN WHO KEPT HOUSE [149]

Written by Kathleen and Michael Hague
Illustrated by Michael Hague
Cloth: HBJ
Paper: Voyager
Published: 1981

The farmer decides to switch roles with his wife and makes a colossal botch of things. Based on a Scandinavian folktale, this is an ever pertinent lesson for all ages. The old-fashioned full-color illustrations are fun, especially the pig.

MARMALADE'S NAP [150]

Written and illustrated by Cindy Wheeler
Cloth: Knopf
Paper: Knopf
Published: 1983

In this tale, just one of a series of small books about a smug and sassy orange cat, Marmalade is looking for a place out of doors to nap on a spring day. Other titles include *Marmalade's Picnic*, *Marmalade's Snowy Day*, and *Marmalade's Yellow Leaf*.

[149]

54

MARTIN'S HATS [151]

Written by Joan Blos
Illustrated by Marc Simont
Cloth: Morrow Junior Books
Paper: Mulberry
Published: 1984

[147]

With his wardrobe of hats to fit every fantasy, Martin is a kind of preschool Walter Mitty. And preschoolers, who generally do love hats, too, respond to or are inspired by Martin. The illustrations are properly fanciful.

MARY HAD A LITTLE LAMB [152]

Written by Mary Josepha Hale
Illustrated by Tomie dePaola
Cloth: Holiday
Paper: Holiday
Published: 1984

A bright and stylized version of one of the best-known songs of early childhood. A musical arrangement is included.

MARY WORE HER RED DRESS, AND HENRY WORE HIS GREEN SNEAKERS [153]

Written and illustrated by Merle Peek
Cloth: Clarion
Published: 1985

Katie's animal friends wear different-colored clothing to her birthday party. The music to this folk song is included, and the verses can be adapted to your family and your preschool birthday parties.

MAX'S FIRST WORD [154]

Written and illustrated by Rosemary Wells
Cloth: Dial
Published: 1979

Max, a lovable rabbit toddler who has a bossy and talkative older sister named Ruby, stars in an outstanding series of board books for very

[154]

young children. Max is curious and quite independent. In addition to *Max's New Suit*, *Max's Ride*, and *Max's Toys: A Counting Book*, there is a series of four "Very First" titles, covering bath, bedtime, birthday, and breakfast, and *Max's Christmas*.

MAY I BRING A FRIEND?   [155]

Written by Beatrice Schenk de Regniers
Illustrated by Beni Montresor
Cloth: Atheneum
Paper: Aladdin
Published: 1964   Prizes: Caldecott Medal

The king and queen keep inviting the little boy to visit, and each time, he brings along a remarkable assortment of animal friends whose manners are not what they should be.

MICE TWICE   [156]

Written and illustrated by Joseph Low
Cloth: McElderry
Paper: Aladdin
Published: 1980   Prizes: Caldecott Honor

Cat invites Mouse to dinner, planning to eat him. Mouse brings an unexpected companion, and a frenzy of competitiveness and surprises ensues, all illustrated with great wit.

THE MILK MAKERS   [157]

Written and illustrated by Gail Gibbons
Cloth: Macmillan
Paper: Aladdin
Published: 1985

Just how does milk get from cow to cup? The answers are given here in clear, accurate illustrations and spare, precise text.

[158]

MILLIONS OF CATS   [158]

Written and illustrated by Wanda Gag
Cloth: Coward
Paper: Sandcastle
Published: 1928   Prizes: Newbery Honor

This is the story of the little old man who went to find a cat to please
the little old woman and brought home hundreds of cats, thousands of
cats, millions of cats. Eventually the cats fight, and only one scrawny,
shy kitten is left to keep the old couple company. A classic picture book
whose text can be recited by hundreds of people, thousands of people,
millions and millions and millions of people. Timeless. Ageless.

[155]

MITCHELL IS MOVING   [159]

Written by Marjorie Weinman Sharmat
Illustrated by Jose Aruego and Ariane Dewey
Cloth: Macmillan
Published: 1978

Moving can be a real problem. Mitchell the dinosaur has decided to
move after sixty years in the same place. His friend Margo decides to
stop him.

THE MIXED-UP CHAMELEON   [160]

Written and illustrated by Eric Carle
Cloth: T. Y. Crowell/HarperCollins
Paper: Harper Trophy
Published: 1975

A chameleon goes to the zoo and imagines becoming a variety of
other creatures. The illustrations—finger-painted collages—are distinctive and in the winning style of Carle's best-loved *The Very Hungry
Caterpillar*.

[158]

MOMMY DOESN'T KNOW MY NAME [161]

Written by Suzanne Williams
Illustrated by Andrew Shacht
Cloth: Houghton Mifflin
Published: 1990

Hannah's mommy's nicknames for her are meant to be sweet and affectionate. But as Hannah considers herself as a chickadee, a pumpkin, a funny monkey, and a mouse, she gets more and more worried. At the end of the day, things are sweetly clarified. The illustrations capture Hannah's frustrations nicely. *But Not Billy* tells the same kind of story about a baby.

MOTHER, MOTHER, I WANT ANOTHER [162]

Written by Maria Poluskin
Illustrated by Diane Dawson
Paper: Crown
Published: 1978

It's bedtime and the little mouse should be settled down, but suddenly she wants another . . . so Mama scurries about trying to figure out what it is she wants. The answer will please. (It's a kiss!)

[163]

MOUSE PAINT [163]

Written and illustrated by Ellen Stoll Walsh
Cloth: HBJ
Published: 1989

Three white mice discover three pots of paint—red, yellow, and blue —and dive in. Presto! This small book is a delightful exploration of color as the mice pitter-pat through puddles and marvel at the changes they make. The funny, cute illustrations are made from cut-paper collage. *Mouse Count* counts mice, natch.

MR. AND MRS. PIG'S
EVENING OUT   [164]

Written and illustrated by Mary Rayner
Cloth: Atheneum
Paper: Aladdin
Published: 1976

Mr. and Mrs. Pig don't take careful notice of the baby-sitter before they leave Mrs. Wolf in charge of their ten piglets. Her true nature emerges late in the evening, and she is about to make a meal of the youngest when she is routed and vanquished, only to reappear in *Garth Pig and the Ice-Cream Lady*. In *Mrs. Pig's Bulk Buy* there is no wolf, but a lightly told moral lesson about what happens when the piglets have all they want of catsup, their favorite food, and more. There is also a collection of family stories, *Mrs. Pig Gets Cross*.

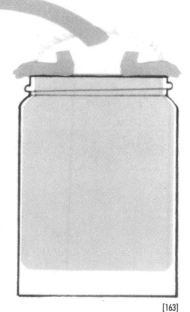

[163]

MR. GUMPY'S OUTING   [165]

Written and illustrated by John Burningham
Cloth: Henry Holt
Published: 1971   Prizes: New York Times Best Illustrated Book

On a hot summer afternoon an ungainly assortment of children and animals pile into Mr. Gumpy's little boat, but of course they don't all fit —with predictable results. Another delightful book about the good fellow and his friends is *Mr. Gumpy's Motor Car*.

MR. RABBIT AND THE
LOVELY PRESENT   [166]

Written by Charlotte Zolotow
Illustrated by Maurice Sendak
Cloth: Harper & Row/HarperCollins
Paper: Harper Trophy
Published: 1962

[165]

Mr. Rabbit helps a gentle little girl gather the components of a truly lovely present for her mother. Part of the book's enduring charm is the generous context for giving in a world that has grown so very commercial even to the young.

Picture Books

MY BOOK   [167]

Written and illustrated by Ron Maris
Paper: Penguin
Published: 1983

The first in a series of cleverly illustrated books using alternating full-page and cut half-pages that reveal details of the illustration. Here the reader follows a child home to bed, where he reads this very book. Other titles include *My Room* and *Is Anyone Home?*

MY GRANDSON LEW   [168]

Written by Charlotte Zolotow
Illustrated by William Pène du Bois
Cloth: Harper & Row/HarperCollins
Paper: Harper Trophy
Published: 1974

Lew's grandfather died when he was quite small, but it turns out that Lew remembers him in vivid fragments while he and his mother talk about remembering.

MY MAMA NEEDS ME   [169]

Written by Mildred Pitts Walter
Illustrated by Pat Cummings
Cloth: Lothrop, Lee & Shepard
Published: 1983

Jason wants to be a good big brother, but he is both excited and scared about the new baby coming home. Then it turns out she sleeps almost all the time, and Jason is relieved.

MY MOM TRAVELS A LOT   [170]

Written by Caroline Feller Bauer
Illustrated by Nancy Winslow Parker
Cloth: Frederick Warne
Paper: Puffin
Published: 1981   Prizes: New York Times Best Illustrated Book

This is a good news/bad news story familiar to all children with parents whose work requires them to travel. It is told in a bright, breezy way, because after all, travel is a fact of life.

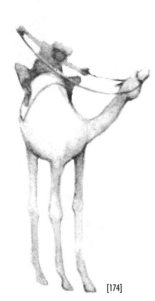

[174]

MY RED UMBRELLA   [171]

Written and illustrated by Robert Bright
Cloth: Morrow Junior Books
Paper: Mulberry
Published: 1959; reissued 1985

A small-hand-size, endearing book about a perky little girl whose red umbrella expands during a shower to shelter a whole menagerie of animals.

NANA UPSTAIRS &
NANA DOWNSTAIRS   [172]

Written and illustrated by Tomie dePaola
Cloth: Putman
Paper: Puffin
Published: 1973

As a grown-up, Tommy remembers the rituals of his visits to the house his active grandmother (Nana Downstairs) shared with his bedridden, ninety-four-year-old great-grandmother (Nana Upstairs), both of whom he loved dearly. Death is a fact, presented and accepted. Even now Tommy sees the Nanas' spirits in shooting stars. A very fine book.

THE NAPPING HOUSE   [173]

Written by Audrey Wood
Illustrated by Don Wood
Cloth: HBJ
Published: 1983   Prizes: New York Times Best Illustrated Book

A silly, sleepy tale set in a blue house in a blue world, in which all the sleeping creatures in the house—child, cat, dog, and more—drift into Granny's bed in a great cuddly heap.

THE NATIVITY   [174]

Illustrated by Julie Vivas
Cloth: HBJ
Published: 1988

Most illustrated versions of the Nativity aim for authenticity of illustration or are set in medieval or Gothic costume, reflecting the great art

[174]

of those periods. In this gloriously relaxed, universally contemporary people's Nativity (using the King James text), the angel Gabriel wears boots and talks to the Virgin Mary over a cup of coffee. She grows truly huge with child. And the baby, oh the baby, he's plump and real and everything sweet the world ever saw. In these light, sandy-toned watercolors, the loose-limbed people have a slightly blurred and disheveled quality. This appealing retelling is especially accessible and plausible to very young children, but it would be difficult to outgrow its charms.

THE NIGHT BEFORE CHRISTMAS   [175]

Written by Clement C. Moore
Illustrated by Anita Lobel
Cloth: Knopf
Paper: Knopf
Published: 1984

The ultimate New York (or, rather, Brooklyn, where Moore lived) edition of the Christmas verse, with illustrations set in an authentic and cozy Victorian brownstone house there with the Brooklyn Bridge in the background. There are many other editions available, from the 1912 version with illustrations by Jessie W. Smith to James Marshall's (cartoonish), Cyndy Szekeres (cuddly), and Wendy Watson's (country).

NO NAP   [176]

Written by Eve Bunting
Illustrated by Susan Meddaugh
Cloth: Clarion
Published: 1990

Instead of taking her nap, Susie exhausts her daddy. When Mommy comes home, the house is a mess and guess who is asleep? A cautionary tale with winning illustrations. The demonic look in Susie's eye when she is the center of the domestic hurricane may be familiar.

[176]

NOT SO FAST, SONGOLOLO [177]

Written and illustrated by Nicki Daly
Cloth: McElderry
Paper: Puffin
Published: 1986

Cheerful, detailed watercolor illustrations accompany the story of little Malusi and his trip to the city with his granny to buy what in South Africa are called tackies and what American children know as sneakers. The simple daily quality of the expedition is part of the book's charm.

[177]

NOTHING EVER HAPPENS
ON MY BLOCK [178]

Written and illustrated by Ellen Raskin
Paper: Aladdin
Published: 1966   **Prizes: New York Times Best Illustrated Book**

A jewel-like example of ironic storytelling with droll illustration. Chester Filbert sits on his stoop, complaining that nothing ever happens on his block, while all around him there is mystery, excitement, and adventure—witches, fires, robbery, mayhem. All ages find it fresh and funny. The trick in reading it aloud is "reading" everything that is happening as well as the text.

[178]

Picture Books

NUTSHELL LIBRARY [179]

Written and illustrated by Maurice Sendak
Cloth: Harper & Row/HarperCollins
Published: 1962

These four little books—*Alligators All Around: An Alphabet; Chicken Soup with Rice: A Book of Months; One Was Johnny: A Counting Book;* and *Pierre: A Cautionary Tale in Five Chapters and a Prologue*—come in a small box, fit in small hands, and are memorable both separately and together. In addition, they are the source of the lyrics to many of the best, catchiest songs in *Really Rosie,* the TV special/video/play, with music by Carole King. The whole family may well end up singing the words from memory.

OH, A-HUNTING WE WILL GO [180]

Written by John Langstaff
Illustrated by Nancy Winslow Parker
Cloth: McElderry
Published: 1974

A very jolly version of the familiar folk song, with piano and guitar accompaniment.

[181]

ON MARKET STREET [181]

Written by Arnold Lobel
Illustrated by Anita Lobel
Cloth: Greenwillow
Paper: Mulberry
Published: 1981

Prizes: Caldecott Honor
New York Times Best Illustrated Book

In this unusual and lavish alphabet book, a boy goes down Market Street buying presents for a friend, beginning with each letter of the alphabet. The letters are figures made of apples, quilts, wigs, and so on.

ONCE A MOUSE . . . [182]

Written and illustrated by Marcia Brown
Cloth: Scribner's
Paper: Aladdin
Published: 1961

Prizes: Caldecott Medal
New York Times Best Illustrated Book

A reconsideration of magic in a successful picture book. A hermit transforms a mouse successively into a car, a dog, a tiger. But the tiger is so proud the hermit pauses.

[184]

ONE FINE DAY [183]

Written and illustrated by Nonny Hogrogian
Cloth: Macmillan
Paper: Aladdin
Published: 1971

Prizes: Caldecott Medal

In this wittily illustrated Armenian folktale, a sly fox steals milk from an old woman. She gets her revenge and his tail.

ONE FISH TWO FISH RED FISH BLUE FISH [184]

Written and illustrated by Dr. Seuss
Cloth: Random House (Beginner Books)
Published: 1960

Designed as an early reader using rhyme and very limited vocabulary, this collection of verses about Seussian creatures at play and rest is wildly successful with toddlers and younger children, and remains endurable to the reading adult who recites it night after night.

[185]

ONE GORILLA: A COUNTING BOOK [185]

Written and illustrated by Atsuko Morozumi
Cloth: Farrar, Straus & Giroux
Published: 1990

Prizes: New York Times Best Illustrated Book

A large gorilla with a sweet, expressive face busies himself in a variety of outdoor settings, allowing young readers to appreciate his charm and grace, and also to count things. There is a surprising lyricism and lushness to the airy illustrations.

[186]

101 THINGS TO DO WITH A BABY   [186]

Written and illustrated by Jan Ormerod

Cloth: Lothrop, Lee & Shepard

Paper: Puffin

Published: 1984

A catalog of activities is also a record of a day in the life of a family with a father, an active older sister, a dear baby, and a black cat. Mother is the loving artist. The three-color illustrations and gentle domestic ideas are both enchanting and encouraging. A book for siblings of many ages.

1 HUNTER   [187]

Written and illustrated by Pat Hutchins

Cloth: Greenwillow

Paper: Mulberry

Published: 1982

A counting book that is both comic and suspenseful, because 1 hunter going through the jungle does not see 2 elephants or 3 giraffes, but they see him. And so on.

ONE MONDAY MORNING   [188]

Written and illustrated by Uri Shulevitz

Cloth: Scribner's

Paper: Aladdin

Published: 1967

In this fine urban fantasy, a little boy who lives in an old apartment building in a downtown somewhere imagines that the king and queen are coming to visit him. But since he's very busy, he misses them on each return visit. Meanwhile their retinue grows, so that while the text remains disarmingly simple, the illustrations grow increasingly complex.

[188]

[189]

THE ORCHARD BOOK OF NURSERY RHYMES [189]

Written by Zena Sutherland
Illustrated by Faith Jacques
Cloth: Orchard Books
Published: 1990

The texts are known so well they are family, as loved and sturdy as they can be. The illustrations in this handsome collection have been charmingly set in eighteenth-century Europe, with lots of details to study and discuss. Gregory Griggs's twenty-seven wigs, for example.

OVER AND OVER [190]

Written by Charlotte Zolotow
Illustrated by Garth Williams
Cloth: Harper & Row/HarperCollins
Published: 1957

Very little children don't understand the passage of time very well. The girl in this story makes a birthday wish for things to happen again and, day by day, then week by week, and month by month, they do. The charming illustrations capture the passing seasons in her year.

PAT THE BUNNY [191]

Written and illustrated by Dorothy Kunhardt
Cloth: Golden/Western
Published: 1942

The original baby's activity book—pat the bunny, feel Daddy's scratchy face, look in the mirror, put your finger through Mummy's ring. Some babies love it, eat several copies before they have even learned to walk. Be reassured that others could care less, and it is not a litmus test of future literary taste either way.

[188]

Picture Books

PEABODY [192]

Written and illustrated by Rosemary Wells
Cloth: Dial
Paper: Pied Piper
Published: 1983
Peabody is Annie's teddy bear and everything is just fine till Annie gets a walking, talking doll. This plays nicely on a story familiar to grown-ups. Like the plain brown nightingale, the familiar teddy proves best.

THE PEARL [193]

Written and illustrated by Helme Heine
Cloth: McElderry
Published: 1985
Playing by the pond one day, Beaver finds a mussel and is sure it contains a pearl. In his dream the pearl causes nothing but dissension and strife among his friends. This cautionary tale by the German artist is illustrated with his usual wit and charm.

PETUNIA [194]

Written and illustrated by Roger Duvoisin
Cloth: Knopf
Paper: Knopf
Published: 1958
Some creatures never do seem to learn, but Petunia, a very silly goose, thinks if she carries a book around the barnyard, she will be wise. There are five stories about her collected in *Petunia, the Silly Goose Stories*.

[195]

PIGGYBOOK [195]

Written and illustrated by Anthony Browne
Cloth: Knopf
Paper: Knopf
Published: 1986
Mr. Piggott and the boys, are, as the note Mrs. Piggott leaves them says, pigs, and she is tired of doing all the "unimportant" household main-

tenance jobs without any help. And lo, they turn into pigs. Clever illustrations underscore the basic feminist/humanist/real-life point about cooperation in the home.

[197]

THE PIGS' WEDDING [196]

Written and illustrated by Helme Heine
Cloth: McElderry
Published: 1979

What do you think would happen at the pigs' wedding? In fact, the answers given in the full-color whimsical illustrations are full of surprises.

POOKINS GETS HER WAY [197]

Written by Helen Lester
Illustrated by Lynn Munsinger
Cloth: Houghton Mifflin
Paper: Houghton Mifflin
Published: 1987

Pookins is spoiled rotten, and by golly, today she wants to be a flower. She gets her way but learns a lesson about cooperation. The author and illustrator have produced a group of funny/wise picture books that make small but important lessons lightly. Other titles include *A Porcupine Named Fluffy* and *It Wasn't My Fault. Tacky the Penguin* is also fine.

POPPY THE PANDA [198]

Written and illustrated by Dick Gackenbach
Cloth: Clarion
Paper: Clarion
Published: 1984

Poppy the Panda, who belongs to Katie O'Keefe, wants a special costume and Katie does her best, but nothing satisfies Poppy until Katie's mother tries her idea. A nice book for preschoolers with strong notions about getting dressed.

POSSUM COME A-KNOCKIN'   [199]

Written by Nancy Van Laan
Illustrated by George Booth
Cloth: Knopf
Published: 1990

The folks are inside doing more or less ordinary things and then this possum in a top hat and vest comes to the back door. The reader is somewhere outside looking at the mayhem that ensues as the cat and dog rouse the household. Manic illustrations. The cumulative rhyme is in an easy-to-read dialect.

POTATOES, POTATOES   [200]

Written and illustrated by Anita Lobel
Paper: HarperCollins
Published: 1984

Two generals are reconciled after a battle over their mother's only remaining potato field. In other words, a fable about war and peace in picture-book form, with illustrations that are suggestive, not preachy.

RACHEL FISTER'S BLISTER   [201]

Written by Amy McDonald
Illustrated by Marjorie Priceman
Cloth: Houghton Mifflin
Published: 1990

If you are going to start with a silly rhyme—say, one that begins "Rachel Fister found a blister on her little left-hand toe," it needs to get sillier and sillier till Queen Alice decrees, in advice "quite precise," the proper cure: a mother's kiss. The illustrations are properly ebullient.

THE RAFFI SINGABLE SONGBOOK   [202]

Written by Raffi
Illustrated by Joyce Yamoroto
Paper: Crown
Published: 1987

Sing along with your records and tapes, boys and girls, mothers and dads. This spiral-bound collection of the Canadian singer's song arrangements is pleasing. There is *The Second Raffi Songbook* as well, and favorites have been illustrated amusingly in separate editions, including *Shake My Sillies Out* and *Down by the Bay*.

[203]

READ-ALOUD RHYMES FOR THE VERY YOUNG   [203]

Written by Jack Prelutsky
Illustrated by Marc Brown
Cloth: Knopf
Published: 1986

A fine, brightly illustrated collection of more than 200 rhymes, mostly familiar, ideal for reading aloud to young children. An introduction by Jim Trelease emphasizes the importance of reading aloud.

THE REAL MOTHER GOOSE   [204]

Written and illustrated by Blanche Fisher Wright
Cloth: Checkerboard
Published: 1916

This selection from the Mother Goose canon comes in a distinctive checkerboard binding and has delightful old-fashioned illustrations. It is, indeed, one that great-grandparents and grandparents first read. It has also been adapted, cut up into smaller selections of verses about animals, children, playtime, and so on.

THE RELATIVES CAME   [205]

Written by Cynthia Rylant
Illustrated by Stephen Gammell
Cloth: Bradbury
Published: 1985   Prizes: Caldecott Honor and New York Times Best Illustrated Book

One summer, a whole slew of relatives gets up before dawn to come on down and visit. They crowd the house, create the happiest kind of chaos and commotion, but eventually have to leave. The spiky illustrations capture the homey confusion and delight of a childhood event that memory does not blur. A real charmer.

[199]

RICHARD SCARRY'S
BEST WORD BOOK EVER   [206]

Written and illustrated by Richard Scarry
Cloth: Golden/Western
Published: 1963

Most adults find this book unappealing—the pages are crowded with details, jumbles of jokes, and anthropomorphized creatures like Lowely Worm involved in running jokes. But they are adults. Children, especially toddlers and preschoolers, consider it almost endlessly interesting, full of things to label, activities to imagine, and jokes to savor again and again. If you remember it from your own childhood and think this edition is slimmer, you are right—it has been abridged, but the dental hygienist is still a walrus. There is also *Richard Scarry's Best Mother Goose Ever.*

ROAR AND MORE   [207]

Written and illustrated by Karla Kuskin
Cloth: Harper & Row/HarperCollins
Paper: Harper Trophy
Published: 1956; reissued 1990

The new full-color edition of this delightful standard title for the very young actually does enhance the short, funny verses about animals and the amusing typographical representation of their sounds.

ROSIE'S WALK   [208]

Written and illustrated by Pat Hutchins
Cloth: Macmillan
Paper: Aladdin
Published: 1968

Rosie the hen goes for a stroll around the barnyard, oblivious to the fox, who keeps botching his attempts to catch her. If the jokes are all telegraphed to the adult eye, that doesn't make them a whit less funny to toddlers and preschoolers.

[208]

ROTTEN RALPH   [209]

Written by Jack Gantos
Illustrated by Nicole Rubel
Cloth: Houghton Mifflin
Paper: Houghton Mifflin
Published: 1976

[211]

This is the first of a series of books about a very naughty cat named Ralph. Sarah, his owner, can never believe how badly he behaves, but oh, the reader can. The illustrations are distinctive and offbeat. Other titles are *Rotten Ralph's Rotten Christmas* and *Worse Than Rotten Ralph*.

THE RUNAWAY BUNNY   [210]

Written by Margaret Wise Brown
Illustrated by Clement Hurd
Cloth: Harper & Row/HarperCollins
Paper: Harper Trophy
Published: 1972

The little bunny plays a pretend game of hide-and-seek and is comforted to realize that his mother will always know how to find him wherever he hides. The illustrations are wonderful—very young children love spotting the bunny in the garden, on the mountain, at the circus. Some grown-ups think the mother's absolute authority is smothering and prefer other, more reassuring measurements of how much a mother loves her child.

THE SANDMAN   [211]

Written and illustrated by Ron Shepperson
Cloth: Farrar, Straus & Giroux
Paper: Sunburst
Published: 1989

Jay stays up one night to see if the sandman will really come. He does. Turns out he's a cross of the best of Paul Bunyan, Pete Seeger, and the Cat in the Hat. It's a night full of wonderful mischief, remembered as if a dream. The text is minimal, the illustrations are wonderfully rich and full of loony details that merit close inspection. The sandman delivers sand in a green wheelbarrow, a baker and a milkman deliver the refreshments, the toy fire truck and firemen seem to be living independent lives.

Picture Books

17 KINGS AND 42 ELEPHANTS   [212]

Written by Margaret Mahy
Illustrated by Patricia McCarthy
Cloth: Dial
Paper: Pied Piper
Published: 1987   Prizes: New York Times Best Illustrated Book

A glorious nonsense verse about royalty and pachyderms trundling through the jungle one mysterious night, illustrated handsomely in batik fabric designs.

SHEEP IN A JEEP   [213]

Written by Nancy Shaw
Illustrated by Margot Apple
Cloth: Houghton Mifflin
Paper: Houghton Mifflin
Published: 1986

What a ride! On a bright, sunny day a flock of sheep set off for a ride in a jeep. The short (83 words), chantable text is great fun for toddlers and preschoolers in particular. The equally delightful, but definitely difficult to speak, sequels are called *Sheep on a Ship* and *Sheep in a Shop*.

SHY CHARLES   [214]

Written and illustrated by Rosemary Wells
Cloth: Dial
Paper: Pied Piper
Published: 1988

It happens that Charles is perfectly happy playing by himself, and social contacts are an endless ordeal. The little mouse can't or won't say thank you in public places, can't or won't cope with dancing lessons or football. But when the baby-sitter falls down the stairs, Charles is able to

[214]

comfort her and call for help on the telephone before resuming his shy silence. A nicely told fable as helpful for their parents as for shy children in need of respect.

SING A SONG OF PEOPLE   [215]

Written by Lois Lenski
Illustrated by Giles Laroche
Cloth: Little, Brown
Published: 1987

Lois Lenski's poem about cultural diversity is set to extraordinary illustrations composed of three-dimensional paper figures depicting downtown Boston in the 1980s. The effect is enchanting even to non-New Englanders.

THE SKY IS FULL OF SONG   [216]

Written by Lee Bennett Hopkins
Illustrated by Dirk Zimmer
Cloth: Harper & Row/HarperCollins
Paper: Harper Trophy
Published: 1983

A very small book for small hands to hold—an anthology of short, seasonal poems, from fall to fall, perfect for early readers, with light and airy wood-block illustrations that complement the verses.

THE SNOWY DAY   [217]

Written and illustrated by Ezra Jack Keats
Cloth: Viking
Paper: Puffin
Published: 1962   Prizes: Caldecott Medal

One snowy day, a little black boy named Peter put on his red snowsuit and explored his city neighborhood. The brightly colored collage illustrations have an undiminished freshness . . . like new-fallen snow itself. Peter also appears in *Goggles, A Letter to Amy, Peter's Chair,* and the delightful *Whistle for Willie.*

[217]

Picture Books

SNUGGLE PIGGY AND THE MAGIC BLANKET [218]

Written by Michele Stepto
Illustrated by John Himmelman
Cloth: Dutton
Paper: Unicorn
Published: 1967

One day Snuggle Piggy's magically beautiful security blanket is left on the line when it begins to rain. He has a satisfying dream adventure to rationalize the situation.

SONG OF THE SWALLOWS [219]

Written and illustrated by Leo Politi
Cloth: Scribner's
Paper: Aladdin
Published: 1949   Prizes: Caldecott Medal

The story of the swallows who come each year to Capistrano is told here through young Juan and old Julian, who lived in the town a long time ago. Although the story remains fresh and interesting, to adult eyes the prizewinning art may seem cartoonish and dated.

SPECTACLES [220]

Written and illustrated by Ellen Raskin
Paper: Aladdin
Published: 1968   Prizes: New York Times Best Illustrated Book

What is ordinary? Iris Fogel sees remarkable things such as couches that look like hippos, until her mother figures out that she is myopic and needs glasses. This book manages to be funny and helpful at the same time.

STONE SOUP [221]

Written and illustrated by Marcia Brown
Cloth: Scribner's
Paper: Aladdin
Published: 1947

This is a large-format, old-fashioned, and very charming version of the familiar story featuring distinctively French peasants and soldiers. No

[223]

one in the village will offer hospitality to three hungry soldiers—the stone soup they prepare teaches the virtue of cooperation.

THE STONECUTTER: A JAPANESE FOLKTALE   [222]

Written and illustrated by Gerald McDermott
Cloth: Viking
Paper: Puffin
Published: 1975
A handsomely told version of a traditional Japanese folktale about a foolish man's grandiose longings and greed. The illustrations are dramatic and somewhat austere.

THE STORY OF FERDINAND   [223]

Written by Munro Leaf
Illustrated by Robert Lawson
Cloth: Viking
Paper: Puffin
Published: 1936
Ferdinand the bull does not want to go into the ring and fight; he really wants to sit under the cork tree and smell the flowers. A funny, wise story more than half a century old, and fresh as the daisy Ferdinand loves so well. (Some things change, but adults will be pleased to see that corks still grow on the cork trees here.)

THE STORY OF JUMPING MOUSE   [224]

Written and illustrated by John Steptoe
Cloth: Lothrop, Lee & Shepard
Paper: Mulberry
Published: 1984   Prizes: Caldecott Honor
A Great Plains Indian legend about how the mouse was transformed and finally found the far-off land, retold in a handsome edition with large, mysterious black-and-white illustrations.

[223]

77

Picture Books

A STORY, A STORY [225]

Written and illustrated by Gail E. Haley

Cloth: Atheneum
Paper: Aladdin
Published: 1970   Prizes: Caldecott Medal

One of the African tales of Anansi the spider. In this episode, dramatically illustrated in full color in a style that evokes African images, he brings to earth all the stories owned by the Sky God.

SWAN SKY [226]

Written and illustrated by Tejima

Cloth: Philomel
Published: 1988   Prizes: New York Times Best Illustrated Book

A companion of sorts to the beautiful and celebratory *Fox's Dream*, this story by a Japanese master, using astonishingly supple woodcuts, tells of the illness and death of a mother swan as spring arrives and her family must leave and fly to their summer home. Do not grieve. On their arrival she appears as the brilliant white blaze of the summer sky. An enthralling and comforting story from nature.

SWIMMY [227]

Written and illustrated by Leo Lionni

Cloth: Pantheon
Paper: Knopf   Prizes: Caldecott Honor
Published: 1963   New York Times Best Illustrated Book

Little Swimmy is alone in the sea. The rest of his school was swallowed by a tuna, but he figures out a camouflage plan for survival. It is a delightful tale told with minimal text and elegant collage illustrations.

THE TALE OF PETER RABBIT [228]

Written and illustrated by Beatrix Potter

Cloth: Frederick Warne
Published: 1902

Flopsy, Mopsy, and Cottontail are good little bunnies, but Peter disobeys and goes to Mr. MacGregor's garden, with nearly disastrous consequences. One of the best known and best loved stories for children,

[228]

Peter Rabbit is dramatic, exciting, and complete all on a very small scale. The watercolor illustrations are exquisite. The original Warne editions, with their smooth paper and trim green binding, small to hold in the hand, were rephotographed and reissued in 1987 and are as readily available and inexpensive as, and far nicer than, any others. But others abound. There are all sorts of auxiliary books and merchandise as well: coloring, cutout, pop-up books, etc. Some are well done, others sloppy and exploitative; choose carefully among them. Peter's immediate relative is, of course, *The Tale of Benjamin Bunny*, but some of the other books in the canon are *The Tale of Squirrel Nutkin, The Tale of Mrs. Tiggy-Winkle, The Tale of Tom Kitten,* and *The Tale of Jemima Puddle-Duck.*

TEDDY BEARS CURE A COLD   [229]

Written and illustrated by Suzanna Gretz
Cloth: Four Winds
Published: 1985
His friends take care of William the teddy bear when he first catches the cold, but he gets so cranky that they leave him mostly alone to let nature take its course. The illustrations are wonderful. Never has a head cold been personified so well as in William's half-lidded, red-nosed face. The same crew of bears (who look like children in teddy bear costumes) also appear in *Teddy Bears Go Shopping, Teddy Bears' Moving Day,* and *Teddy Bears' ABC,* and board books for toddlers *I'm Not Sleepy, Ready for Bed,* and *Hide and Seek.*

THE TEENY-TINY WOMAN   [230]

Written and illustrated by Paul Galdone
Cloth: Clarion
Paper: Clarion
Published: 1984
The teeny-tiny woman hides the teeny-tiny bone she finds in the teeny-tiny churchyard. A slightly scary and mostly funny old English ghost story, retold with enthusiasm. Other versions have been illustrated by Tomie dePaola and Jane O'Conner.

[228]

79

Picture Books

TELL ME A STORY, MAMA [231]

Written by Angela Johnson
Illustrated by David Soman
Cloth: Orchard Books
Published: 1989

It's bedtime, snuggle time, and the little girl asks for a story about when her mother was little, and then proceeds to help, indeed to tell it herself. The child's version is beguiling.

TEN, NINE, EIGHT [232]

Written and illustrated by Molly Bang
Cloth: Greenwillow
Paper: Mulberry
Published: 1983   Prizes: Caldecott Honor

This is both a bedtime and a counting book. The story, told in lush and soothing illustrations, is about the bedtime rituals of one little girl and her father.

[232]

THIS IS BETSY [233]

Written and illustrated by Gunilla Wolde
Cloth: Random House
Published: 1982

Small, bright books about an engaging preschooler's ordinary experiences. Titles in the series include *Betsy's Baby Brother, Betsy's First Day at Nursery School, Betsy and the Doctor,* as well as *Betsy's First Day at Day Care* and *Betsy and the Chicken Pox.* The illustrations are simple and appealing. Check with a library for titles in paperback.

THE THREE BILLY GOATS GRUFF [234]

Written and illustrated by Paul Galdone
Cloth: Clarion
Paper: Clarion
Published: 1973

The troll in this large-format version of the familiar folktale is truly loathsome. Happily, the billy goats are quite fearless as they trit-trot over that bridge to the meadow full of sweet grass and bright daisies.

There are many other editions, but the one by Marcia Brown also has a classic quality.

[233]

THE THREE LITTLE PIGS   [235]

Written and illustrated by Margot Zemach
Cloth: Farrar, Straus & Giroux
Paper: Sunburst
Published: 1988

In this pretty and amusing version of the familiar story, the wolf wears a frock coat while the pigs are downright ragtag. There are, of course, many other editions, including an exuberant one by Paul Galdone, a roisterous slapstick one by James Marshall, and one by William G. Hooks, in which the clever pig is a female. The deconstructed truth has been revealed in *The True Story of the 3 Little Pigs.*

THE THREE ROBBERS   [236]

Written and illustrated by Tomi Ungerer
Cloth: Atheneum
Paper: Aladdin
Published: 1962

This eternally modern, alarming, funny-scary story is in its original large format. The three fierce black robbers gallop across the pages unchecked until the girl named Tiffany changes their lives. The natural audience for the story is made up of school-age children and adults.

THROUGH MOON AND STARS AND NIGHT SKY   [237]

Written by Ann Warren Turner
Illustrated by James Graham Hale
Cloth: Harper & Row/HarperCollins
Published: 1990

Every child loves his or her birth or arrival story. The family of this adopted Asian child retell the story of his arrival on a huge plane that came through the night sky. He found parents, house, red dog, and quilt waiting. The prose is lyric, the tone universally reassuring.

[235]

THY FRIEND OBADIAH [238]

Written and illustrated by Brinton Turkle
Paper: Puffin
Published: 1969   Prizes: Caldecott Honor

One of a number of books about the Starbuck family of Nantucket, nineteenth-century Quakers, featuring Obadiah and his sister, Rachel. The illustrations are full of period detail that are easy to discuss. The others are *Rachel and Obadiah, Obadiah the Bold,* and *The Adventures of Obadiah.*

TIKKI TIKKI TEMBO [239]

Written by Arlene Mosel
Illustrated by Blair Lent
Cloth: Henry Holt
Paper: Henry Holt
Published: 1968

This story about how Chinese children came to have short names has been chanted by generations of nursery-school children. Help can be summoned for brother Chang, but for Tikki Tikki Tembo, it's more problematic. Teenagers and adults, too, remember and find themselves absently mumbling that wonderful rolling name: "Tikki Tikki Tembo No Sa Rembo Chari Bari Ruchi Pip Peri Pembo."

[238]

TOMIE dePAOLA'S MOTHER GOOSE [240]

Written and illustrated by Tomie dePaola
Cloth: Putnam
Published: 1985

A buoyant collection of some two hundred familiar verses and rhymes illustrated in dePaola's characteristic bright and stylized manner.

TORTILLITAS PARA MAMMA: AND OTHER SPANISH NURSERY RHYMES [241]

Written by Margot C. Griego
Illustrated by Barbara Cooney
Cloth: Henry Holt
Paper: Henry Holt
Published: 1981

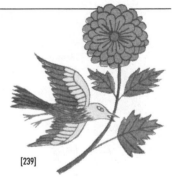
[239]

Enchanting folkloric illustrations accompany a selection of delightful rhymes from Latin America. The words are given in both Spanish and English and are accompanied by suggestions for finger play.

TOUCH! TOUCH! [242]

Written by Riki Levinson
Illustrated by True Kelley
Cloth: Dutton
Published: 1987

This adorable person in overalls and sailor hat is a total terror as he lurches through the house with hands covered with cake batter. It's a funny, messy domestic adventure, the sort that will please toddlers and tickle their slightly older siblings as well.

A TRIP TO THE DOCTOR [243]

Written by Margot Linn
Illustrated by Catherine Siracusa
Cloth: Harper & Row/HarperCollins
Published: 1988

Each double-page spread in this foldout-page book consists of a question about a visit to the doctor, with three possible answers. There is at least one laugh for even a very small child on each page. Who is going to weigh and measure Joey? The nurse. What will he stand on? A stool, a skateboard, or the scale? The doctor has a friendly puppy hand puppet.

THE TUB PEOPLE [244]

Written by Pam Conrad
Illustrated by Richard Egielski
Cloth: Harper & Row/HarperCollins
Paper: Harper Trophy
Published: 1989

The tub people are little dolls who look startlingly like Fisher-Price toys, live on the bathtub ledge, and play in the water. One day the little tub boy is sucked down the drain. Never fear, he is rescued. The illustrations are large, round, stolid, and although charming, seem static to an adult eye at first or even thirtieth reading. But very young children hear the emotions described in the text, concentrate, and believe in those pictures and believe in them intensely.

THE TWELVE DAYS OF CHRISTMAS [245]

Written and illustrated by Jan Brett
Cloth: Dodd, Mead/Putnam
Published: 1986

This version of the Christmas carol is bright and gay, with jewel-like, detailed illustrations embellished with the artist's characteristic style of folk-art borders and embroidery-like patterns. There are other editions, including a mysteriously romantic one by Louise Brierley, and *Emma's Christmas*, which is an amusing variation.

UP GOES THE SKYSCRAPER [246]

Written and illustrated by Gail Gibbons
Cloth: Four Winds
Published: 1986

A wonderfully clear account of how a skyscraper is built, from drawing up the plans and digging the foundation to moving the tenants into their offices. Recommended for adults who accompany small children on city walks and don't know the difference between an H beam and an I beam.

[246]

[246]

[245]

THE VERY BUSY SPIDER   [247]

Written and illustrated by Eric Carle
Cloth: Philomel
Published: 1985
The spider spins her web in raised lines, making this remarkable picture book accessible for both sighted and blind children.

THE VERY HUNGRY CATERPILLAR   [248]

Written and illustrated by Eric Carle
Cloth: Philomel
Paper: Philomel
Published: 1969
The very hungry caterpillar eats his way through his life cycle and the cutout pages of this classic picture book until he becomes a butterfly. If you are going to buy it, this is a book to have in the original hardback edition, with its large format and stiff pages, because little fingers need to poke through the holes in the apple, pear, strawberry, and other edibles. The miniature paperback edition just isn't strong enough or large enough.

WAITING FOR MAMA   [249]

Written by Beatrice Schenk de Regniers
Illustrated by Victoria de Larrea
Cloth: Clarion
Published: 1984
A little girl sits under a tree, as she is told to, and imagines a whole lifetime passing by while she waits for her mother to finish an errand. She might grow up, get married, have children, even grandchildren, before the shopping is finally done.

[248]

WASHDAY ON NOAH'S ARK   [250]

Written and illustrated by Glen Rounds
Cloth: Holiday
Paper: Holiday
Published: 1985

If you stop to think about it, the question of how they did the washing on Noah's Ark is a reasonable and difficult one. The answer propounded here, which involves a living laundry line, is hilarious, as are the illustrations.

WAVING: A COUNTING BOOK   [251]

Written and illustrated by Peter Sis
Cloth: Greenwillow
Published: 1988

There is so much friendly activity in this delightful urban counting book. The action begins as Mary and her mother wave at "1 taxi." Then, "2 bicyclists waved back at her" and "3 boys walking dogs waved at the bicyclists." Soon the streets are full of people, not to mention the interesting neighborhood buildings and things to look at and talk about in addition to the accumulating numbers. In *Beach Ball,* Mary runs off after a striped ball and her mother follows her through illustrations that convey concepts including number, alphabet, size. There's even a maze.

[252]

WE'RE GOING ON A BEAR HUNT   [252]

Written by Michael Rosen
Illustrated by Helen Oxenbury
Cloth: McElderry
Published: 1989

The whole family sets out, but catching a bear isn't like going to the corner for a quart of milk. Oh, no! Slog through grass, mud, snow, forest, river, on to the cave, and then—whoops!—rush back home again.

THE WEDDING PROCESSION OF THE RAG DOLL AND THE BROOM HANDLE AND WHO WAS IN IT [253]

Written by Carl Sandburg
Illustrated by Harriet Pincus
Cloth: HBJ
Paper: Voyager
Published: 1967

A glorious setting for an excerpt from the *Rootabaga Stories* about a fine procession that includes Spoon Lickers, Dirty Bibs, Musical Soup Eaters, and others. The angular illustrations are eccentric and funny. Perfect for bedtime reading aloud together.

WENDY WATSON'S MOTHER GOOSE [254]

Written and illustrated by Wendy Watson
Cloth: Lothrop, Lee & Shepard
Published: 1990

The verses are so familiar, an artist has great freedom in organizing a setting for the rhymes we call Mother Goose. This selection is placed in cozy New England: pretty towns, pleasant woods, chubby folks in comfortable houses. Lots of snow.

WHAT DO YOU SAY, DEAR?/ WHAT DO YOU DO, DEAR? [255]

Written by Sesyle Joslin
Illustrated by Maurice Sendak
Cloth: Harper & Row/HarperCollins
Paper: Harper Trophy
Published: 1958

Prizes: Caldecott Honor
New York Times Best Illustrated Book

As the syndicated etiquette columnist Miss Manners has reminded us regularly, good manners are a matter of constant practice. These two books, out of print for many years, are wonderfully instructive. By

[252]

placing those basic responses every child must learn in ludicrous, impossible situations, the whole subject becomes positively palatable. "What do you say when you bump into a crocodile on a busy street?"

WHAT'S INSIDE?　[256]

Written and illustrated by Satoshi Kitamura
Cloth: Farrar, Straus & Giroux
Paper: Sunburst
Published: 1985

This imaginative and handsomely illustrated alphabet book, set in what looks like a run-down district of London, involves clever puzzles and concealment as each page not only contains two letters and words using them, but the next letters to come.

WHEN THE NEW BABY COMES I'M MOVING OUT　[257]

Written and illustrated by Martha Alexander
Cloth: Dial
Paper: Pied Piper
Published: 1971

Oliver's problem is pretty clear, but he learns to cope. There is a related title, also low-key and comic, *Nobody Asked Me If I Wanted a Baby Sister.*

WHEN THE TIDE IS LOW　[258]

[261]

Written by Sheila Cole
Illustrated by Virginia Wright-Frierson
Cloth: Lothrop, Lee & Shepard
Published: 1985

A little girl is very anxious to get to the beach, but it's not time yet, and meanwhile, as she swings up and down on her swing, her mother answers her questions about what they will see "when the tide is low." The illustrations add to the spirit of this subtle and informative book.

WHEN YOU WERE A BABY [259]

Written and illustrated by Ann Jonas
Cloth: Greenwillow
Paper: Mulberry
Published: 1982

A book for toddlers and preschoolers who find great pleasure, and also reassurance, in being reminded of the times when they were little and helpless. All examples end with "but now you can . . ."

WHERE ARE YOU GOING, LITTLE MOUSE? [260]

Written by Robert Kraus
Illustrated by Jose Aruego and Ariane Dewey
Cloth: Greenwillow
Paper: Mulberry
Published: 1986

[260]

Having decided that no one loves him, Little Mouse sees nothing left to do but run away from home. He gets to the nearest phone booth, and his parents come to the rescue. Earlier books *Whose Mouse Are You?* and *Come Out and Play, Little Mouse* complete the trilogy.

WHERE THE WILD THINGS ARE [261]

Written and illustrated by Maurice Sendak
Cloth: Harper & Row/HarperCollins
Paper: Harper Trophy
Published: 1963

Prizes: Caldecott Medal
New York Times Best Illustrated Book

This is the story of the night Max wore his wolf suit and was sent to bed supperless, only to dream a strange, wild, violent, and glorious dream and then return to where he is loved best of all. It is perhaps the greatest picture book of permission for young children, acknowledging and allowing the terrible temper and urge for independence that they feel but cannot fully act upon. The illustrations remain fresh and funny/scary, only time passes.

[261]

Picture Books

WHERE'S SPOT? [262]

Written and illustrated by Eric Hill
Cloth: Putnam
Published: 1980

Sally cannot find her puppy, Spot, and goes searching, and behind the flap on each double-page illustration is something silly—there's a striped snake in the clock, a funny lion under the stairs. Perfectly wonderful nonsense, satisfying to children of most early ages. This is the first and the best in a large and generally successful series. Other good titles are *Spot's First Walk*, *Spot's First Christmas*, and *Spot Goes to School.*

WHERE'S THE BEAR? [263]

Written by Charlotte Pomerantz
Illustrated by Byron Barton
Cloth: Greenwillow
Published: 1984

This story of how a bear is sighted in the forest and how the villagers respond is brilliantly told in just seven words of text. The bold illustrations capture a breathless, exciting chase. Great fun to read aloud with the very young.

WHERE'S THE BABY? [264]

Written and illustrated by Pat Hutchins
Cloth: Greenwillow
Published: 1988

That humorously hideous family first seen in *The Very Worst Monster* is back, and this time, little Hazel helps her mother and grandmother

[262]

follow the baby monster's muddy tracks as he wreaks havoc through the entire house. Very pleasing to preschoolers with younger siblings.

WHISKERS & RHYMES   [265]

Written and illustrated by Arnold Lobel
Cloth: Greenwillow
Paper: Mulberry
Published: 1985
In this collection of delightful nonsense verses the conceit is that they are all illustrated by cats—dandified cats in old-fashioned costumes, perhaps visiting from the eighteenth century.

WHO SAID RED?   [266]

Written by Mary Serfozo
Illustrated by Keiko Narahashi
Cloth: McElderry
Paper: Aladdin
Published: 1988
The simple text here is a happy rhyming chat between two children, siblings perhaps, about color, very specific colors like "cherry, berry, very red" and "slicker yellow" and "green bean green" and the happy, mysterious rainbow illustrations are full of funny things. It's a beguiling book for the very young and pleasing to say aloud again and again. The pretty watercolor illustrations have an airy charm. In *Who Wants One?* they continue their conversation and discuss numbers—"One butterfly, one raisin bun/One rainbow coming with the sun."

WHO SANK THE BOAT?   [267]

Written and illustrated by Pamela Allen
Cloth: Coward
Paper: Sandcastle
Published: 1983
A cow, a donkey, a sheep, a pig, and a mouse decide to go out rowing in a boat that is, however, very small. The joke is unmistakable, even to very small children.

[262]

WILLIAM'S DOLL   [269]

Written by Charlotte Zolotow
Illustrated by William Pène du Bois
Cloth: Harper & Row/HarperCollins
Paper: Harper Trophy
Published: 1972

It was shocking, years ago, that William wanted a doll to play with. Certainly, his father and his brother objected. But William got his doll and, in playing with him, imagined how he would one day be a father. Time has passed since this book was published, and what we read today seems modest and wry.

WILLIAM THE VEHICLE KING   [268]

Written by Laura P. Newton
Illustrated by Jacqueline Rogers
Cloth: Bradbury
Published: 1987

Vroom, vroom, rrrhhhhhoar. This book is for and about every little boy obsessed with his racing cars. William, who gets a demonic look in his eye as he sees potential racecourses on the rug, has half a dozen prize vehicles and a wonderful time playing with them. The delightful full-color illustrations look up at William from the floor.

THE WINTER BEAR   [270]

Written by Ruth Craft
Illustrated by Erik Blegvad
Cloth: McElderry
Paper: Aladdin
Published: 1975

Three children take a walk in the country on a cold, snowy day and, of course, find a bear. The illustrations have a delicacy that reflects thin winter light.

THE YEAR AT MAPLE HILL FARM [271]

Written and illustrated by Alice and Martin Provensen
Paper: Aladdin
Published: 1978

The seasons go by on the old-fashioned farm in upstate New York, where the authors live. The illustrations are deceptively simple and provide much to discuss with toddlers and older children.

YELLOW AND PINK [272]

Written and illustrated by William Steig
Cloth: Farrar, Straus & Giroux
Paper: Michael di Capua/Farrar, Straus & Giroux
Published: 1984

Two small wooden figures lie on their backs on a sheet of newspaper in a meadow and debate the origins of the universe. Their creator appears at the end. Although the text is very simple, this is one of the most sophisticated of Steig's books and is most effective with children old enough to find it thought provoking. Adults like it, too.

YONDER [273]

Written by Tony Johnston
Illustrated by Lloyd Bloom
Cloth: Dial
Paper: Pied Piper
Published: 1988

Sometime in the last century, somewhere in the wilderness, a young farmer brings a new wife home. The couple plant a plum tree, say a prayer, then set about being fruitful and multiplying. A tree is planted

for each child, and by the time the old farmer dies and a tree is planted to mark that event too, there is a large orchard. The rhythmic text is simple, returning to the phrase "Yonder," meaning "there, just over there." The oil-painting illustrations, especially the five double-page spreads capturing the seasons and the growth of the plum tree, are perfectly lovely.

YOU BE GOOD AND I'LL BE NIGHT   [274]

Written by Eve Merriam
Illustrated by Karen Lee Schmidt
Cloth: Morrow Junior Books
Published: 1989
The title of these playful bedtime verses captures the affectionate spirit that gives the collection such appealing charm. Lots of small, gentle jokes, for small lap listeners, and beguiling illustrations as well.

Story Books

Here are books with ample, sometimes lavish illustration and strong stories as well. Younger children can often listen to the text and then read the books for themselves with pleasure, but the books are best suited to children in the early grades. Precocious readers have not graduated from the pleasures of story books, either, and find special satisfaction in the combination of pictures and text.

ANANSI THE SPIDER: A TALE FROM THE ASHANTI [275]

Written and illustrated by Gerald McDermott
Cloth: Henry Holt
Published: 1973   Prizes: Caldecott Honor

In this witty illustrated story about Anansi, the West African spider-hero, he has six sons who combine their talents to save their father.

THE ACCIDENT [276]

Written by Carol Carrick
Illustrated by Donald Carrick
Cloth: Clarion
Paper: Clarion
Published: 1976

This is the pivotal book in a series of three about a boy named Christopher and his dog, Bodger. In *Lost in the Storm*, the boy must wait out a storm before searching for his dog. In *The Accident*, his dog is hit by a truck and killed, and Christopher must grieve. In *The Foundling*, Christopher concludes his mourning. The stories are all sensitively and thoughtfully done, worthwhile if read separately or serially. The illustrations are low-key and unobtrusive.

ALEXANDER AND THE TERRIBLE, HORRIBLE, NO GOOD, VERY BAD DAY [277]

Written by Judith Viorst
Illustrated by Ray Cruz
Cloth: Atheneum
Paper: Aladdin
Published: 1972

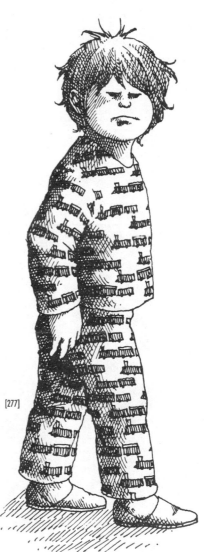

[277]

It is somehow soothing for readers of all ages—i.e., children and their parents—to know that there just are those terrible horrible rotten days that are miserable from beginning to end, no matter what. Everything that can go wrong does, and Alexander is simply furious. The two-color illustrations fairly quiver with the boy's mounting frustrations.

Positively a modern classic for good cause. Other books about Alexander and his brothers are *I'll Fix Anthony* and *Alexander, Who Used to Be Rich Last Sunday*.

ALFIE GIVES A HAND   [278]

Written and illustrated by Shirley Hughes
Cloth: Lothrop, Lee & Shepard
Paper: Mulberry
Published: 1984

Alfie is the quintessential four-year-old—kind, well-meaning, but not quite as brave as he would like to be. His adventures are small and perfectly told. In this episode, he takes his blanket to a birthday party but eventually puts it down in order to help care for a little girl even shyer than he. The deft full-color illustrations sweetly capture characters, as well as the domestic settings, in a comfortable, slightly run-down urban neighborhood. Other titles in the series include *Alfie Gets in First, Alfie's Feet,* and *An Evening at Alfie's.* His little sister, Annie Rose, stars in books for younger children: *Bathwater's Hot* and *All Sizes and Shapes.* There is also a large-format *Alfie and Annie Rose Story Book.*

ALWAYS, ALWAYS   [279]

Written by Crescent Dragonwagon
Illustrated by Arich Zeldich
Cloth: Macmillan
Published: 1984

A low-key story about a little girl whose parents are divorced. She spends her summers with her father in Colorado and the school year with her mother in New York and has learned to accept the situation. And she even finds some merit in it.

[277]

ALWAYS ROOM FOR ONE MORE [280]

Written by Sorche Nic Leodhas
Illustrated by Nonny Hogrogian
Cloth: Henry Holt
Paper: Henry Holt
Published: 1965   Prizes: Caldecott

In this retelling of a story that occurs in many cultures, it is given as a
highlands tale about Lachie MacLachlan, whose hospitality extends to
every traveler who passes by until the walls of his house burst. The
three-color illustrations have a misty quality of mountain air.

AMAHL AND THE NIGHT VISITORS [281]

Written by Gian Carlo Menotti
Illustrated by Michele Lemieux
Cloth: Morrow Junior Books
Published: 1986

This popular modern Christmas opera tells of the three kings stopping
en route to Bethlehem at the home of a poor, crippled shepherd boy.
Evocative full-color illustrations add an aura of mystery and reverence
to this telling.

THE AMAZING BONE [282]

Written and illustrated by William Steig
Cloth: Farrar, Straus & Giroux
Paper: Penguin
Published: 1976   Prizes: Caldecott Honor

Steig stories are always different, always identifiable by their wit and
loony reasonableness. The heroine here, Pearl, who happens to be a
piglet, finds a talking bone that has fallen out of a witch's basket.

[278]

99

AMERICAN FOLK SONGS FOR CHILDREN   [283]

Written by Ruth Crawford Seeger
Illustrated by Barbara Cooney
Paper: Zephyr
Published: 1970

A collection of ninety songs you probably know but you can't remember all the words to anymore. This standard collection has user-friendly suggestions about adapting songs for play and dancing, and altering the words for your family.

ANIMAL FACT, ANIMAL FABLE   [284]

Written by Seymour Simon
Illustrated by Diane de Groat
Paper: Crown
Published: 1979

In this nature book, the illustrations are low-key and the text is clear. One page asserts a common myth about an animal: turn it over and find a truthful answer that may surprise a young reader.

ANNA BANANA AND ME   [285]

Written by Lenore Blegvad
Illustrated by Erik Blegvad
Cloth: McElderry
Paper: Aladdin
Published: 1985

The boy who tells this story is afraid of a lot of things, unlike his utterly brave friend Anna Banana. They are playing in New York's Central Park at a socially benign time. The illustrations capture Anna's daring and the narrator's anxieties and eventual triumph.

[287]

ANNIE AND THE OLD ONE [286]

[287]

Written by Miska Miles
Illustrated by Peter Parnell
Cloth: Joy Street/Little, Brown
Paper: Joy Street/Little, Brown
Published: 1971   Prizes: Newbery Honor

A little Indian girl recognizes that her grandmother is going to die and learns to accept the cycle of life and death. The story is told with delicacy and caring, and the fine illustrations are a perfect complement.

ANNIE AND THE WILD ANIMALS [287]

Written and illustrated by Jan Brett
Cloth: Houghton Mifflin
Paper: Houghton Mifflin
Published: 1985

It's midwinter somewhere in the north country when Annie's cat, Taffy, disappears. The story of what is really happening is told in the borders. In the meantime, at the center of each double page, Annie tries to make friends with a series of wild animals who emerge from the woods as winter fades into damp, mossy spring. At the end, Taffy reappears with her kittens. The illustrations are exquisitely detailed and have a folkloric and Scandinavian quality. In *The Mitten,* the motifs are Ukrainian and a white mitten is lost in the snow.

ARNOLD OF THE DUCKS [288]

Written and illustrated by Mordicai Gerstein
Cloth: Harper & Row/HarperCollins
Paper: HarperCollins
Published: 1983

Here's a grand fantasy about Arnold, who is living happily with Mrs. Leda Duck and her ducklings, dressing in feathers and learning to swim, even to fly. He is, however, a little boy, and eventually he returns to a more conventional family.

Story Books

ARTHUR'S NOSE [289]

Written and illustrated by Marc Brown
Cloth: Joy Street/Little, Brown
Paper: Joy Street/Little, Brown
Published: 1976

This is the first of a popular series of gently comic books that appeal to children in the early grades, and their younger siblings as well, and it sets the tone. Arthur is a young aardvark who deals with life's daily issues in an appealing way. Here he learns to accept his most distinctive features. Other titles include *Arthur's Eyes* (about getting glasses), *Arthur's Tooth* (about losing the first one), and *Arthur's Halloween* (about not being so frightened). There are also books about Arthur's kid sister, D. W.

ASHANTI TO ZULU: AFRICAN TRADITIONS [290]

Written by Margaret Musgrove
Illustrated by Leo and Diane Dillon
Cloth: Dial
Paper: Pied Piper
Published: 1976

Prizes: Caldecott Medal
New York Times Best Illustrated Book

A remarkable alphabet book that also describes and brilliantly illustrates aspects of African culture. The captions are small gems of anthropological reporting. Among the tribes described are the Dogon, the Fanta, and the Kung. This is a picture book definitely for older children and adults. The library may have it shelved with large-format and travel books, but keep looking; it's worth it.

[289]

AUNT NINA AND HER NEPHEWS AND NIECES [291]

Written by Franz Brandenberg
Illustrated by Aliki
Cloth: Greenwillow
Published: 1983

Aunt Nina invites her six nephews and nieces to celebrate her cat Fluffy's birthday. It turns out to be the birthday of Fluffy's six kittens as well. *Aunt Nina's Visit* is another book about the same large family.

BA-NAM [292]

Written and illustrated by Jeanne M. Lee
Cloth: Henry Holt
Published: 1987

This is a story about the special day on which the Vietnamese honor their ancestors and the day Nan is finally old enough to go to the graveyard with her family. The full-color illustrations convey great poignance. For school-age children.

BABUSHKA: AN OLD
RUSSIAN FOLKTALE [293]

Written and illustrated by Charles Mikolaycak
Cloth: Holiday
Paper: Holiday
Published: 1984   Prizes: New York Times Best Illustrated Book

An affecting retelling of a traditional Russian tale about an old woman who was too busy to go when she was invited to visit the baby Jesus and now searches endlessly for him. The darkly lit illustrations are dramatic.

THE BAKER'S DOZEN: A COLONIAL
AMERICAN TALE [294]

Written by Heather Forest
Illustrated by Susan Gaber
Cloth: HBJ
Published: 1988

[290]

In Albany, N.Y., in colonial times, a baker named Van Amsterdam grew greedy and cheated on his St. Nicholas cookies. Soon his fortunes failed. However, when he learned the value of generosity both in his measurements and his attitude and gave thirteen cookies to the dozen, he prospered. Snowy illustrations capture the wintry feeling of December days long ago.

THE BALANCING GIRL [295]

Written by Bernice Rabe
Illustrated by Lillian Hoban
Cloth: Dutton
Paper: Unicorn
Published: 1981

This remarkable book is about Margaret, who is confined to a wheel-chair and has developed her own special skill at balancing things. She uses her talent to benefit her whole school in an imaginative way. Thus, a book about a physically disabled child conveys a message about social tolerance that is accessible for a preschool child. *Margaret's Moves,* for older readers, takes up the story a few years later, as Margaret deals with new problems and especially her brother, Rusty. Margaret is a determined, optimistic, yet believable character.

BEA AND MR. JONES [296]

Written and illustrated by Amy Schwartz
Cloth: Bradbury
Paper: Puffin
Published: 1982

Bea is tired of kindergarten and Mr. Jones is tired of being an advertising executive, so they swap jobs. The results are very satisfying. The distinctive line drawings, old-fashioned but somewhat cartoonish, are very amusing, especially Bea and Mr. Jones with their smug, fat faces.

THE BEACHCOMBER'S BOOK [297]

Written by Bernice Kohn
Illustrated by Arabella Wheatley
Paper: Puffin
Published: 1976, reissued 1987

This compendium of information and projects is the perfect take-along paperback for a beach vacation or a beach house. Although aimed at grade-school children, it includes a lot of information a browsing parent might find fascinating, too. *Shell,* by Alex Arthur, in the "Eyewitness" series, is an outstanding companion.

THE BEAST OF MONSIEUR RACINE [298]

Written and illustrated by Tomi Ungerer
Cloth: Farrar, Straus & Giroux
Paper: Sunburst
Published: 1971

A retired tax collector finds a strange, friendly, rather squooshy creature in his garden. Approaching it scientifically, Monsieur Racine takes it to the Academy of Sciences in Paris, where it breaks apart, revealing the two children from next door. The quirky fable suggests a Gallic worldliness in inimitable style.

BEAUTY AND THE BEAST [299]

Written and illustrated by Warrick Hutton
Cloth: McElderry
Published: 1986

There are many versions of this familiar story, set in different countries and historical periods. This one, by a contemporary British artist who works wonders with pale watercolor washes and pen-and-ink drawings, is quite eerie, even haunting. Beauty's eyes and expressions capture first fear and finally love. The Beast's horror is ambiguous.

[299]

BEDTIME FOR FRANCES [300]

Written by Russell Hoban
Illustrated by Garth Williams
Cloth: Harper & Row/HarperCollins
Paper: Harper Trophy
Published: 1960

Frances is a bright, willful, whimsical little badger who often makes up songs about aspects of her days—bedtime, sibling rivalry, friendship,

[296]

candy. Her adventures in this and the other books in the series (the others are illustrated by Lillian Hoban) reflect the small and specific concerns of children in preschool and the early grades but transcend bibliotherapy. *A Baby Sister for Frances, Best Friends for Frances, A Birthday for Frances, Bread and Jam for Frances*, and *Egg Thoughts and Other Frances Songs* are all delightful. Whenever you hear people talk about a Chompo bar, they have been reading Frances. The Frances books have more text than pictures, but because they read aloud so well, they appeal to children of a wide age range—roughly from toddlers to third grade.

THE BERENSTAIN BEARS' TROUBLE WITH MONEY [301]

Written and illustrated by Stan and Jan Berenstain
Paper: Random House
Published: 1983

The popular bears are featured in a series of "First Time" books that address issues of family life. In this case, the young bears must work to earn money to play video games, and the story provides reasonable guidance on a familiar problem. While parents may feel that the writing is both pedantic and didactic, children accept moral instruction from the bears they would reject coming directly from the real authority figures in their lives. Other titles in the series that may already be familiar from Saturday-morning cartoon adaptations include *The Berenstain Bears, Too Much Junk Food, Too Much TV, Mama's New Job*, and *The Messy Room*.

[299]

BEST FRIENDS [302]

Written and illustrated by Steven Kellogg
Cloth: Dial
Paper: Pied Piper
Published: 1985

Kathy and Louise are best friends. While Louise is away for the summer, Kathy meets a new neighbor whose dog is expecting puppies, with some unforeseen and poignant results. Detailed and imaginative full-color illustrations add depth and humor.

THE BEST TOWN IN THE WORLD　[303]

Written by Byrd Baylor
Illustrated by Ronald Himler
Cloth: Scribner's
Published: 1983

[304]

A prose poem that celebrates a place in the American Southwest where all the wildflowers had "butterflies to match" and "of course you knew everyone's name and everyone knew yours." The full-color sun-dappled illustrations are romantic.

THE BIG GREEN BOOK　[304]

Written by Robert Graves
Illustrated by Maurice Sendak
Cloth: Macmillan
Paper: Aladdin
Published: 1962

Jack is an orphan who finds the big green book full of magic spells in the attic. He promptly turns himself into a little old man, then tricks his tedious aunt and uncle, terrifies the dog, and puts away the book before further mischief can be done. A distinguished collaboration of author and illustrator. The black-and-white drawings, especially the full page of the dog running from a rabbit, are dandy.

THE BIONIC BUNNY SHOW　[305]

Written by Marc and Laurene Brown
Illustrated by Marc Brown
Cloth: Joy Street/Little, Brown
Paper: Joy Street/Little, Brown
Published: 1984

In the story of the making of an episode of the *Bionic Bunny Show*, this witty picture book debunks the myth of the effortless superhero and also shows how television programs are made. A glossary of television terms is included, and the illustrations are funny and detailed.

[304]

THE BOOK OF PIGERICKS: PIG LIMERICKS   [306]

Written and illustrated by Arnold Lobel
Cloth: Harper & Row/HarperCollins
Paper: Harper Trophy
Published: 1983

A piggy feast: thirty-eight original limericks (very hard to accomplish; try writing some) illustrated with glowing good humor. The cast of Lobelian porkers is splendidly costumed.

THE BOY WHO WAS FOLLOWED HOME   [307]

Written by Margaret Mahy
Illustrated by Steven Kellogg
Cloth: Dial
Paper: Pied Piper
Published: 1975

This is an inspired (kind of) shaggy hippopotamus story. One day an amiable hippo follows a proper little boy home from school. Then there is another. The hippos multiply daily until there are forty-three of them. The story has a compelling logic, a ridiculous witch, some magic, and an unexpected and funny final twist. The illustrations are hilarious. This is the only Mahy picture book currently available in the United States in which the illustrations are the equal of the text.

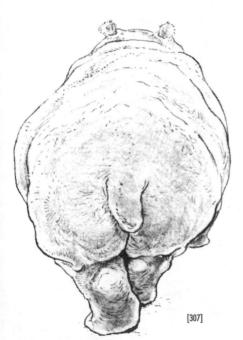

[307]

THE BRAMBLY HEDGE BOOKS   [308]

Written and illustrated by Jill Barklem
Cloth: Philomel
Published: 1980

There are four small books in this endearing series about some very English mice who dress in nineteenth-century period costumes and live in an elaborately detailed world—*Autumn Story, Spring Story, Summer Story,* and *Winter Story.*

BRATS [309]

Written by X. J. Kennedy
Illustrated by James Watts
Cloth: McElderry
Published: 1986

A bright collection of forty-two short original poems about an assortment of brats—obnoxious, rude, noisy, and various other combinations of familiar and unpleasant. The illustrations are apt and amusing. There is also *Fresh Brats,* another forty-one bits of mischief.

[310]

BRAVE IRENE [310]

Written and illustrated by William Steig
Cloth: Farrar, Straus & Giroux
Paper: Sunburst
Published: 1986   Prizes: New York Times Best Illustrated Book

Irene Bobbin, the dressmaker's daughter, volunteers to deliver the duchess's new ball gown and sets off in a fierce snowstorm. The wicked wind blows the dress out of the box, Irene musters on, and there is a happy ending. This is vintage Steig. As with his other story books, lap listeners are almost as interested as children who can read the story for themselves.

THE BUCK STOPS HERE: THE PRESIDENTS OF THE UNITED STATES [311]

Written and illustrated by Alice Provensen
Cloth: HarperCollins
Published: 1990

In a large, full-page format, poster-style illustrations present, almost as a panorama or banner, the first forty-one American presidents, who virtually parade past the reader. Each entry carries a rhymed couplet and a set of facts, both familiar and obscure, that are embedded in the illustration. It is a stunning book for browsing, merely amusing to youngest children, genuinely absorbing for middle-school children who are fluid readers but are just grasping historical sequence, and thoroughly entertaining for adults as well. It is a fine companion to *The Book of Americans.*

[307]

BUFFALO WOMAN [312]

Written and illustrated by Paul Goble
Cloth: Bradbury
Paper: Aladdin
Published: 1984

The young hunter's bride, scorned by his people, returns to her own—the Buffalo Nation. He follows and proves his love for her and their son with the son's help. The hunter is then transformed into a buffalo, too, and honor is given to all. Dramatic, eloquent, and beautifully illustrated in highly stylized full-color illustrations, this is a profound love story. Children in the early grades find it particularly thrilling.

BUGS [313]

Written by Nancy Winslow Parker and Joan Richards Wright
Illustrated by Nancy Winslow Parker
Cloth: Greenwillow
Paper: Mulberry
Published: 1987

Humorous verses introduce sixteen common insects, including fleas, flies, and mosquitoes, which make this first book of entomology an engaging browsing book. It is a good early independent reading book for young scientists, as is the fascinating *Frogs, Toads, Lizards and Salamanders*, by the same team. The illustrations are clear, precise but cartoonish, enough to allow the phobic a chance to enjoy the subject.

CALEB AND KATE [314]

Written and illustrated by William Steig
Cloth: Farrar, Straus & Giroux
Paper: Sunburst
Published: 1978

[316]

After yet another spat, Caleb goes into the forest to get away from Kate. A witch casts a spell, and he's turned into a dog. Caleb returns to Kate, who accepts him as a pet, until the day when thieves arrive. . . . Impossible, of course. Wonderful, too—especially for children in the early grades.

CAPTAIN SNAP AND THE CHILDREN OF VINEGAR LANE [315]

Written and illustrated by Marcia Sewall
Cloth: Orchard Books
Published: 1989

Captain Snap looks like one mean old codger and doesn't like children. But it is the neighborhood children who come to his aid when he is ill, and their rewards, in friendship and crafts, are quite wonderful. The angular illustrations give the story a special energy.

CATWINGS [316]

Written by Ursula K. Le Guin
Illustrated by S. D. Schindler
Cloth: Orchard Books
Paper: Scholastic
Published: 1988

Mrs. Jane Tabby's four new little kittens seem to have, er, um, wings. They live in an unsafe urban area and their harassed mother does her best, but ultimately sends them to the country alone. The laconic, matter-of-fact prose is utterly believable. The delicate ink-and-watercolor illustrations are faintly Victorian and thoroughly enchanting and suited to the small, palm-size shape of the book. *Catwings Return* is a sequel but has not got quite the same magic.

[316]

CELEBRATIONS [317]

Written by Myra Cohn Livingston
Illustrated by Leonard Everett Fisher
Cloth: Holiday
Paper: Holiday
Published: 1985

Simple, appealing poems to mark the traditions, symbols, and memories of an assortment of days throughout the year. The author and illustrator have collaborated on other special collections, including *A Circle of Seasons*, *Earth Songs*, *Sea Songs*, *Sky Songs*, and *Space Songs*.

A CHAIR FOR MY MOTHER [318]

Written and illustrated by Vera B. Williams
Cloth: Greenwillow
Paper: Mulberry
Published: 1982

Prizes: Caldecott Honor

This is the first of three stories about Rosa, her mother, who works in the Blue Tile Diner, and her grandmother. Burned out of their home, they relocate and start saving for a comfortable chair. The chair, lush and pink and covered with roses, is, like the book, unusual and fine. The illustrations, with their distinctive borders and themes, are wry rather than whimsical. The two other equally enchanting titles are *Something Special for Me* and *Music, Music Everywhere.*

THE CHALK DOLL [319]

Written by Charlotte Pomerantz
Illustrated by Frané Lessac
Cloth: Lippincott/HarperCollins
Published: 1989

Rose is home in bed with a cold and her mother is settling her for a nap, telling about when she was a little girl in Jamaica. They were too poor for store-bought dolls, but she made a fine rag doll, who even had high-heeled shoes. You don't need to be sick, or even at home, to remember the story.

THE CHANGING CITY [320]

Written and illustrated by Jorg Muller
Cloth: McElderry
Published: 1977

In a series of delicately detailed paintings, the Swiss artist shows the changes over a twenty-three-year period in a European city. This is a case of an illustrated book whose most appropriate audience is older children, who can consider the implications of the changes the artist presents and then make value judgments about them. The companion volume is *The Changing Countryside.* There is a similarly illustrated study of an American town called *New Providence.*

A CHILD IS BORN:
THE CHRISTMAS STORY   [321]

[318]

Written by Elizabeth Winthrop
Illustrated by Charles Mikolaycak
Cloth: Holiday
Published: 1983

The story of the birth of Christ, told in simple language. The strong, lush illustrations show remarkably believable people with contemporary, realistic features. The author and illustrator have used the same techniques effectively in *He Is Risen* about Easter. *B Is for Bethlehem* tells the story as a pageant (perfect for classroom adaptation), with wonderful airy illustrations.

A CHILD'S GARDEN OF VERSES   [322]

Written by Robert Louis Stevenson
Illustrated by Tasha Tudor
Cloth: Checkerboard
Published: 1981

This edition of sixty-six of the verses from one of the most famous collections of poems for children is illustrated in a sweet and rosy way. Artists who have taken different approaches include Michael Foreman, Erik Blegvad, Jesse W. Smith, and Brian Wildsmith.

A CHILD'S TREASURY OF POEMS   [323]

Written by Mark Daniel
Cloth: Dial
Published: 1986

A charming collection of familiar English poems, mostly by nineteenth-century authors—Tennyson, Stevenson, Wordsworth, Rossetti. The lavish period illustrations of appropriate paintings and engravings are reproductions from works in museums and private collections. Many of the illustrations are unfamiliar but seem especially apt. This is a presentation gift/read-aloud collection for all ages.

EL CHINO   [324]

Written and illustrated by Allen Say
Cloth: Houghton Mifflin
Published: 1990

The American dream—of unlimited possibility, and finding your true self somehow, somewhere—is told quietly and powerfully in this almost cinematic account of Bong Way, who became Billy Wong. A Chinese-American athlete "too short for basketball," he found his sport, and goal, in the bullring in Spain. In becoming a matador he also reclaimed his Chinese heritage. It is a stunning story book with beautiful, spare illustrations that burst into brilliant color when Billy Wong sees the bullring. It can be read at many levels, even by young children, but is perhaps most rewarding for middle-graders, who are grappling with questions of identity.

CHITA'S CHRISTMAS TREE   [325]

Written by Elizabeth Fitzgerald Howard
Illustrated by Floyd Cooper
Cloth: Bradbury
Published: 1989

This description of a Christmas in Baltimore at the end of the nineteenth century has been drawn from the family recollections of Elizabeth McCard Shipley, the real Chita and the only child of one of the first black doctors in the city. The illustrations are full of rich domestic detail, but it is the beguiling Chita who is the star.

THE CHOSEN BABY   [326]

Written by Valentine P. Wasson
Illustrated by Glo Coalson
Cloth: Lippincott/HarperCollins
Published: 1939; reprinted 1977

A gentle book about adoption for very young children that has been in print for decades.

CHRISTINA KATERINA AND THE TIME SHE QUIT THE FAMILY   [327]

Written by Patricia Lee Gauch
Illustrated by Elsie Primavera
Cloth: Putnam
Published: 1987

Family life sometimes gets to be too much. One morning when it does, Christina Katerina just up and quits the family. "Call me Agnes," she says, and spends the next days doing just what she wants. Her savvy mother handles the situation neatly. Our heroine also appears in *Christina Katerina and the Box.*

[324]

CHRISTMAS IN THE BARN   [328]

Written by Margaret Wise Brown
Illustrated by Barbara Cooney
Cloth: T. Y. Crowell/HarperCollins
Paper: Harper Trophy
Published: 1949

A gentle and careful collaboration between author and artist make this traditional version of the Nativity particularly pleasing for very young children.

THE CHURCH MOUSE   [329]

Written and illustrated by Graham Oakley
Cloth: Atheneum
Paper: Aladdin
Published: 1972

Arthur, a rather intelligent mouse, arranges to have all the other mice in an English market town move into the church he shares with Sampson, the benign marmalade church cat. Their adventures, all illustrated in droll detail, continue in *The Church Mice and the Moon, The Church Mice Adrift, The Church Mice in Action, The Church Mice at Christmas,* and *The Church Mice Spread Their Wings.* In addition to youngsters, the church mice, as a group, may have many adult admirers.

CINDERELLA   [330]

Written by Charles Perrault
Illustrated by Marcia Brown
Cloth: Scribner's
Paper: Aladdin
Published: 1954

Prizes: Caldecott Medal

A fine translation in an appealing illustrated edition of the familiar story about the dutiful daughter and the glass slipper. There are also unusual editions illustrated by Susan Jeffers, Roberto Innocenti, Errol Le Cain and, for a comic variation, James Marshall.

THE CLOWN OF GOD   [331]

Written and illustrated by Tomie dePaola
Cloth: HBJ
Paper: Voyager
Published: 1978

This lovely retelling of a French folktale about a juggler's gift to the Christ Child has appealing, stylized illustrations recalling Pierrot.

COME A TIDE   [332]

Written by George Ella Lyon
Illustrated by Stephen Gammell
Cloth: Orchard Books
Published: 1990

Grandma, who is old, wise, and lives at the top of the hill someplace in the Appalachians, knows that after a four-day spring rain, "It'll come a tide." Because of the lighthearted, almost lyric text and the exuberant, funny illustrations, what happens during a recurring natural disaster —flooding—becomes a great adventurous romp.

[332]

COMPANY'S COMING [333]

Written by Arthur Yorinks
Illustrated by David Small
Cloth: Crown
Paper: Scholastic
Published: 1988

Two creatures from space land in Moe and Shirley's backyard the day
the relatives are expected for dinner. The laconic story is a joke about
suspicion and hospitality—the visitors' first request is for the bathroom,
they are polite, the humans are hysterical. The illustrations, which suggest that the space creatures are cockroaches and their vehicle a bar-
becue, are hilarious. Young children don't get it, and the natural (and
appreciative) audience is older children, teenagers, and adults.

[333]

THE CRACK-OF-DAWN WALKERS [334]

Written by Amy Hest
Illustrated by Amy Schwartz
Cloth: Macmillan
Published: 1984

A little girl explains about how she and her brother take turns accom-
panying their grandfather on his early-morning walks. The setting is
winter in a city, the time is not so long ago, and the affection between
the two characters, in text and the black-and-white illustrations, is palpable. In *The Midnight Eaters* another, similar little girl and her grandmother share private midnight snacks and memories.

THE CRANE WIFE [335]

Written by Sumiko Yagawa
Illustrated by Suekichi Akaba
Paper: Mulberry
Published: 1981   Prizes: New York Times Best Illustrated Book

Translated by Katherine Paterson, the prizewinning American writer,
this is a beautiful version of a favorite, heartbreaking Japanese folktale.
It tells about the farmer who marries a beautiful and mysterious
stranger. She weaves fine cloth and warns him never to watch her, and
for good reason: She is really the crane he rescued from death, and if
he sees her, she must leave him.

117

d'AULAIRES' BOOK OF GREEK MYTHS [336]

Written and illustrated by Ingri and Edgar Parin d'Aulaire
Cloth: Doubleday
Paper: Zephyr
Published: 1962

The best-known modern book of the Greek myths adapted for children. The stories are organized around Zeus and his family, minor gods, and mortal descendants. The complex illustrations, full of symbols and evoking the classical tradition, are distinguished. The prose is straightforward and easy to read aloud. The stories are, of course, thrilling. The *Macmillan Book of Greek Myths,* an attractive compilation, has fewer stories but is also very readable. There are dozens of story books of individual myths, of varying quality. For night-after-night bedtime reading, the larger collections are recommended.

[334]

d'AULAIRES' NORSE GODS AND GIANTS [337]

Written and illustrated by Ingri and Edgar Parin d'Aulaire
Cloth: Doubleday
Paper: Zephyr
Published: 1967

This is a generous collection of the ancient Norse myths, including those describing creation and daily life, set out in a lavishly illustrated large-format volume. Wonderful to read aloud.

DAKOTA DUGOUT [338]

Written by Ann Turner
Illustrated by Ronald Himler
Cloth: Macmillan
Paper: Aladdin
Published: 1985

A memoir of the life of a young bride living in a sod house on the Dakota prairie in the late nineteenth century. The black-and-white illustrations set off the text with distinction.

[336]

THE DANCING GRANNY   [339]

Written and illustrated by Ashley Bryan
Paper: Aladdin
Published: 1977

A bright and engaging retelling of an African folktale about the spider Anansi, who in this story lures Granny Anika into a dance so he can steal her crops. But, of course, she outwits Anansi.

A DAY WITH WILBUR ROBINSON   [340]

Written and illustrated by William Joyce
Cloth: HarperCollins
Published: 1990

If you stick with the words, it is just a slight story about how the narrator goes over to a friend's house and spends the night. The pictures, however, show a wacky household with tigers and trains, relatives dropping in from outer space, and frogs playing violins. It's great fun because it's not the least bit humble and there's no place like Wilbur's home.

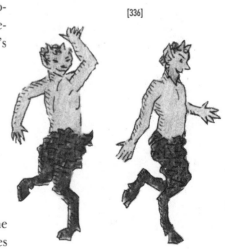

[336]

THE DESERT IS THEIRS   [341]

Written by Byrd Baylor
Illustrated by Peter Parnall
Cloth: Scribner's
Paper: Aladdin
Published: 1975

For readers who live in or near the desert, or in other parts of the world and wonder, this is a lyrical introduction to many of the creatures

119

who live there in the dry, sere places. There is an ecological message about species' adaptation to climate. The illustrations are fine line drawings.

THE DEVIL AND MOTHER CRUMP   [342]

Written by Valerie Scho Carey
Illustrated by Arnold Lobel
Cloth: Harper & Row/HarperCollins
Paper: Harper Trophy
Published: 1987

Mother Crump was so mean and so stingy—but also so smart—that she even tricked the devil himself. She is something like the "mean old lady" everyone knows and tells stories about. A folkloric fable with thoughtful illustrations that young readers and listeners both enjoy.

DINOSAURS DIVORCE: A GUIDE FOR CHANGING FAMILIES   [343]

Written by Marc and Laurene Krasny Brown
Illustrated by Marc Brown
Cloth: Joy Street/Little, Brown
Paper: Joy Street/Little, Brown
Published: 1986

Set in a cartoon world with a cast of dinosaurs, this story book for children of all ages deals with the trauma of divorce. The text is straightforward, and although silly and funny, the illustrations are also sophisticated enough to allow older children to return to the book for its sound and reassuring advice without feeling embarrassed.

[343]

DINOSAURS, BEWARE! [344]

Written by Stephen Krensky and Marc Brown
Illustrated by Marc Brown
Cloth: Joy Street/Little, Brown
Paper: Joy Street/Little, Brown
Published: 1982

A basic guide to household safety—everything from playing with fire to telephone manners—but the households pictured are those of ridiculously entertaining dinosaurs, who set some truly bad examples to avoid.

[345]

DOCTOR DE SOTO [345]

Written and illustrated by William Steig
Cloth: Farrar, Straus & Giroux
Paper: Sunburst
Published: 1982   Prizes: Newbery Honor

Doctor De Soto, a mouse, has a dental practice on a busy city street. As a rule, he does not accept patients threatening to his species, but he makes an exception for a fox with an emergency, and outsmarts the fox, whose gratitude is ultimately questionable. A glorious book with matchlessly witty full-color illustrations.

DUFFY AND THE DEVIL [346]

Written by Harve Zemach
Illustrated by Margot Zemach
Cloth: Farrar, Straus & Giroux
Paper: Sunburst
Published: 1973   Prizes: Caldecott Medal

This is a wry Cornish version of Rumpelstiltskin. Duffy is the servant girl Squire Lovel believes can spin and knit so well. But then the devil takes back the garments he made, much to the squire's embarrassment. Bright, cheerful full-color illustrations. *The Judges* is also a witty tale of justice.

[346]

ELOISE [347]

Written by Kay Thompson
Illustrated by Hilary Knight
Cloth: Simon & Schuster
Published: 1955

You remember me, Eloise. I'm six and rather adorable and I live in the Plaza Hotel in New York City. I have lots of fun there: I order from room service and ride the elevators and check out what's happening all over the hotel. I'm terribly clever. A timeless favorite about a terrorizing child.

THE ENORMOUS CROCODILE [348]

Written by Roald Dahl
Illustrated by Quentin Blake
Cloth: Knopf
Paper: Penguin
Published: 1978

A droll story about an enormous crocodile who dares to leave the river and go to the town to find little children to eat. He poses as a coconut tree, a merry-go-round, and a picnic bench and is foiled each time by other animals. Witty illustrations.

EVERETT ANDERSON'S GOODBYE [349]

Written by Lucille Clifton
Illustrated by Ann Grifalconi
Cloth: Henry Holt
Published: 1983

Everett Anderson, a little black boy, must deal with his father's death. His feelings are eloquently evoked in simple poems and underscored in gentle pencil illustrations. Two other Everett Anderson books have been reissued—*Some of the Days of Everett Anderson* and *Everett Anderson's Nine Month Long.*

EVERYBODY NEEDS A ROCK [350]

Written by Byrd Baylor
Illustrated by Peter Parnall
Cloth: Scribner's
Paper: Aladdin
Published: 1974

[351]

Here is a guide to finding your own special rock, a bit of the earth to have and hold. Incidentally, the search for a special talisman teaches a good deal about the universe. The dramatic line drawings are engrossing in this seamless and persuasive collaboration between author and illustrator.

EVERYONE KNOWS WHAT A DRAGON LOOKS LIKE   [351]

Written by Jay Williams
Illustrated by Mercer Mayer
Cloth: Four Winds
Published: 1976   Prizes: New York Times Best Illustrated Book

Of course, the truth is everyone doesn't know what a dragon looks like, even in the Chinese kingdom wittily portrayed in this traditional tale. The story skillfully pokes fun at people's presumptions and prejudices.

[351]

EVOLUTION   [352]

Written by Joanna Cole
Illustrated by Aliki
Cloth: T. Y. Crowell/HarperCollins
Paper: Harper Trophy
Published: 1987

A carefully distilled explanation for early-grade children of the idea of evolution of complex plants and animals from one-celled beings. Cheerful children romp through the illustrations.

FABLES   [353]

Written and illustrated by Arnold Lobel
Cloth: Harper & Row/HarperCollins
Paper: Harper Trophy
Published: 1980   Prizes: Caldecott Medal

These are short original fables with unexpected and definitely contemporary morals—pleasing to adult readers as well as children for their gentle wit and full-color illustrations.

FIREFLIES [354]

Written and illustrated by Julie Brinckloe
Cloth: Macmillan
Paper: Aladdin
Published: 1985

A favorite summer memory is captured in soft, mysterious two-color illustrations. A boy finishes his supper, grabs a jar, and rushes out into the dusk to catch fireflies.

FLOSSIE & THE FOX [355]

Written by Patricia C. McKissack
Illustrated by Rachel Isadora
Cloth: Dial
Paper: Pied Piper
Published: 1986

Based on a Tennessee folktale. L'il Flossie Finley carries a basket of eggs through the woods and purely outwits a pesky, furry red figure who insists he is a fox. Flossie is a purely spunky and delightful heroine. The full-color sun-dappled illustrations are very appealing.

THE FOOL OF THE WORLD AND THE FLYING SHIP [356]

Written by Arthur Ransome
Illustrated by Uri Shulevitz
Cloth: Farrar, Straus & Giroux
Paper: Sunburst
Published: 1968

Prizes: Caldecott Medal

The Fool of the World is a peasant who wins the hand of the czar's daughter by paying close attention to good advice and taking advantage of the skills of the Listener, the Swift-goer, the Drinker, and others. The old folktale is illustrated with great charm and wit.

[355]

FRANCIS: THE POOR MAN
OF ASSISI   [357]

Written and illustrated by Tomie dePaola
Cloth: Holiday
Paper: Holiday
Published: 1982

An episodic life of the well-loved saint, illustrated in a characteristic, stylized fashion by an artist with a folkloric touch.

FRANNIE'S FRUITS   [358]

Written by Leslie Kimmelman
Illustrated by Petra Mathers
Cloth: Harper & Row/HarperCollins
Published: 1989

This is a sweet slice-of-summer story told by the daughter of the family who run a fruit and vegetable stand they have named for their dog. Not a lot happens on a perfect day: customers, familiar and unfamiliar, come and go, and at sunset the family goes home. The illustrations are distinctively whimsical and full of delightful, unexpected detail (a sign says "TAKE A PEACH TO THE BEACH").

THE FROG PRINCE CONTINUED   [359]

Written by Jon Scieszka
Illustrated by Steve Johnson
Cloth: Viking
Published: 1991

So they got married, and then what happened? Well, it wasn't easy for a princess to be married to a former frog. He kept hopping around the furniture and occasionally flicked his tongue. This thoroughly logical sequel picks up the story when the prince goes off into the deep dark woods to find a witch who can leave her duties in other stories and help him. The clever story is matched by brilliantly stylish illustrations.

[359]

125

FROM PATH TO HIGHWAY: THE STORY OF THE BOSTON POST ROAD [360]

Written and illustrated by Gail Gibbons
Cloth: T. Y. Crowell/HarperCollins
Published: 1986

An illustrated history of one of the earliest and most important roadways on the East Coast of the continent. This account begins with the Indian footpath that cut through deep woodlands and became the four-lane highway that exists today.

FROM THE HILLS OF GEORGIA: AN AUTOBIOGRAPHY IN PAINTINGS [361]

Written and illustrated by Mattie Lou O'Kelley
Cloth: Little, Brown
Paper: Little, Brown
Published: 1983

Primitive-style full-color paintings tell the story of the author's childhood in the early years of this century. This is a book to pore over conversationally, as each painting is filled with details that make the past more immediate and imaginable.

GALIMOTO [362]

Written by Karen Lynn Williams
Illustrated by Catherine Stock
Cloth: Lothrop, Lee & Shepard
Paper: Mulberry
Published: 1990

Kondi lives in a village on the shores of Lake Malawi. An imaginative and energetic boy, he spends an entire day collecting the bits of scrap he needs to build his very own *galimoto*. The word in Kondi's language, Chichewa, means both car and a kind of push toy. The text is precise and pleasing; the illustrations are delightfully rich and detailed. Watching Kondi collect his wires and snippets may inspire other young inventors.

THE GARDEN OF ABDUL GASAZI [363]

Written and illustrated by Chris Van Allsburg

Cloth: Houghton Mifflin

Published: 1979

Prizes: Caldecott Honor
New York Times Best Illustrated Book

A cautionary tale about a boy who lets the dog he is supposed to be caring for wander into the garden of a magician who specifically warns strangers not to enter. The first of a dazzling series of sophisticated story books by an artist whose drawings are technically unparalleled but whose vision is often chilly.

GEORGE AND MARTHA [364]

Written and illustrated by James Marshall

Cloth: Houghton Mifflin

Paper: Houghton Mifflin

Published: 1972

Prizes: New York Times Best Illustrated Book

The first in a hilarious series of stories about two dear friends (who happen to be large, awkward hippos) with prominent buck teeth and a knack for finding themselves in farcical situations. Other titles include *George and Martha Back in Town, George and Martha One Fine Day, George and Martha Tons of Fun,* and *George and Martha Rise and Shine.* The latest in the series, *George and Martha Round and Round,* is just as funny and serious as the first.

GEORGIA MUSIC [365]

Written by Helen Griffith
Illustrated by James Stevenson

Cloth: Greenwillow

Paper: Mulberry

Published: 1986

A little girl spends sweet private summers in Georgia with her grandfather, until he becomes ill and comes to live with her family. When others fail, the child is able to penetrate his depression with her memories. Thoughtful, not maudlin, with remarkably complementary text and illustrations. *Grandaddy's Place* tells the story of their first meeting.

GIANTS OF LAND, SEA & AIR: PAST AND PRESENT [366]

Written and illustrated by David Peters
Cloth: Knopf
Published: 1986

This is a huge and enthralling compilation of detailed illustrations of all sorts of giant creatures that have really lived—from sharks to whales, mammoths, and dinosaurs. They are shown in a scaled relationship with a pair of human beings, who appear on each double-page spread either jogging or swimming. This is a book that younger children can enjoy; older children find it engrossing, and adults, irresistible.

THE GIFT OF THE SACRED DOG [367]

Written and illustrated by Paul Goble
Cloth: Bradbury
Paper: Aladdin
Published: 1978

The beautifully illustrated legend tells about the arrival of the sacred dog, the horse, which totally changed the buffalo-hunting ways of the Plains Indians. The brilliant colors and stylized design make the horses especially vivid.

[370]

THE GINGERBREAD RABBIT [368]

Written by Randall Jarrell
Illustrated by Garth Williams
Cloth: Macmillan
Paper: Aladdin
Published: 1964

A distinguished American poet wrote this story about a gingerbread rabbit who escaped the oven only to meet a fox who would eat him raw. The illustrations capture the spirit of the chase.

THE GIRL WHO LOVED THE WIND   [369]

Written by Jane Yolen
Illustrated by Ed Young
Cloth: Harper & Row/HarperCollins
Paper: Harper Trophy
Published: 1972

[370]

In a kingdom to the east, a wealthy merchant thought he could protect his precious daughter from all temptations, but Danina heard the wind. The illustrations to this haunting fable are in a style that evokes but does not exactly copy Persian miniatures.

THE GIRL WHO LOVED WILD HORSES   [370]

Written and illustrated by Paul Goble
Cloth: Bradbury
Paper: Aladdin
Published: 1978   Prizes: Caldecott Medal

The romantic and compelling Plains Indian legend of a girl who so identifies with the wild horses that eventually she goes and joins them is beautifully illustrated in this prizewinning book. The artist's style abstracts traditional Indian design motifs.

THE GIVING TREE   [371]

Written and illustrated by Shel Silverstein
Cloth: Harper & Row/HarperCollins
Published: 1964

A much-loved story tells about a boy and a tree, one growing, the other giving generously. It is, perhaps, corny but not mawkish.

[370]

Story Books

THE GLORIOUS FLIGHT: ACROSS THE CHANNEL WITH LOUIS BLÉRIOT   [372]

Written and illustrated by Alice and Martin Provensen
Cloth: Viking
Paper: Puffin
Published: 1983   Prizes: Caldecott Medal

In this spectacular book—history and art are in winning combination. It is the story of Louis Blériot, a Frenchman, and the flying machine he built to cross the English Channel. The illustrations convey both science and social period.

GO AWAY, BAD DREAMS!   [373]

Written by Susan Hill
Illustrated by Vanessa Julian-Ottie
Paper: Random House
Published: 1985

Tom's mother helps him figure out how his imagination works to create some of his bad dreams, and then he is able to chase them away. This British import has a slightly stiff upper lip quality, but it may be helpful to a school-age child with simple nightmare troubles.

GOLDIE THE DOLLMAKER   [374]

Written and illustrated by M. B. Goffstein
Paper: Sunburst
Published: 1969

Goldie the dollmaker, who appears in delicate, careful drawings, is an artist who lives alone and makes dolls. She chooses the wood, carves the dolls carefully, then paints them with precision. It is an unusually satisfying story about love and work.

THE GOOD GIANTS AND
THE BAD PUKWUDGIES   [375]

Written by Jean Fritz
Illustrated by Tomie dePaola
Cloth: Putnam
Paper: Sandcastle
Published: 1982

A folkloric account, drawn from Indian legends, about the formation of Cape Cod. The giant Mauship, his wife, Quant, and their five sons coexist with creatures, who sometimes appear as mosquitoes or fireflies, called the pukwudgies. The author is a distinguished historian for children, the artist a prizewinner. Once the geography lesson is pointed out, the map of the Cape comes clear.

GORKY RISES   [376]

Written and illustrated by William Steig
Cloth: Farrar, Straus & Giroux
Paper: Sunburst
Published: 1980   **Prizes: New York Times Best Illustrated Book**

Another zany Steig fable, this one tells about Gorky, a young frog, who fools around in the kitchen one summer morning when his parents are out. He makes a potion that, wondrously, later causes him to rise and fly through the soft afternoon.

[374]

A GREAT BIG UGLY MAN CAME UP AND TIED HIS HORSE TO ME   [377]

Written and illustrated by Wallace Tripp
Cloth: Little, Brown
Paper: Little, Brown
Published: 1973

A collection of hilarious poems and nonsense, illustrated in deadpan fashion by an artist who challenges the reader's attention by inserting famous people, past and present, in improbable settings. Great fun to read with children, but they happily read it alone. *Grandpa Griggs* is another grand collection.

THE GREAT WALL OF CHINA   [378]

Written and illustrated by Leonard Everett Fisher
Cloth: Four Winds
Published: 1986

The story of the Great Wall told in brief text and very dramatic black-and-white illustrations, decorated with Chinese characters. *Pyramid of the Sun, Pyramid of the Moon*, and *The Wailing Wall* tell of two other man-made walls of great cultural significance.

[381]

HANDTALK: AN ABC OF FINGER SPELLING AND SIGN LANGUAGE   [379]

Written by Remy Charlip and Mary Beth Miller
Illustrated by George Ancona
Cloth: Four Winds
Paper: Aladdin
Published: 1974

The photographs in this introductory guidebook to sign language are so clear—both the gestures and the exaggerated expression of the models—that very young children as well as sophisticated adults can understand the finger spelling. The full-color companion volume, *Handtalk Birthday*, has a bubbly spirit and aura of goodwill that are as irresistible as they are unexpected.

HANSEL AND GRETEL   [380]

Written by Rika Lesser
Illustrated by Paul O. Zelinsky
Cloth: Dodd, Mead/Putnam
Paper: Sandcastle
Published: 1984   Prizes: Caldecott Honor

This lush version of one of the most familiar of the Grimm stories is
based on the first transcription of the tale. The oil paintings that illus-
trate it are in the style of eighteenth-century European landscape painting. There are, of course, many other editions of the story, including
those illustrated by Susan Jeffers, who favors large, wide-eyed faces;
Lisbeth Zwerger, whose style is very delicate and subtle; Paul Galdone,
who uses broad, cartoonish lines; and Margot Tomes, whose quirky
pen-and-ink characters have psychological weight. James Marshall's
version has a slapstick quality.

[380]

HATTIE AND THE WILD WAVES   [381]

Written and illustrated by Barbara Cooney
Cloth: Viking
Published: 1990

The daughter of well-to-do German-Americans in Brooklyn at the turn
of the century, Hattie wants to be a painter. As the large household
progresses pleasantly through the seasons and years bemused by her,
Hattie remains determined, and eventually she succeeds in enrolling in
the art institute. The illustrations and text capture the affectionate
family and their comfortable days with such charm and nuances of
insight it is not surprising to learn that Hattie, who really did become a
painter, is based on the author's mother.

HAVE YOU EVER SEEN . . . ?
AN ABC BOOK   [382]

Written and illustrated by Beau Gardner
Cloth: Dodd, Mead/Putnam
Published: 1986

An alphabet book of graphic tricks and optical illustrations. The designs are very bright and angular and very clever.

HAWK, I'M YOUR BROTHER [383]

Written by Byrd Baylor
Illustrated by Peter Parnall
Cloth: Scribner's
Paper: Aladdin
Published: 1976

In the Southwest, a bare land of mountains and wide sky, a boy named Rudy dreams of flying like a hawk over Santos Mountain. He captures a young hawk and eventually sets it free. The adults are wise and understanding. A very affecting book that is thrilling to read out loud, with spare evocative illustrations.

HER MAJESTY, AUNT ESSIE [384]

Written and illustrated by Amy Schwartz
Cloth: Bradbury
Paper: Penguin
Published: 1984

The little girl who narrates this story can just tell that her aunt Essie, who has moved into her family's apartment (located in an inner-city neighborhood in perhaps the 1940s), used to be a queen. Aunt Essie's style, habits, and gentleman caller make it clear—and believable. It is an affectionate look at eccentricity in family life.

HERSHEL AND THE HANUKKAH GOBLINS [385]

Written by Eric Kimmel
Illustrated by Trina Schart Hyman
Cloth: Holiday
Published: 1989   Prizes: Caldecott Honor

The setting is an Eastern European village, and the plot borders on Halloween Hanukkah. It seems that goblins are occupying the synagogue on the hill. Along comes plucky Hershel of Ostropol, and he cleverly outwits the definitely spooky demons on the successive nights of Hanukkah.

[383]

HEY, AL   [386]

Written by Arthur Yorinks
Illustrated by Richard Egielski
Cloth: Farrar, Straus & Giroux
Paper: Sunburst
Published: 1986   Prizes: Caldecott Medal

Al, a janitor, and Edie, his dog, live together in a small room on the
West Side of Manhattan. When they are offered a chance to go to a
paradisiacal island, they discover that the life of luxury, lush as it may
be, has too high a price. They manage to escape and are grateful to
return home. The brilliant full-color illustrations—from the cramped
apartment to the tropical island—are just right.

HIGHER ON THE DOOR   [387]

Written and illustrated by James Stevenson
Cloth: Greenwillow
Published: 1987

Three slim story books, *When I Was Nine, Higher on the Door,* and *July,*
constitute an artist's notebook memoir, and they capture in spare
watercolor illustrations what seems to have been an idyllic childhood in
a suburb of New York City before World War II. Life was straightforward and orderly, with recurring amusements and problems. These
memorable books can be read separately or all together.

[383]

HILDILID'S NIGHT   [388]

Written by Cheli Duran Ryan
Illustrated by Arnold Lobel
Cloth: Macmillan
Published: 1971   Prizes: Caldecott Honor

Hildilid is an old woman who is determined to put off the night.
Among other things, she tries to sweep it out, tie it up, burn it. She
fails, of course, but a sleep-resisting child enjoys the effort.

Story Books

HOMES IN THE WILDERNESS: A PILGRIM'S JOURNAL OF THE PLYMOUTH PLANTATION IN 1620 BY WILLIAM BRADFORD AND OTHERS OF THE MAYFLOWER COMPANY [389]

Written and illustrated by Margaret Wise Brown
Cloth: Linnet Books/Shoestring Press
Paper: Linnet Books/Shoestring Press
Published: 1939; reissued 1988

This simply written adaptation of the actual Pilgrim diaries has a thrilling immediacy. The clear drawings and maps help place the modern reader.

HORTON HATCHES THE EGG [390]

Written and illustrated by Dr. Seuss
Cloth: Random House
Published: 1940

To be truly successful, nonsense has to be unrelenting and, by its own lights, logical, and in his early books Dr. Seuss was a master of the genre. Horton the elephant agrees to hatch an egg and he sticks to his promise through a year of hilarious trials and outrageous tribulations. Then his kindness and devotion are truly rewarded. There is also an early reader, *Horton Hears a Who*, a large-format picture book.

HOW MANY DAYS TO AMERICA? [391]

Written by Eve Bunting
Illustrated by Beth Peck
Cloth: Clarion
Published: 1988

At the end of this account of the recent arrival on United States shores of an open boat filled with refugees from an unnamed island, a welcoming soul offers two children heaping dinner plates and an explanation: "Long ago, unhappy people came here to start new lives. . . . They celebrated by giving thanks." It's a good thing to remember.

HOW MUCH IS A MILLION? [392]

Written by David M. Schwartz
Illustrated by Steven Kellogg
Cloth: Lothrop, Lee & Shepard
Paper: Scholastic
Published: 1985

A series of lighthearted conceptualizations and visualizations of really big numbers, such as how big a bowl you would need to hold a million goldfish, say. The giddy full-color illustrations hold up under intense scrutiny. *If You Made a Million* goes at that big idea another way, but the illustrator is the same.

HOW MY PARENTS LEARNED TO EAT [393]

Written by Ina Friedman
Illustrated by Allen Say
Cloth: Houghton Mifflin
Paper: Puffin
Published: 1984

A little girl describes her parents' courtship ritual, which was caring and thoughtful, as her father was an American sailor stationed in Japan and her mother was a proper young Japanese lady. The illustrations are subtly reminiscent of nineteenth-century Japanese woodcuts.

HOW PIZZA CAME TO QUEENS [394]

Written and illustrated by Dayal Kaur Khalsa
Cloth: Clarkson N. Potter
Published: 1989   Prizes: New York Times Best Illustrated Book

It's the 1950s in Queens, N.Y., and Mrs. Pelligrino comes from Italy to spend the summer with the Penny family. Mae, the Penny girls' best friend, tells about the sad visitor who sniffs the air and says "No pizza," and how the children find the ingredients to bring joy to their foreign guest and feed the neighborhood. Droll illustrations suit the story. Of course, it also makes you want a taste. *Pizza Man* is a photojournalism story about a contemporary pizza maker. [394]

HOW THE GRINCH STOLE CHRISTMAS [395]

Written and illustrated by Dr. Seuss
Cloth: Random House
Published: 1957

Dr. Seuss's sermon on the true meaning of Christmas features one of the best Scrooges of the twentieth century, that wretched, selfish Grinch. The animated version is shown on television regularly but, like *The Night Before Christmas,* it's more fun to read aloud than watch.

HOW YOU WERE BORN [396]

Written by Joanna Cole
Cloth: Morrow Junior Books
Paper: Mulberry
Published: 1984

When the appropriate time comes, this is a fine book to read with young children who want to know how babies grow inside the mother and are born. The text is clear and accurate; the photographs are beautiful, rather than alarming, for readers from toddler to middle-grade level.

I HAD A FRIEND NAMED PETER: TALKING TO CHILDREN ABOUT THE DEATH OF A FRIEND [397]

Written by Janice Cohn
Illustrated by Gail Owens
Cloth: Morrow Junior Books
Published: 1987

[395]

This is bibliotherapy, but there is no natural way for the subject to arise, and yet it does. Betsy's friend Peter was killed by an automobile. This is the story of how her parents and nursery school helped Betsy understand what happened. Very young children find death, even the death of a peer, unimaginable and there is no right way to address it. However, this book has an introduction by a social worker who has some thoughtful suggestions.

I KNOW A LADY [398]

Written by Charlotte Zolotow
Illustrated by James Stevenson
Cloth: Greenwillow
Published: 1984

In this collaboration between author and artist, a child describes the old lady in her small-town neighborhood who offers perfect friendship to the children as well as small seasonal gifts like homemade cookies or lemonade. The illustrations evoke New England and a nostalgic sense of a social order —of the way things ought to be.

I LIKE THE MUSIC [399]

Written by Leah Komaiko
Illustrated by Barbara Westman
Cloth: Harper & Row/HarperCollins
Paper: Harper Trophy
Published: 1987

The girl who tells this story likes urban street music; she's hip and cool. Her grandmother, who is pretty hip herself, takes the child to her first outdoor symphony concert, with happy results. The full-color illustrations are festive.

[395]

I'LL FIX ANTHONY [400]

Written by Judith Viorst
Illustrated by Arnold Lobel
Cloth: Harper & Row/HarperCollins
Paper: Aladdin
Published: 1969

A tale of revenge intended—it is about all the things the narrator wants to do to get even with his older brother. "When I am six" like Anthony, he'd better just watch out.

I'M TERRIFIC [401]

Written by Marjorie Weinman Sharmat
Illustrated by Kay Chorao
Cloth: Holiday
Paper: Scholastic
Published: 1977

In this gently comic story, Jason Bear tries many ways of being different until he accepts himself.

IF YOU ARE A HUNTER
OF FOSSILS [402]

Written by Byrd Baylor
Illustrated by Peter Parnall
Cloth: Scribner's
Paper: Aladdin
Published: 1980

Here is a splendid introduction to paleontology, with spare, poetic prose and pictures showing how rocks reveal secrets of past life.

IN COAL COUNTRY [403]

Written by Judith Hendershot
Illustrated by Thomas Allen
Cloth: Knopf
Published: 1987

Papa returns from the coal mine blue-eyed, of course, but black-faced from coal dust, grinning at his daughter, who has come to meet him and is seen, in an evocative illustration, reflected in the glass of his head lamp. The text, which recalls growing up in a coal-mining town in the 1950s, is unsentimental and proud; the rich illustrations seem properly smudged with the omnipresent dust.

[402]

IN THE NIGHT KITCHEN [404]

Written and illustrated by Maurice Sendak
Cloth: Harper & Row/HarperCollins
Paper: Harper Trophy
Published: 1970

Prizes: Caldecott Honor
New York Times Best Illustrated Book

[403]

Mickey's dream adventure carries him into the night kitchen, where the bakers are making cake for the morning. The brilliant illustrations are also about movies and New York City in the 1930s. Some adults have found the story—not to mention Mickey's frontal nudity—alarming, but children, especially boys, adore the nocturnal adventure.

THE INCREDIBLE PAINTING OF FELIX CLOUSSEAU [405]

Written and illustrated by Jon Agee
Cloth: Farrar, Straus & Giroux
Paper: Sunburst
Published: 1988

[405]

At a grown-up level, the story of Felix Clousseau and the literal triumph of his paintings, which come to life and leave the salon in Paris, is about art and the establishment. From a young child's perspective it's purely funny, and the droll pictures make more of shades of gray than anyone might reasonably imagine. Older children may find a lot to think about behind the jokes.

IRA SLEEPS OVER [406]

Written and illustrated by Bernard Waber
Cloth: Houghton Mifflin
Paper: Houghton Mifflin
Published: 1972

A first sleepover, even if it is at the house of a close friend like Reggie, who lives right next door to Ira, is a big event. Here it is handled tenderly, and the story is told almost entirely in pricelessly accurate sounding dialogue. The important question is whether a boy takes his teddy bear along. *Ira Says Goodbye* takes place a few years later, when Reggie's family decides to move, and deals as sensitively with a different problem of separation.

THE IRON LION   [407]

Written by Peter Dickinson
Illustrated by Pauline Baynes
Cloth: Bedrick
Published: 1984

A sly modern fairy tale about Mustapha, a charming, impoverished prince who is determined to restore the family fortune and marry the emperor's daughter, Yasmin. He makes the iron lion laugh, becomes his friend, and cures his rustiness. The lavish and exotic full-color illustrations combining Persian miniatures and medieval illumination are both exquisite and funny.

ISLAND BOY   [408]

Written and illustrated by Barbara Cooney
Cloth: Viking
Paper: Puffin
Published: 1988

Consider the life of Matthais Tibbetts, who lived a full, rich one mostly on a small island off the coast of Maine. His parents and eleven siblings all abandoned the island for easier places, but Matthais returned from a career at sea and settled in. The brilliantly spare New England voice telling the story is calm and controlled. The haunting illustrations are washed with the blues of sea and sky. It is a companion, in its way, to *Miss Rumphius*.

ISLAND WINTER   [409]

Written and illustrated by Charles Martin
Cloth: Greenwillow
Published: 1983

A pleasant catalog of month-to-month life off-season on an island almost surely off the northeastern coast of the United States. The illustrations detail the family and community life and happy activities of a third-grader named Heather and her seven friends. Other titles in the series include *For Rent, Island Rescue,* and *Summer Business*.

IT COULD ALWAYS BE WORSE [410]

Written and illustrated by Margot Zemach

Cloth: Farrar, Straus & Giroux

Paper: Sunburst

Published: 1977

Prizes: Caldecott Honor
New York Times Best Illustrated Book

A poor man thinks his crowded household in an Eastern European town is so intolerably crowded that he goes to the rabbi to ask for advice. Amazingly, amusingly, astonishingly, his life gets worse, and the man learns to count his blessings. A familiar folktale, told and illustrated with charm. Another version of the same story is *Too Much Noise*.

IT HAPPENED IN PINSK [411]

Written by Arthur Yorinks
Illustrated by Richard Egielski

Cloth: Farrar, Straus & Giroux

Paper: Sunburst

Published: 1983

Irv Irving, a cranky Russian shoe salesman, literally loses his head before breakfast and runs around Pinsk looking for it. The full-color illustrations are folkloric, Slavic, and stylishly zany all at once.

JELLY BELLY [412]

Written by Dennis Lee
Illustrated by Juan Wijngaard

Cloth: Bedrick

Paper: Bedrick

Published: 1985

A collection of raucous and rowdy verses illustrated with gusto.

[408]

Story Books

JERUSALEM, SHINING STILL   [413]

Written by Karla Kuskin
Illustrated by David Frampton
Cloth: Harper & Row/HarperCollins
Paper: Harper Trophy
Published: 1987

The wood-block illustrations that accompany this poetic account of the history of Jerusalem are as golden, spare, and appealing as the text. Good to read aloud for families of all faiths.

JONAH AND THE GREAT FISH   [414]

Written and illustrated by Warwick Hutton
Cloth: McElderry
Published: 1984   **Prizes: New York Times Best Illustrated Book**

The story of Jonah is interpreted here by a contemporary British artist, whose watercolor illustrations, unusually rich and textured, carry the narrative with greater power than the spare text taken from the King James Bible.

JOSEPH WHO LOVED
THE SABBATH   [415]

Written by Marilyn Hirsh
Illustrated by Devis Grebu
Cloth: Viking
Paper: Puffin
Published: 1986

The traditional Jewish story about Joseph, the devout but poor man who bought the finest things to celebrate the Sabbath and was eventually rewarded for his devotion, has been airily illustrated by an Israeli artist.

JUMANJI [416]

Written and illustrated by Chris Van Allsburg

Cloth: Houghton Mifflin

Published: 1981

Prizes: Caldecott Medal
New York Times Best Illustrated Book

Two restless, cranky children find a board game in the park. They take it home and somehow unleash jungle creatures in the house. Complex, haunting pencil illustrations create a real sense of threat and excitement before a safe return to reality.

KATIE MORAG AND THE TWO GRANDMOTHERS [417]

Written and illustrated by Mairi Hedderwick

Cloth: Little, Brown

Published: 1986

The setting is a remote Scottish island, and young Katie Morag figures out how to reconcile her island granny, bluff and hearty, and her refined mainland granny, who comes to visit. Another title, about the birth of her brother, is *Katie Morag and the Tiresome Ted.*

THE KING HAS HORSE'S EARS [418]

Written by Peggy Thomson
Illustrated by David Small

Cloth: Simon & Schuster

Paper: Simon & Schuster Books for Young Readers

Published: 1988

Only his barber knew. The rest of the world thought that King Horace had everything, even if he was privately miserable and, in truth, silly. At the end of the story, it turns out that his queen thinks his large horse's ears are perfectly lovely. The moral fable is so wittily illustrated that it gets well past bibliotherapy and amuses the least self-conscious young readers, as well as those with anxieties about themselves.

KING ISLAND CHRISTMAS   [419]

Written by Jean Rogers
Illustrated by Rie Munoz
Cloth: Greenwillow
Published: 1985

The Eskimo community of King Island has to rescue its new priest and get him from his stranded ship in the Bering Sea to the village in time for Christmas. An unusual story with glorious illustrations in the myriad blues of the north.

THE KNEE-HIGH MAN: AND OTHER TALES   [420]

Written by Julius Lester
Illustrated by Ralph Pinto
Cloth: Dial
Paper: Pied Piper
Published: 1972

A collection of six animal stories from the American black folklore tradition. The author has also retold many of the Uncle Remus stories.

LIKE JAKE AND ME   [421]

[423]

Written by Mavis Jukes
Illustrated by Lloyd Bloom
Cloth: Knopf
Paper: Knopf
Published: 1984   Prizes: Newbery Honor

Alex, who is quiet and rather shy, probably like his father, is trying to cope with his stepfather, Jake, a brash cowboy. The turning point comes when Alex rescues Jake from a wolf spider. This well-written story about the formation of new families carries special conviction. The illustrations are insightful.

THE LITTLE BOOKROOM   [422]

Written by Eleanor Farjeon
Illustrated by Edward Ardizzone
Cloth: David Godine
Paper: Godine
Published: 1984   Prizes: H. C. Andersen

This collection of illustrated stories is perhaps the best known title by the British author and artist. Both of them were renowned and beloved earlier in this century and are worth seeking out.

THE LITTLE HOUSE   [423]

Written and illustrated by Virginia Lee Burton
Cloth: Houghton Mifflin
Paper: Houghton Mifflin
Published: 1942   Prizes: Caldecott Medal

Here is the now classic story of a little house that was built on a hill long ago, and how, as time passed, the city closed in upon it. Eventually, the little house was rescued and brought back to rural peace and calm. With its windows, door, and stoop that together look like a smiling face, the little house is back where it belongs—on a country hilltop. Beneath the charm and sweetness there is a profound anti-urbanism to both text and illustration, which adults can see clearly but may choose not to mention.

[423]

LITTLE RABBIT'S LOOSE TOOTH   [424]

Written by Lucy Bate
Illustrated by Diane de Groat
Cloth: Crown
Paper: Crown
Published: 1975

The title tells all but does not convey the charm of the heroine and the dialogue as she moves through one of life's crises inevitably faced by six-year-olds—the first loose tooth. Little Rabbit reappears addressing another threatening issue in *Little Rabbit's Baby Brother*.

THE LITTLE RED LIGHTHOUSE AND THE GREAT GRAY BRIDGE   [425]

Written by Hildegarde Hoyt Swift
Illustrated by Lynd Ward
Cloth: HBJ
Paper: Voyager
Published: 1942

There really is a little red lighthouse that sits in the shadow of the George Washington Bridge, which spans the Hudson River in New York City. This has been a picture-book favorite for generations.

LITTLE RED RIDING HOOD   [426]

Written by the Brothers Grimm
Illustrated by Trina Schart Hyman
Cloth: Holiday
Paper: Holiday
Published: 1983   Prizes: Caldecott Honor

The illustrator of this version of the classic tale has a distinctive style—lush, romantic, anxious, and at the same time tense—that suits the story well. There are many other editions, including cartoonish ones illustrated by Paul Galdone, James Marshall, and Harriet Pincus, and a very provocative one illustrated with photographs by Sarah Moon. Consider the age of the reader when choosing—younger children find the lighter, more cartoonish versions easier to handle.

LITTLE SISTER AND THE MONTH BROTHERS   [427]

Written by Beatrice Schenk de Regniers
Illustrated by Margot Tomes
Cloth: Clarion
Paper: Clarion
Published: 1976

[427]

In this bright retelling of the Russian fairy tale about how the Month brothers help little sister meet the seasonally impossible demands of her greedy stepmother, the illustrations are witty and washed with moody grays.

LITTLE TIM AND THE BRAVE SEA CAPTAIN   [428]

Written and illustrated by Edward Ardizzone
Paper: Puffin
Published: 1979

Now available only in paperback, this beloved English story-book adventure tells how young Tim stows away on a steamship and nearly goes down with the captain in a storm. The watercolor illustrations capture the changing moods of the sea beautifully. It's a thrilling book with a happy ending. Other Tim books include *Tim and Ginger*, *Tim and Charlotte*, and *Tim and Towser*.

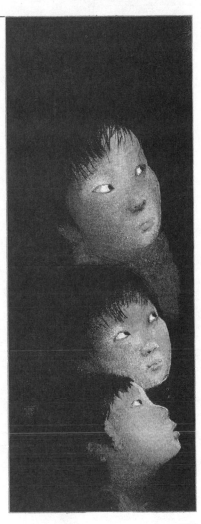

[429]

LON PO PO: A RED-RIDING HOOD STORY FROM CHINA   [429]

Written and illustrated by Ed Young
Cloth: Philomel
Published: 1989   Prizes: Caldecott Medal

Mysterious watercolor illustrations make this story of the three Chinese sisters who mistake the wolf for Po Po, their grandmother, very appealing. They realize their mistake, and the next day they cleverly lure the predator up into the gingko tree.

LORD OF THE DANCE: AN AFRICAN RETELLING   [430]

Written and illustrated by Veronique Tadjo
Cloth: Lippincott/HarperCollins
Published: 1989

The Senufo people who live in the Ivory Coast have always worshiped spirits represented by sacred masks. The text here is a transposition of a Christian hymn, "Lord of the Dance," that is retold as the mask's song and that conveys the beliefs that guide Senufo tradition and modern life. The brilliantly colored illustrations are spare and the symbolism is accessible for young readers.

LOUHI, WITCH OF NORTH FARM [431]

Written by Toni de Gerez
Illustrated by Barbara Cooney
Cloth: Viking
Paper: Puffin
Published: 1986

Here is a story from the epic Finnish cycle the Kalevala about naughty Louhi, the witch. In this episode, she steals both the sun and moon and locks them away in Copper Mountain. Vainamoinen the Great Knower outwits her, of course. The text and the carefully detailed illustrations, in a muted northern palette, perfectly complement each other.

LOUIS THE FISH [432]

Written by Arthur Yorinks
Illustrated by Richard Egielski
Cloth: Farrar, Straus & Giroux
Paper: Sunburst
Published: 1980

A perfectly executed, scaly fantasy in which Louis, a respectable, aproned butcher, turns into a large fish—a salmon, actually. And he looks really ridiculous lying in bed under the covers, wearing striped pajamas over his fins. It's the kind of zany story that often appeals to parents as much as to children.

LULLABIES AND NIGHT SONGS [433]

Written by William Engvick
Illustrated by Maurice Sendak
Cloth: Harper & Row/HarperCollins
Paper: Harper Trophy
Published: 1965

The music for these forty-eight songs, whose lyrics are taken from nursery rhymes and poems, is by Alec Wilder. The color illustrations are by another master, Maurice Sendak. If you are musical enough to pick out the graceful melodies, this is worth having at home.

[432]

THE LULLABY SONGBOOK [434]

Written by Jane Yolen
Illustrated by Charles Mikolaycak
Cloth: HBJ
Published: 1986

This is a pleasing collection of bedtime songs, old and new, from around the world, with charming illustrations and simple piano and guitar arrangements.

LYLE, LYLE, CROCODILE [435]

Written and illustrated by Bernard Waber
Cloth: Houghton Mifflin
Paper: Houghton Mifflin
Published: 1965

The crocodile who first moved in with the Primm family in *The House on East 88th Street* now wants to make friends with Loretta the cat. The family copes, of course. Other titles in the series include *Lovable Lyle, Lyle and the Birthday Party,* and *Lyle Finds His Mother.*

MAGGIE DOESN'T WANT
TO MOVE [436]

Written by Elizabeth Lee O'Donnell
Illustrated by Amy Schwartz
Cloth: Four Winds
Published: 1987

[432]

This is bibliotherapy, but so laced with wit and humor—and further enhanced by winsome, comic illustrations—it is a good story book. Simon, who is seven, insists that he doesn't really mind moving; it's Maggie, his little sister, who would miss the slide at the playground and his teacher, Mrs. Acosta, and the neighborhood. But when they go to visit the new house, new neighborhood, and new school, Simon thinks maybe Maggie might change her mind. *Teddy Bears' Moving Day* is another appealing book on the same subject.

THE MAGIC SCHOOL BUS AT THE WATERWORKS [437]

Written by Joanna Cole
Illustrated by Bruce Degen
Cloth: Scholastic
Paper: Scholastic
Published: 1986

With her outlandish outfits and diffident manner, Ms. Frizzle may be the strangest teacher in the school, but the trip she takes her class on—going into the reservoir system and through the waterworks and back to school—is magical. Everyone, even Arnold, the anxious whiner, has a wonderful time and helps tell part of the tale. The straight scientific information is delivered in sidebar notes. The book is a model of witty, imaginative, and accurate science writing, with equally amusing and imaginative illustrations. The series includes *The Magic School Bus: Inside the Earth; The Magic School Bus: Inside the Human Body;* and *The Magic School Bus: Lost in the Solar System.*

THE MAN WHO COULD CALL DOWN OWLS [438]

Written by Eve Bunting
Illustrated by Charles Mikolaycak
Cloth: Macmillan
Published: 1984

This is a fable about a sorcerer, deep in the woods, who calls down the owls each night. An evil stranger envies his power. The black-and-white illustrations are full of mystery and slightly scary shadows.

THE MAN WHOSE MOTHER WAS A PIRATE [439]

Written by Margaret Mahy
Illustrated by Margaret Chamberlin
Cloth: Viking
Paper: Puffin
Published: 1986

He's an office-worker wimp, his mother was a pirate, and now she wants to go home to the sea. So, with only a wheelbarrow and a kite, Sam takes her. The illustrations to this grand story are broad and funny; the text, however, is far better still, and includes lyrical praise of the sea. This book is worth reading aloud again and again just for the pleasure of the language.

MANY MOONS   [440]

Written by James Thurber
Illustrated by Louis Slobodkin
Cloth: HBJ
Paper: Voyager
Published: 1943   Prizes: Caldecott Medal

There was once a little princess who wanted the moon—and she got it. A classic story with pale, subtle, haunting illustrations. There is also a newer edition, with illustrations by Marc Simont.

MARGUERITE, GO WASH YOUR FEET!   [441]

Written and illustrated by Wallace Tripp
Cloth: Houghton Mifflin
Paper: Houghton Mifflin
Published: 1985

A collection of funny verse from Shakespeare to Spike Milligan, with suitably sharp illustrations, many of which contain cartoonish renditions of famous people.

[440]

MAZEL AND SHLIMAZEL   [442]

Written by Isaac Bashevis Singer
Illustrated by Margot Zemach
Cloth: Farrar, Straus & Giroux
Paper: Sunburst
Published: 1967

This story, told in the manner of an Eastern European folktale, is about the contest between good and evil, which take the forms of the happy and good Mazel and the wicked old Shlimazel. The illustrations perfectly complement the fable.

A MEDIEVAL FEAST   [443]

Written and illustrated by Aliki
Cloth: T. Y. Crowell/HarperCollins
Paper: Harper Trophy
Published: 1983

What happens when the king announces that he and his attendants plan to visit the lord of the manor? In this remarkably accomplished historical story book, the detailed illustrations, in the medieval style, show both the structure of manor life and the elaborate preparations that must take place before the king arrives—how the food is prepared and served, the entertainment organized, and so on. Joe Lasker's *Merry Ever After* and *A Tournament of Knights* are fine companion titles.

MERRY EVER AFTER: THE STORY OF TWO MEDIEVAL WEDDINGS   [444]

Written and illustrated by Joe Lasker
Paper: Puffin
Published: 1976   Prizes: New York Times Best Illustrated Book

The celebration of two weddings offers a fine explanation of class and custom in the Middle Ages. The illustrations are detailed and high-spirited. *A Tournament of Knights* by the same author is another good story book about medieval life, as is *A Medieval Feast* by Aliki.

MIKE MULLIGAN AND HIS STEAM SHOVEL   [445]

Written and illustrated by Virginia Lee Burton
Cloth: Houghton Mifflin
Paper: Houghton Mifflin
Published: 1939

A classic picture book with a message that has pleased generations of young readers. Mike Mulligan and his steam shovel, Mary Anne, are being declared obsolete, but fiercely determined, they find one last job in a small town. They dig their way to a new career and a happy ending.

MING LO MOVES THE MOUNTAIN   [446]

Written and illustrated by Arnold Lobel
Paper: Scholastic
Published: 1982

Ming Lo asks the wise man's help in moving the mountain away from his house because of the falling debris that annoys his cranky wife. The wise man puffs away on his water pipe and eventually comes up with the perfect solution that convinces Ming Lo and, more important, his wife that indeed the mountain has moved.

MINN OF THE MISSISSIPPI   [447]

Written and illustrated by Holling C. Holling
Cloth: Houghton Mifflin
Paper: Houghton Mifflin
Published: 1951

A classic book about the great river. The margins are filled with detailed illustrations of flora and fauna, and the text remains engrossing, although the waterway has changed dramatically over the forty years since the book was originally published.

MIRANDY AND BROTHER WIND   [448]

Written by Patricia C. McKissick
Illustrated by Jerry Pinkney
Cloth: Knopf
Published: 1988   Prizes: Caldecott Honor

The cakewalk contest is coming and Mirandy, who plans on winning, needs a special partner. She decides on Brother Wind, but he's unreliable and she ends up with Ezel, who adores her, instead. The story, inspired by a photograph of the author's grandparents taken in 1906, when, as teenagers, they won a similar contest, is wise and humorous. It captures the spirit of small-town festivals and the voices of older folks giving advice. The illustrations fairly dance.

[445]

MISS NELSON IS MISSING!   [449]

Written by Harry Allard
Illustrated by James Marshall
Cloth: Houghton Mifflin
Paper: Houghton Mifflin
Published: 1977

The first in a trio of raucous books about the students in Room 207, their dear teacher, Miss Nelson, and her mean, hideous, lunatic substitute, Miss Viola Swamp. Other titles are *Miss Nelson Has a Field Day* and *Miss Nelson Is Back.* These are especially loved by second- and third-graders.

MISS RUMPHIUS   [450]

Written and illustrated by Barbara Cooney
Cloth: Viking
Paper: Puffin
Published: 1982

Miss Rumphius was told as a child that she must do something to make the world more beautiful. She traveled, had adventures, and found her calling as the Lupine Lady, sowing the seed of the blue and purple flowers by the seacoast where she lives. She is very old now, and quite magical. A small, jewel-like picture book that carries its moral imperative lightly. It is a kind of companion to *Island Boy.*

MOLLY'S PILGRIM   [451]

Written by Barbara Cohen
Illustrated by Michael J. Deraney
Cloth: Lothrop, Lee & Shepard
Paper: Bantam
Published: 1983

The Pilgrim doll that Molly makes for her third-grade Thanksgiving class assignment reflects her experiences as a recent immigrant and the only Jewish child in the class. An unusual and provocative book, it was made into an award-winning short film.

MOON TIGER   [452]

Written by Phyllis Root
Illustrated by Ed Young
Cloth: Henry Holt
Published: 1985

A dream of adventure and revenge. Jessica Ellen and her little brother are sent to bed. She dreams that the moon tiger will carry her off to the Arctic and to jungles and, finally, of course, home. Intense, vibrant illustrations in startling colors make this an unusual bedtime book.

[449]

MOSS GOWN   [453]

Written by William H. Hooks
Illustrated by Donald Carrick
Cloth: Clarion
Published: 1987

This story, drawn from Carolina folklore and set in the antebellum South, mixes elements of *King Lear* and *Cinderella*. Candace is rejected by her father for loving him "as much as meat loves salt." Magically transformed to Moss Gown, she becomes the mistress of a great plantation and years later is reconciled with her father. The language is rich and the illustrations are mysterious.

MOTHER GOOSE: A COLLECTION OF CLASSIC NURSERY RHYMES   [454]

Written and illustrated by Michael Hague
Cloth: Henry Holt
Published: 1984

A collection of the illustrator's favorites from the Mother Goose canon. The lush style is often reminiscent of the work of artists from an earlier era.

157

THE MOUNTAINS OF TIBET   [455]

Written and illustrated by Mordicai Gerstein
Cloth: Harper & Row/HarperCollins
Paper: Harper Trophy
Published: 1987   Prizes: New York Times Best Illustrated Book

The life cycle of a boy who grows up to become a woodcutter in a valley in Tibet is told in a brilliant story-book adaptation of the Tibetan Book of the Dead. At his death, the woodcutter has the choice of becoming part of heaven or living another life. The illustrations help carry the story from that faraway valley into the cosmos itself and back to the valley. It is an awesomely accomplished book that can be read repeatedly by both children and adults.

THE MOUSEHOLE CAT   [456]

Written by Antonia Barber
Illustrated by Nicola Bayley
Cloth: Macmillan
Published: 1990

The story comes from a Cornish legend about a fishing village called Mousehole, meaning a safe cove. Mowser, the sleek, striped cat who is the hero of the tale, lives with old Tom the fisherman, who treats him very well. This telling has lyrically beautiful illustrations that evoke sea and storm and especially the Great Storm-Cat, which threatens the town in myriad shades of blue. And the fish—oh so many gleaming fish.

[456]

MRS. MOSKOWITZ AND THE SABBATH CANDLESTICKS   [457]

Written and illustrated by Amy Schwartz
Paper: Jewish Publication Society
Published: 1984

Mrs. Moskowitz and her cat, Fred, have moved to a new apartment. Finding her Sabbath candlesticks in a packing box prompts the widow into unpacking and making their new quarters into a welcoming home. The round, chunky illustrations and an unselfconscious text explain Jewish Sabbath rituals in an affecting way.

MUFARO'S BEAUTIFUL DAUGHTERS: AN AFRICAN TALE [458]

Written and illustrated by John Steptoe
Cloth: Lothrop, Lee & Shepard
Paper: Scholastic
Published: 1987   **Prizes: Caldecott Honor**

This West African tale tells about Mufaro's two beautiful but totally different daughters—Manyara, who is ambitious and mean, and Nyasha, who is kind and helpful. Guess which one ends up marrying the king? The illustrations are sumptuous.

MUMMIES MADE IN EGYPT [459]

Written and illustrated by Aliki
Cloth: T. Y. Crowell/HarperCollins
Paper: Harper Trophy
Published: 1979

This is a well-organized and very well illustrated introduction to ancient Egyptian beliefs and funerary practices, especially, of course, the fascinating mummies.

[457]

MY FIRST PICTURE DICTIONARY [460]

Written by Katherine Howard
Illustrated by Huck Scarry
Paper: Random House
Published: 1978

A slim, simply arranged paperback that is both a useful dictionary— over two hundred words are illustrated in cheerful fashion—but also an introduction to the idea of dictionaries and reference books.

MY LITTLE ISLAND [461]

Written and illustrated by Frané Lessac
Cloth: Lippincott/HarperCollins
Paper: Harper Trophy
Published: 1985

The lucky narrator describes a wonderful holiday visit to an island in the Caribbean that he takes with his best friend, who was born there. Their holiday trip is captured in exuberant, brightly colored primitive-style paintings. Lucky boys.

THE MYSTERIES OF
HARRIS BURDICK [462]

Written and illustrated by Chris Van Allsburg
Cloth: Houghton Mifflin
Paper: Dell
Published: 1984   Prizes: New York Times Best Illustrated Book

Strange, even weird, fragments of text, illustrated in totally unexpected ways by a master draftsman. This is a contemporary picture book that speaks to teenagers and adults as strongly as to older children. A book for discussion and to use in making up games and plays.

NED AND THE JOYBALOO [463]

Written by Hiawyn Oram
Illustrated by Satoshi Kitamura
Cloth: Farrar, Straus & Giroux
Paper: Sunburst
Published: 1989

Ned's Joybaloo is "big and beautiful, with a funny leathery nose and its breath full of paper roses." The fantasy creature is his companion in escape from the ordinary, and what blissful escape it is. But when the time comes for Ned to go on alone, the Joybaloo helps him with the separation. The artist and writer collaborated on *Angry Arthur,* which is similarly satisfying. The accomplished watercolor drawings are best when freest—as when Ned and the Joybaloo go sailing through the deep blue sky.

A NEW COAT FOR ANNA [464]

Written by Harriet Ziefert
Illustrated by Anita Lobel
Cloth: Knopf
Paper: Knopf
Published: 1986

Someplace in Europe after World War II, Anna's mother bargains and barters with a sheep farmer, a spinner, a weaver, and a tailor so that Anna will have a new coat the following winter. This story, accompanied by appealing illustrations, is of greatest interest to early-grade children, especially girls, but holds the attention of younger listeners.

THE NIGHTINGALE   [465]

Written by Hans Christian Andersen
Illustrated by Lisbeth Zwerger
Cloth: Picture Book
Paper: Scholastic
Published: 1986

The Viennese illustrator's version of the familiar story of the emperor and the real and mechanical songbirds is very fragile and subtle. The emperor and his court seem, somehow, like China dolls, possibly made of porcelain. There are pretty, very different versions illustrated by Demi (delicate); Beni Montresor (lush); and Nancy E. Burkert (large faces).

NO STAR NIGHTS   [466]

Written by Anna Egan Smucker
Illustrated by Steve Johnson
Cloth: Knopf
Published: 1989

A little girl remembers growing up in a steel-mill town in West Virginia in the 1950s. "We couldn't see the stars in the nighttime sky because the furnaces of the mill turned the darkness into a red glow." Her affectionate sketch of a time of hard work and domestic tranquillity is splendidly framed, even sharpened, by the deeply colored illustrations.

NOAH AND THE GREAT FLOOD   [467]

Written and illustrated by Warwick Hutton
Cloth: McElderry
Published: 1977

The familiar Bible story is told here by the contemporary English artist, whose watercolors capture the sea and storm with startling power.

[463]

NOAH'S ARK [468]

Written and illustrated by Peter Spier
Cloth: Doubleday
Paper: Zephyr
Published: 1977

Prizes: Caldecott Medal
New York Times Best Illustrated Book

The only text in this prizewinning version of the story of Noah is a seventeenth-century Dutch poem describing the menagerie. The rest of this account is narrative illustration. There are double-page spreads showing minute details of the construction of the ark and habits of the animals, contrasted with double-page spreads of the tiny boat on wind-tossed, rainy seas. The crowding, chaos, and tension of the ark just before the end are palpable. This book holds the attention of a wide age range, from toddlers through the middle-graders. For what happened next, see *Aardvarks, Disembark.*

NTOMBI'S SONG [469]

Written by Jenny Seed
Illustrated by Anno Berry
Cloth: Beacon Press
Paper: Beacon Press
Published: 1989

Ntombi, a brave and clever six-year-old South African girl, has a special song she sings to cheer herself up. It comes in handy. One morning she is sent to the store all by herself to buy sugar, an expedition that promises (and delivers) great adventures. The illustrations capture the spunky heroine deftly. The author and the illustrator are both from South Africa.

OL' PAUL, THE MIGHTY LOGGER   [470]

Written and illustrated by Glen Rounds
Cloth: Holiday
Paper: Holiday
Published: 1936

Here's a dandy collection of stories about the giant logger's adventures and achievements. Rounds is the author/illustrator of another Bunyan tale, called *The Morning the Sun Refused to Rise,* which is also comic and farfetched. There are other Paul Bunyan stories in print, including Stephen Kellogg's exuberant full-color picture-book version and a reissue of a distinguished, more sober volume, illustrated by Rockwell Kent.

OLD HENRY   [471]

Written by Joan Blos
Illustrated by Stephen Gammell
Cloth: Morrow Junior Books
Paper: Mulberry
Published: 1987

Old Henry just doesn't keep house the way his neighbors think he ought to, but when he up and leaves, they find they miss him. A small morality play about tolerance, illustrated with great wit in a style reminiscent of *The Relatives Came.*

THE OLD SYNAGOGUE   [472]

Written and illustrated by Richard Rosenblum
Cloth: Jewish Publication Society
Published: 1989

[472]

Some European Jews who came to the United States in the late nineteenth century founded a neighborhood synagogue in the city where they settled. The story of the synagogue, the neighborhood, and, implicitly, the unnamed city is told in detailed drawings and spare text. As time passed, things changed   the sidewalk hustle and bustle faded, people moved away, the synagogue fell into disuse, the neighborhood into decay. But this is a story of both religious and urban renewal, and a contemporary wave of migrants arrived, people who wanted both to live in the city and renew their faith. The slim book is rich in messages and morals.

ONE DAY IN PARADISE   [473]

Written and illustrated by Helme Heine
Cloth: McElderry
Published: 1986
Beautiful watercolor illustrations by a distinguished German artist make this charming version of the biblical story of creation unique. It shows God as the kindliest and most dignified of elderly gardeners.

ONE SUMMER AT GRANDMOTHER'S HOUSE   [474]

Written and illustrated by Poupa Montaufier
Cloth: Carolrhoda
Published: 1986
A memoir, illustrated with charming primitive-style paintings, of a summer the author spent with her grandmother Oma in the Alsace region of France. There are lots of garden and domestic details to discuss.

OUTSIDE OVER THERE   [475]

Written and illustrated by Maurice Sendak
Cloth: Harper & Row/HarperCollins
Paper: Harper Trophy
Published: 1981

Prizes: Caldecott Honor
New York Times Best Illustrated Book

Sendak's most visually lavish book has a spare text and addresses potent, emotional issues—siblings and abandonment. Ida is left in charge of her baby sister, who is kidnapped. Ida determines to rescue the baby and enters a baffling dream world from which they both emerge with new understanding. The painterly illustrations, full of elaborate symbolism and literary, musical, and historical references, are worth studying closely. As with Sendak's other books, children tend to see them differently as they grow older rather than outgrow them.

[477]

OWL MOON   [476]

Written by Jane Yolen
Illustrated by John Schoenherr
Cloth: Philomel
Published: 1987

Prizes: Caldecott Medal

This is the sort of book that makes city children achingly wish to live in the country. The very idea of going out late on a moonlit winter's night with your father and calling for owls is quite magical, as is this story, with its snowy, night-lit illustrations.

OX-CART MAN   [477]

Written by Donald Hall
Illustrated by Barbara Cooney
Cloth: Viking
Paper: Puffin
Published: 1979

Prizes: Caldecott Medal
New York Times Best Illustrated Book

The rich context of history can be conveyed in stories for young children, as this splendid book clearly shows. The text is by a distinguished writer and poet; the beautiful prizewinning illustrations are in the folk tradition. Their collaborative evocation of a year of domestic life in a nineteenth-century rural New England area is rich with detail and insight. It reads aloud very well.

[477]

PADDLE-TO-THE-SEA   [478]

Written and illustrated by Holling C. Holling
Cloth: Houghton Mifflin
Published: 1941

This book is both very old-fashioned to look at and thrillingly modern in its idea and organization. A boy living in the Great Lakes region sets a toy Indian lad into a canoe and sends them downstream. The story follows the waterways to the ocean. Half a century has passed since it was written and a great deal has changed—technology the least of it—and yet the book is compelling.

PAMELA CAMEL   [479]

Written and illustrated by Bill Peet
Cloth: Houghton Mifflin
Paper: Houghton Mifflin
Published: 1984

Circus life makes Pamela Camel cross and irritable. She runs away along a railroad track, where she happens upon a broken tie, recognizes the danger it represents, and later is able to prevent a wreck by bravely stopping a train. A hero, she returns to the circus a star. There are several dozen books by Bill Peet in print. They are lightly told, often rhymed, fables, with illustrations that suggest his background as a Walt Disney studios artist. They are endearing, unpretentious, and satisfying. Among the best are *Kermit the Hermit; Buford, the Little Bighorn; Ella;* and *The Pinkish, Bluish, Purplish Egg.*

[479]

PANDA   [480]

Written and illustrated by Susan Bonners
Cloth: Delacorte
Paper: Young Yearling
Published: 1978

In addition to the charming watercolor illustrations of pandas, there is solid information about the habits and behavior of the shy mammals from the mountains of southwest China. *A Penguin Year* is also appealing.

PAPER JOHN   [481]

Written and illustrated by David Small
Cloth: Farrar, Straus & Giroux
Paper: Sunburst
Published: 1987

Paper John is a mysterious fellow who makes wonderful things, including his own house, out of folded paper. He does battle with a devil who has only one trick, but it is the potent one of controlling the winds and it threatens to destroy Paper John and the town as well. Handsomely illustrated.

[480]

PA'S BALLOON AND OTHER
PIG TALES   [482]

Written and illustrated by Arthur Geisert
Cloth: Houghton Mifflin
Published: 1984

Pa takes the whole pig family flying in a hot-air balloon, and they have a series of adventures, set out in hand-colored copper-plate prints. The thrill of being airborne is almost palpable.

THE PATCHWORK QUILT   [483]

Written by Valerie Flournoy
Illustrated by Jerry Pinkney
Cloth: Dial
Published: 1985

As she cut and stitched pieces from old family clothes, Tanya's grandmother told the little girl about the quilt she was making. Then, Grandmother became ill, and now the family works together to complete her masterpiece. The full-color illustrations capture the richness and strength of Tanya's loving family as well as the quilt.

PATRICK'S DINOSAURS   [484]

Written by Carol Carrick
Illustrated by Donald Carrick
Cloth: Clarion
Paper: Clarion
Published: 1983

Patrick listens carefully to his big brother Hank's description of dinosaurs and then scares himself with some fantasies about what it would be like if they were around today. In the even funnier *Return of Patrick's Dinosaurs*, he claims they are back, and the illustrations show clearly how the creatures enrich the ordinary things in life.

PAUL BUNYAN   [485]

Written and illustrated by Steven Kellogg
Cloth: Morrow Junior Books
Paper: Mulberry
Published: 1984

A rambunctious version of the legend of the mighty logger and his blue ox, Babe. The illustrations are exuberant. The author/illustrator has also retold the story of Pecos Bill.

A PEACEABLE KINGDOM:
THE SHAKER ABECEDARIUS   [486]

Written and illustrated by Alice and Martin Provensen
Cloth: Viking
Paper: Puffin
Published: 1978   **Prizes: New York Times Best Illustrated Book**

This splendid abecedarius (or alphabet book) shows a grand procession of real and imaginary animals parading in a setting that is also a vision

[486]

of Shaker society. Parents who choose can go on to explain more about the American religious sect whose designs are so prized today.

PERFECT THE PIG   [487]

Written and illustrated by Susan Jeschke
Cloth: Henry Holt
Paper: Scholastic
Published: 1981

Sometimes getting what you wish for leads to serious complications. Perfect the Pig wishes for wings, but the results are not what he expected, even though he and his friend Olive end up just where they want to be in this charming and roundabout story.

PETER AND THE WOLF   [488]

Written by Sergei Prokofiev
Illustrated by Jorg Muller
Cloth: Knopf
Published: 1986

This version of the story with music that is so often a child's real introduction to the orchestra is persuasively placed in a lush theatrical setting—a European opera house. The relationship of the musical instruments to the characters thus becomes clear, and even the role of the conductor makes sense. There are other good editions around, by such illustrators as Charles Mikolaycak and Warren Chappell. There is also a pop-up version by Barbara Cooney.

PETER THE GREAT   [489]

Written and illustrated by Diane Stanley
Cloth: Four Winds   [486]
Paper: Aladdin
Published: 1986

A brightly told and well-illustrated biography of one of Western history's truly larger than life figures. This is especially appealing to boys who are not yet fluid readers but are interested in real people and history.

THE PHILHARMONIC GETS DRESSED [490]

Written by Karla Kuskin
Illustrated by Marc Simont
Cloth: Harper & Row/HarperCollins
Paper: Harper Trophy
Published: 1982

As a winter day ends, 105 people bathe, get dressed, and go to work. They are members of an orchestra who live in and around a big city. The text and illustrations are both witty and economical and offer a great deal to talk about at bedtime (or any other time, for that matter). The equally delightful companion book is *The Dallas Titans Get Ready for Bed.*

PIGS FROM A TO Z [491]

Written and illustrated by Arthur Geisert
Cloth: Houghton Mifflin
Paper: Houghton Mifflin
Published: 1986   **Prizes: New York Times Best Illustrated Book**

A rich and imaginative alphabet book in which seven piglets build a tree house. The illustrations are in fact intricate etchings. This alphabet book seems especially appealing to boys.

[490]

THE PILGRIMS OF PLIMOTH [492]

Written and illustrated by Marcia Sewall
Cloth: Atheneum
Published: 1986

The narrator gives a detailed and appreciative account of daily life in the Plymouth colony as well as a brief history of its establishment, culminating, of course, with Thanksgiving. The oil painting illustrations are unusually evocative, luminous canvases with precise details. The sequel, *People of the Breaking Day*, describes daily life in the same period from the Indian point of view. These scrupulously researched and thoughtful books approach illustrated history seriously and are appreciated by children in the lower and middle grades.

PINKERTON, BEHAVE [493]

Written and illustrated by Steven Kellogg
Cloth: Dial
Paper: Pied Piper
Published: 1979

Even as a puppy, Pinkerton (who is really a Great Dane) is as big as a pony, as eager as a monkey, not to mention amiable, awkward, and full of mischief and goodwill. In *A Rose for Pinkerton,* the family gives him a kitten, who, it turns out, wants to be a Great Dane, too. There are also *Tallyho, Pinkerton* and *Prehistoric Pinkerton,* all with illustrations in the author's recognizable wild, funny style.

THE POLAR EXPRESS [494]

Written and illustrated by Chris Van Allsburg
Cloth: Houghton Mifflin   Prizes: Caldecott Medal
Published: 1985   New York Times Best Illustrated Book

An unseen adult narrator remembers a mysterious Christmas Eve when he rode the special train to the North Pole and was selected by Santa Claus to receive the first Christmas gift. Haunting illustrations in rich, subtle colors make this a very special book indeed.

THE PORCELAIN CAT [495]

Written by Michael Patrick Hearn
Illustrated by Leo and Diane Dillon
Cloth: Little, Brown
Published: 1987

There are rats in the sorcerer's library, so he wants to cast a spell to bring his porcelain cat to life and chase them. To cast the right spell, Nickon, his assistant, must first go out into the night to fetch a vial of basilisk blood. Nickon meets a witch, a centaur, and an undine. The structure is a classic fairy tale; the illustrations are mysterious and full of surprises for searching eyes. The result is a very satisfying read-it-again story.

[490]

171

A PRAIRIE BOY'S WINTER   [496]

Written and illustrated by William Kurelek
Cloth: Houghton Mifflin
Paper: Houghton Mifflin
Published: 1973   **Prizes: New York Times Best Illustrated Book**

A prairie farm in winter during the 1930s is vividly recalled in a book distinguished by the quality of both prose and full-page illustrations. The companion volume is *A Prairie Boy's Summer*.

PRINCESS FURBALL   [497]

Written by Charlotte Huck
Illustrated by Anita Lobel
Cloth: Greenwillow
Paper: Scholastic
Published: 1989

This variation on "Cinderella" tells how the beautiful and clever princess escapes marrying an ogre and captures the heart of the true prince. She tells her father she must have "three bridal gifts—one dress as golden as the sun, another as silvery as the moon, and a third as glittering as the stars. In addition . . . a coat made out of a thousand different kinds of fur," and then she sets off on her own. The illustrations are all appealing; those set outdoors in the winter are haunting.

THE PURPLE COAT   [498]

Written by Amy Hest
Illustrated by Amy Schwartz
Cloth: Four Winds
Published: 1986

Every year Gabrielle's grandfather makes her a new navy blue coat in his tailor shop in the city. This year, Gabrielle wants a purple coat and her mother says no. Grandfather finds a way. The quirky, cartoonish illustrations are precise and full of details to explore, especially those of the tailor shop.

PUSS IN BOOTS   [499]

Written by Charles Perrault
Illustrated by Fred Marcellino
Cloth: Farrar, Straus & Giroux
Published: 1990   Prizes: Caldecott Honor

The miller left his youngest son a cat, but oh, what a cat! This version
of the well-loved French tale first told by Charles Perrault is particularly
sumptuous—the lush, period-perfect illustrations gleam with silk and
velvet. The cat who brings such good fortune is sly and fine. Another,
wordless, version of the story, by John Goodall, is particularly pleasing
to share with younger children.

RABBIT MAKES A MONKEY OUT OF
LION: A SWAHILI TALE   [500]

Written by Verna Aardema
Illustrated by Jerry Pinkney
Cloth: Dial
Paper: Pied Piper
Published: 1989

Lion learns the hard way that "rabbits are just too hard to catch" in this
laugh-out-loud East African trickster story. The watercolor illustrations
have a velvety softness.

THE RANDOM HOUSE BOOK OF
MOTHER GOOSE   [501]

Written and illustrated by Arnold Lobel
Cloth: Random House
Published: 1986

This generous edition of the canon, including 306 verses, shows a fine
artist at the top of his roly-poly form. An ebullient collection, with
selections appropriate for all ages.

THE RANDOM HOUSE BOOK OF POETRY FOR CHILDREN   [502]

Written by Jack Prelutsky
Illustrated by Arnold Lobel
Cloth: Random House
Published: 1983

This large and distinctly optimistic anthology of poetry, includes many familiar gems and has zestful illustrations of distinctly Arnold Lobelish owls, cats, and frogs, among other creatures.

THE RED BALLOON   [503]

Written and illustrated by Albert Lamorisse
Cloth: Doubleday
Paper: Zephyr
Published: 1957   **Prizes: New York Times Best Illustrated Book**

It's Paris just a shiver of time back in the past. The book, like the film on which it is based, captures the adventures of a little boy and his best friend, a glorious red balloon that follows him everywhere. An enduring favorite, illustrated with color photographs from the film.

RICHARD SCARRY'S WHAT DO PEOPLE DO ALL DAY?   [504]

Written and illustrated by Richard Scarry
Cloth: Random House
Published: 1968

Well, what do people do? Here, in typical Scarry fashion (i.e., very busy pictures featuring many of his regular cast of animals), is a series of stories about building houses, baking bread, laying roads, going on a railroad, going on a boat, and more. Preschoolers can pore over the pages for hours, and many's the adult who has been intrigued at the clarity of the explanations. The present edition is abridged, alas.

[504]

ROSALIE [505]

Written by Joan Hewett
Illustrated by Donald Carrick
Cloth: Lothrop, Lee & Shepard
Published: 1987

Rosalie is an old dog. She can't run and her hearing isn't so good, but every member of the family loves her and makes adjustments for her infirmities. If your family has an elderly pet, this might be comfortingly familiar.

[505]

ROTTEN ISLAND [506]

Written and illustrated by William Steig
Cloth: David Godine
Published: 1984

This is a revised edition of a splendid fantasy, first published in the 1960s, about a horrible, ghastly, ugly, vicious island populated with hideous monsters, disgusting creatures, thorny plants, and awful things. A flower appears one day and sets off an earth-shattering brawl. The wondrously imaginative illustrations are printed in fluorescent color. It is one of Steig's best books.

THE RUMOR OF PAVEL AND PAALI: A UKRAINIAN FOLK TALE [507]

Written by Carole Kismaric
Illustrated by Charles Mikolaycak
Cloth: Harper & Row/HarperCollins
Published: 1988

Pavel is the selfish, wicked twin, Paali, the kind one in this harsh and haunting tale retold in stirring text and stunning pictures. Blinded by his brother for two measures of moldy grain, Paali overhears the evil spirits listing their accomplishments. He undoes their work and lives happily. Pavel's greed is, of course, punished.

[506]

RUMPELSTILTSKIN   [508]

Written and illustrated by Paul O. Zelinsky
Cloth: Dutton
Published: 1986   Prizes: Caldecott Honor

A version of the familiar folktale placed in a medieval setting—turreted castles, peasants in the fields, executed in technically accomplished oil paintings. The straw and gold truly gleam. The text is from Grimm. Adults may be distracted by the resemblance between Rumpelstiltskin and the late comedian Marty Feldman. The illustrator has done an equally lavish setting of "Hansel and Gretel" in the style of seventeenth-century Dutch landscape painting. There are other Rumpelstiltskins, including an almost cartoonishly high-spirited one illustrated by Paul Galdone, and a similarly medieval one by Gennady Spirin, the Soviet artist.

ST. GEORGE AND THE DRAGON   [509]

Written by Margaret Hodges
Illustrated by Trina Schart Hyman
Cloth: Little, Brown
Paper: Little, Brown   Prizes: Caldecott Medal
Published: 1984   New York Times Best Illustrated Book

Based on Spenser's *Faerie Queen,* this is a retelling of St. George's three-day battle with the dragon. The prizewinning illustrations are in the style of illuminated manuscripts; the text has been simplified but remains courtly. *The Kitchen Knight* is equally well told.

SAYING GOODBYE TO GRANDMA   [510]

[508]

Written by Jane Resh Thomas
Illustrated by Marcia Sewall
Cloth: Clarion
Published: 1988

A young girl tells about going with her parents to her grandmother's funeral. Her account captures the stunned uncertainty about what happens very well—family commotion, games with her cousins, a visit to the funeral home, the service itself. The understated illustrations fit perfectly.

SAYONARA, MRS. KACKLEMAN [511]

Written and illustrated by Maira Kalman
Cloth: Viking
Published: 1989

Lulu takes her little brother, Alexander, on a totally madcap tour of
Japan. There are the Tokyo subway, the noodle shops, a rock garden,
and details of food, games, and films. Lulu is something of a know-it-
all; Alexander has great aplomb. The artist's style is a pastiche of wit
imposed on chaos and too busy for many younger children but rewarding to pore over as sly jokes reveal themselves. In *Hey, Willy, See the
Pyramids*, Lulu and Willy take another trip.

[511]

SECRETS OF A SMALL BROTHER [512]

Written by Richard J. Margolis
Illustrated by Donald Carrick
Cloth: Macmillan
Published: 1984

A collection of poems, pointed and poignant, about what it is like being
a younger brother. The pencil illustrations are a perfect complement
to the verses.

THE SELFISH GIANT [513]

Written by Oscar Wilde
Illustrated by Lisbeth Zwerger
Cloth: Picture Book
Published: 1984

The Christian parable about children seeking access to a giant's garden
is illustrated here by an unusually talented Viennese artist who takes
an oblique view of the tale in her delicate watercolor paintings. She has
also illustrated Wilde's *The Canterville Ghost*. The story reads aloud well
and has a lasting appeal for adults as well as for children.

THE SELKIE GIRL   [514]

Written by Susan Cooper
Illustrated by Warwick Hutton
Cloth: McElderry
Paper: Aladdin
Published: 1986

The haunting tale, from the Irish and Scots islands, of the young lad who loves and marries the maiden who is really a seal is beautifully told in this distinguished collaboration. The author and illustrator also worked together on the Welsh tale *The Silver Cow*, and *Tamlin*.

THE SEVEN CHINESE BROTHERS   [515]

Written by Margaret Mahy
Illustrated by Jean and Mou-Sien Tseng
Cloth: Scholastic
Published: 1990

Seven seemingly identical siblings are endowed with some spectacular physical prowess, which comes in handy here. They protect the slave laborers working on the Great Wall as the dread Chinese emperor Chin Shih Huang attempts to brutally consolidate his power. Basically, this is the same story as in *The Five Chinese Brothers*, but without racial stereotyping, and with great dollops of wit in the text.

[514]

SHADOW   [516]

Written by Blaise Cendrars
Illustrated by Marcia Brown
Cloth: Scribner's
Paper: Aladdin
Published: 1982

Prizes: Caldecott Medal

The text, translated from the French, describes the mysterious eeriness of the shadow figure in African tribal life. The illustrations are dramatic collages.

SHAKA KING OF THE ZULUS [517]

Written by Diane Stanley and Peter Vennema
Illustrated by Diane Stanley
Cloth: Morrow Junior Books
Published: 1988   Prizes: New York Times Best Illustrated Book

In life, Shaka (1787–1828) was a brilliant military leader, heroic by any measure, and then, near the end of his twelve-year reign as king and mighty leader, quite horribly, cruelly insane. This stunning large-format story-book biography decorated with Zulu artifacts and shields has a clear, dispassionate text that deals tactfully with the most terrifying parts of the life. The book is accessible as a read-aloud to young-grade children but most exciting to middle-graders, for whom historical figures are becoming real.

[517]

SHAKER LANE [518]

Written and illustrated by Alice and Martin Provensen
Cloth: Viking
Paper: Puffin
Published: 1987

This is a cautionary tale about real-estate development and environmental preservation most artfully disguised as a handsome children's book about a somewhere place called Shaker Lane. It tells about the folks who have always lived there, the newcomers, and the changes that come along in very modern times. The illustrations are so simple and so sophisticated at the same time that readers of many ages can find different but equally rewarding stories and lessons in it.

THE SIGN IN MENDEL'S WINDOW [519]

Written by Mildred Phillips
Illustrated by Margot Zemach
Cloth: Macmillan
Published: 1985

A retelling of an old Jewish story about Mendel, who rents half his butcher shop to Tinker the thinker, who tries to swindle everyone. Folk wisdom, wryly told, with illustrations that capture Mendel's bemusement.

SING A SONG OF POPCORN: EVERY CHILD'S BOOK OF POEMS [520]

Compiled by Beatrice Schenk de Regniers
Cloth: Scholastic
Published: 1988

This jolly collection of mostly familiar poetry to read aloud or quietly is organized thematically and illustrated with great style and wit by nine American artists, all winners of the Caldecott Medal. A family treat.

SIR CEDRIC [521]

Written and illustrated by Roy Gerrard
Cloth: Farrar, Straus & Giroux
Paper: Sunburst
Published: 1984   Prizes: New York Times Best Illustrated Book

A gallant tale of knights of old, in this case the very round Sir Cedric the Good, who travels with his horse, Walter, and cucumber sandwiches. He wins the hand of the fair Fat Matilda. Very amusing, with lavish, detailed illustrations. *Sir Cedric Rides Again* continues the story and introduces their daughter, Edwina the Pest.

THE SLEEPING BEAUTY [522]

Written and illustrated by Trina Schart Hyman
Cloth: Little, Brown
Paper: Little, Brown
Published: 1977

This adaptation of the Grimm brothers' tale is distinguished by the artist's characteristically intense and dramatic illustrations. Other fine versions have been illustrated by Arthur Rackham, Warwick Hutton, Warren Chappell, and Mercer Mayer.

A SNAKE IS TOTALLY TAIL [523]

Written by Judi Barrett
Illustrated by Lonni Sue Johnson
Cloth: Atheneum
Paper: Aladdin
Published: 1983
Epigrams that encapsulate twenty-eight animals, suitably illustrated.
Bees, of course, buzzzz.

SOME SWELL PUP OR ARE YOU SURE YOU WANT A DOG? [524]

Written by Matthew Margolis and Maurice Sendak
Illustrated by Maurice Sendak
Cloth: Farrar, Straus & Giroux
Paper: Sunburst
Published: 1976
Before you consider bringing a puppy into your home, you should consult this guidebook for young owners. The information, presented in comic-strip form, comes from a dog trainer and stresses the need for patience and kindness in training a dog. The illustrations are vintage Sendak and show clearly that he is a dog lover.

SOMETHING ON MY MIND [525]

Written by Nikki Grimes
Illustrated by Tom Feelings
Paper: Pied Piper
Published: 1978
Poems about thoughts, hopes, and fears of black children, with sensitive illustrations.

THE SOMETHING [526]

Written and illustrated by Natalie Babbitt
Cloth: Farrar, Straus & Giroux
Paper: Sunburst
Published: 1970

A soothing book about a common anxiety. Mylo, a hairy sort of cave-monsterish little fellow, worries about something coming through his window at night. His mother gives him some clay and he eventually manages to make a statue of it. Later, he is not afraid when he meets the something in a dream. The black-and-white line drawings are simultaneously amusing and comforting.

SPACE CASE [527]

Written by Edward Marshall
Illustrated by James Marshall
Cloth: Dial
Paper: Pied Piper
Published: 1980

A creature from outer space named Space Case comes to visit Buddy and his family one Halloween. The sequel is *Merry Christmas, Space Case*. These silly adventures, like those of *The Stupids*, appeal strongly to children, especially boys, in the early grades.

[528]

SPINKY SULKS [528]

Written and illustrated by William Steig
Cloth: Farrar, Straus & Giroux
Paper: Sunburst
Published: 1988

For reasons too silly to bear much inspection, Spinky has gone into a world-class sulk, and nothing his parents or his reprehensible siblings or even his grandmother do is going to persuade him to come out of the yard. In this glorious, hilarious, painfully wonderful book, text and illustrations are seamlessly united to convey the palpable rage of a real tantrum and the delicacy needed to negotiate a way out.

SPIRIT CHILD: A STORY OF
THE NATIVITY   [529]

Written by John Bierhorst
Illustrated by Barbara Cooney
Paper: Mulberry
Published: 1984

An Aztec version of the Nativity, translated into modern English. The exciting text is matched by the fine illustrations that incorporate Aztec motifs.

STEVIE   [530]

Written and illustrated by John Steptoe
Cloth: Harper & Row/HarperCollins
Paper: Harper Trophy
Published: 1969

The frustrations of family life: a young black boy tells about the problems a younger foster brother caused in the house and then acknowledges gruffly that he misses him very much. This was a stunning and innovative book when first published and remains poignant and appealing to new generations of readers.

THE STORY ABOUT PING   [531]

Written by Marjorie Flack
Illustrated by Kurt Wiese
Cloth: Viking
Paper: Puffin
Published: 1933

Ping lives with his extended family on a boat on the great Yangtze River. One day, to avoid getting a spanking for being last back on board at the end of the day, Ping ventures off. Miraculously, he finds his way home. After more than half a century, this remains a compelling, even thrilling, story of nearly universal appeal to children just discovering the wide world beyond their own daily routines.

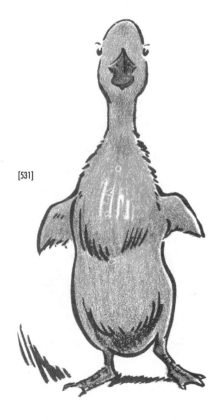
[531]

Story
Books

THE STORY OF BABAR   [532]

Written and illustrated by Jean De Brunhoff
Cloth: Random House
Paper: Knopf
Published: 1933

This is the classic French tale of a baby elephant, cruelly orphaned, who reaches the city, is civilized, even acquiring a handsome green suit, and eventually returns home to be king. The cast of characters includes his wife, Queen Celeste, their children, their relatives, and the splendid Old Lady. Some readers have seen the politics of colonialism in the stories, but that has not deterred children in many countries from adoring them. The series includes *The Travels of Babar, Babar and His Children,* and *Babar the King.* The originals are good-looking large-format books with script rather than type, reproduced in *Babar's Anniversary Album,* an edition that includes six of the stories. There are some other, less satisfying Babar titles and a variety of paperback adaptations that are diluted but popular nonetheless.

THE STORY OF MRS. LOVEWRIGHT AND PURRLESS HER CAT   [533]

Written by Lore Segal
Illustrated by Paul O. Zelinsky
Cloth: Knopf
Published: 1985   Prizes: New York Times Best Illustrated Book

Mrs. Lovewright, who lives alone, inherits a kitten and plans on being cozy with it. But Purrless, who grows to giant size, has a different, sometimes bruising definition of cozy. Adults may detect a wry parable on marriage here, but children take the story more literally. The stylized illustrations are raucous.

[532]

184

THE STORY OF THE DANCING FROG [534]

Written and illustrated by Quentin Blake
Paper: Knopf
Published: 1985

A young widow befriends a frog who can dance. She puts him on the stage, and he becomes world famous before retiring to domestic life, or so claims the mother who tells the story. The loose, cartoonish illustrations add to the silly fun.

THE STORY OF THE NUTCRACKER BALLET [535]

Written by Deborah Hautzig
Illustrated by Diane Goode
Paper: Knopf
Published: 1986

Based on the version George Balanchine created for the New York City Ballet that is now standard holiday fare around the country, this behind-the-scenes look is perfect for before and after that annual outing. Warren Chappell's *The Nutcracker* is still in print.

[532]

STREGA NONA [536]

Written and illustrated by Tomie dePaola
Cloth: Prentice Hall
Paper: Treehouse
Published: 1975   Prizes: Caldecott Honor

The first of the inspired story books about the magic witch of Calabria in which we meet Strega Nona and her doltish helper Big Anthony and are introduced to Strega Nona's powers. Delightful to read aloud. Among the others in the series, *Merry Christmas, Strega Nona* is outstanding.

STRINGBEAN'S TRIP TO THE SHINING SEA [537]

Written by Vera B. Williams
Illustrated by Vera B. and Jennifer Williams
Cloth: Greenwillow
Paper: Scholastic
Published: 1988   Prizes: New York Times Best Illustrated Book

This sophisticated account of a trip the boy nicknamed Stringbean took with his uncle to the West Coast is told in witty postcards that come complete with cancellation stamps and photo or illustration credits. It is at once a very simple and very complicated book, appealing strongly to middle- and upper-grade schoolchildren, who are often good readers, enjoy working on elaborate projects, and know at least a little about geography and travel.

THE STUPIDS HAVE A BALL [538]

Written by Harry Allard
Illustrated by James Marshall
Cloth: Houghton Mifflin
Paper: Houghton Mifflin
Published: 1978

The Stupids manage to justify their name in the series of silly, clamorous books by the Allard/Marshall team that also produced the manic *Miss Nelson* tales. In this installment, they celebrate the fact that Buster and Petunia have failed every school subject—including recess. Don't miss *The Stupids Step Out* and *The Stupids Die*.

SUSANNA OF THE ALAMO: A TRUE STORY [539]

Written by John Jakes
Illustrated by Paul Bacon
Cloth: HBJ
Paper: Voyager
Published: 1986

Susanna Dickinson played a crucial role in the early history of Texas because she and her baby survived the siege of the Alamo in 1836, and

Susanna brought General Santa Anna's warning and challenge to Sam Houston. Her story was lost or overlooked for a long time, and this book helps straighten out the record.

SWAN LAKE [540]

Written by Margot Fonteyn
Illustrated by Trina Schart Hyman
Cloth: HBJ
Published: 1989

You can virtually hear the music as you go through the great ballerina's telling of one of the best-known stories in the standard classical repertory. She makes it a very human story told from the perspective of a prince named Siegfried, who falls in love with a maiden imprisoned in a swan's body, and incorporates stage details echoed in the lush period illustrations. The gestures, poses, and costumes all suggest the ballet.

THE TALE OF THE MANDARIN DUCKS [541]

Written by Katherine Paterson
Illustrated by Leo and Diane Dillon
Cloth: Lodestar
Published: 1990   Prizes: New York Times Best Illustrated Book

[541]

Once in imperial Japan a cruel lord took a fancy to a beautiful wild drake and had it captured and brought to his estate. The drake, pining for his mate, is helped to escape by the lord's chief steward, Shozo. The clever ducks find a way for Shozo and his love, the kitchen maid, to escape into the forest. The lush and beautiful illustrations, styled after Japanese ukyo-e paintings, are in the mottled colors of ducks' plumage.

TALES OF A GAMBLING GRANDMA [542]

Written and illustrated by Dayal Kaur Khalsa
Cloth: Potter
Published: 1986

A little girl considers her gambling grandmother, who came from Russia, married Louis the plumber, and played poker. Grandmother

taught many lessons, including card games and some strong social values. The primitive-style illustrations are as whimsical and refreshing as the story itself.

TALES OF PAN   [543]

Written and illustrated by Mordicai Gerstein
Cloth: Harper & Row/HarperCollins
Published: 1986

A giddy, boisterous, infectious, and therefore utterly suitable collection of stories about the Greek god Pan and his mischievous ways. The colorful line-drawing illustrations are as light as confetti.

THE TALKING EGGS: A FOLKTALE FROM THE AMERICAN SOUTH   [544]

Written by Robert D. San Souci
Illustrated by Jerry Pinkney
Cloth: Dial
Paper: Pied Piper
Published: 1989   **Prizes: Caldecott Honor**

Blanche, a kind little girl, gives a drink of water to a strange old woman at the well, who, naturally, turns out to be a good witch. Doing as she is told, Blanche takes the plain eggs that talk from the old woman's henhouse and is richly rewarded. Her greedy sister, who sets off to find similar loot, is treated appropriately. The jewel-toned pencil and watercolor illustrations serve the story well.

[542]

TELEPHONE TIME: A FIRST BOOK OF TELEPHONE DO'S AND DON'TS   [545]

Written by Ellen Weiss
Illustrated by Hilary Knight
Paper: Random House
Published: 1986

Ringalina the Telephone Fairy has some "sound" advice for the whole family about using the telephone—taking messages, what to do in emergencies, and safety. There are also amusing examples of some social monsters such as the Tie-Uppasaurus. The illustrations are perky and bright.

TELL ME A MITZI   [546]

Written by Lore Segal
Illustrated by Harriet Pincus
Cloth: Farrar, Straus & Giroux
Paper: Sunburst
Published: 1970

Three memorable stories about Mitzi and her little brother, Jacob: their
secret attempt to visit Grandma, the whole family's cold, and an encounter with a presidential procession. The funny, awkward illustrations combine fantasy and vivid detail in a way that complements the
text perfectly. There is a related title, *Tell Me a Trudy*, illustrated by
Rosemary Wells.

[547]

THE TENTH GOOD THING
ABOUT BARNEY   [547]

Written by Judith Viorst
Illustrated by Erik Blegvad
Cloth: Atheneum
Paper: Aladdin
Published: 1971

When Barney the cat dies, his young owner struggles to think of good
things about his pet, and to understand both the finality of death and
the unity of life. This is a splendid book, deservedly a classic, suitable
for readers of all ages. In its simplicity and the genuine comfort it
offers, it is one of the best books for children about death.

THE THIRD STORY CAT   [548]

Written and illustrated by Leslie Baker
Cloth: Little, Brown
Paper: Little, Brown
Published: 1987

Alice is a calico cat whose world is the third-floor apartment in which
she lives. One day, when the kitchen window is open, Alice goes out to
see the world. The watercolor illustrations are beguiling, and sharp-
eyed observers will be certain that the neighborhood Alice explores is
located in center-city Philadelphia.

THE THREE BEARS & FIFTEEN OTHER STORIES [549]

Written and illustrated by Anne Rockwell
Cloth: T. Y. Crowell/HarperCollins
Paper: Harper Trophy
Published: 1975

A collection of classic stories from La Fontaine, Aesop, the Grimm brothers, and others, economically told, with bright, witty illustrations. Good for beginning readers as well as for reading aloud.

THREE DAYS ON A RIVER IN A RED CANOE [550]

Written and illustrated by Vera B. Williams
Cloth: Greenwillow
Paper: Mulberry
Published: 1981

Just what the title promises—an account of the trip a little girl, her cousin, and their mothers took, complete with instructions on how to set up a tent, make a fire, and cook. A charming travelogue.

THROUGH GRANDPA'S EYES [551]

Written by Patricia MacLachlan
Illustrated by Deborah Ray
Cloth: Harper & Row/HarperCollins
Paper: Harper Trophy
Published: 1980

On his visits to his grandparents, John has learned to appreciate that although Grandpa is blind, he sees and moves through a rich and detailed world.

THUNDER CAKE [552]

Written and illustrated by Patricia Polacco
Cloth: Philomel
Published: 1990

Grandmother's farm is in Michigan, but she came from the Ukraine, and her way of dealing with her granddaughter's fear of an approach-

[549]

ing thunderstorm is . . . to bake a cake. The storm looms wonderfully in the watercolor illustrations as the little girl scurries about gathering the ingredients, a task that involves postponing and conquering her fears. The recipe for the cake, including the surprise ingredient, is at the end.

[552]

TODAY WAS A TERRIBLE DAY   [553]

Written by Patricia Reilly Giff
Illustrated by Susanna Natti
Cloth: Viking
Paper: Puffin
Published: 1984

Ronald Morgan is a hapless hero and suffers from acute bumbling and the problems of the second grade. His struggles continue in *Watch Out, Ronald Morgan!* and *Ronald Morgan Goes to Bat,* which are almost as funny as *The Almost Awful Play,* in which Ronald is the star, sort of, of the class play. He is Winky the Cat.

TOMIE dePAOLA'S FAVORITE NURSERY TALES   [554]

Written and illustrated by Tomie dePaola
Cloth: Putnam
Published: 1986

A bright companion volume to dePaola's *Mother Goose* that includes more than twenty-five well-loved stories such as "Rumpelstiltskin," "The Frog Prince," and "The Emperor's New Clothes."

[554]

THE TOMTEN AND THE FOX [555]

Written by Astrid Lindgren
Illustrated by Harald Wilberg
Cloth: Coward
Paper: Sandcastle
Published: 1961

The Tomten is a Swedish troll who guards farms. In this version of a traditional tale, the author of *Pippi Longstocking* tells about the wise and canny Tomten who wards off the fox who slinks silently around in the moonlight. The midwinter illustrations are snowy and fine. Other Tomten stories include *The Tomten* and *The Christmas Tomten*.

TOUGH EDDIE [556]

Written by Elizabeth Winthrop
Illustrated by Lillian Hoban
Cloth: Dutton
Published: 1985

Everyone thinks Eddie is a tough little boy until his sister mentions his doll house. He sorts out his pals and deals with the problems of sexual stereotyping in a believable way. The illustrations are engaging.

[559]

THE TOWN MOUSE AND THE COUNTRY MOUSE [557]

Written and illustrated by Lorinda Bryan Cauley
Cloth: Putnam
Paper: Sandcastle
Published: 1984

This charming retelling of the familiar fable from Aesop is set lovingly in the nineteenth century, with fine domestic and culinary detail. The illustrator has also done a jolly version of *The Owl and the Pussycat* and a satisfying *Three Blind Mice*.

THE TREK [558]

Written and illustrated by Ann Jonas
Cloth: Greenwillow
Paper: Mulberry
Published: 1985

Walking to school isn't what grown-ups might think. Why, there are wild creatures hidden almost everywhere, and in these clever illustrations you can see them. Don't be afraid, though. You will get there safely.

THE TRUE STORY OF
THE 3 LITTLE PIGS [559]

Written by Jon Scieszka
Illustrated by Lane Smith
Cloth: Viking
Published: 1989

A chap calling himself Alexander T. Wolf ("You can call me Al") wants to straighten out the record about what happened with those pigs. Mr. Wolf claims he's been victimized by the press. His version—how he had a cold (the huffing and puffing) and went to the neighbors to borrow some sugar and sneezed—is funny enough. What make this account dazzling as well as hilarious are the excited, jazzy illustrations. If you have mastered the traditional story, and there are wonderful versions available, this is great fun. It is also good to read with middle-grade children learning about "point of view."

[559]

[558]

193

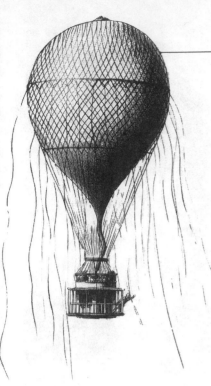

[562]

TURKEYS, PILGRIMS AND INDIAN CORN: THE STORY OF THE THANKSGIVING SYMBOLS [560]

Written by Edna Barth
Illustrated by Ursula Arndt
Cloth: Clarion
Paper: Clarion
Published: 1975

This is a simple introduction to the symbols and ideas of Thanksgiving. It is one of a series of books about holidays that includes *Witches, Pumpkins and Grinning Ghosts; Lilies, Rabbits, and Painted Eggs;* and *Shamrocks, Harps, and Shillelaghs.*

THE TWELVE DANCING PRINCESSES: RETOLD FROM A STORY BY THE BROTHERS GRIMM [561]

Illustrated by Errol Le Cain
Paper: Puffin
Published: 1981

A very pretty, ornamented version of the story of the princesses who dance the nights away and fool all their prospective suitors until a poor soldier manages to follow them to their subterranean pleasure grounds. There are several other hardcover editions, including a lush one illustrated by Keiko Craft.

THE TWENTY-ONE BALLOONS [562]

Written and illustrated by William Pène du Bois
Cloth: Viking
Paper: Puffin
Published: 1947   **Prizes: Newbery**

Here is a wonderfully illustrated account of what happens when Professor William Waterman Sherman is found in the middle of the ocean with what is left of twenty-one balloons. This delightful fantasy continues to appeal.

THE TWO OF THEM [563]

Written and illustrated by Aliki
Cloth: Greenwillow
Paper: Mulberry
Published: 1979

This is a quiet story about a grandfather who loved his granddaughter from the time she was born, and how, when he died, she was able to remember things he had made for her and the time they had spent together, and thus absorb their special relationship.

[565]

TWO WAYS TO COUNT TO TEN: A LIBERIAN FOLKTALE [564]

Written by Ruby Dee
Illustrated by Susan Meddaugh
Cloth: Henry Holt
Published: 1988

In this African folktale the jungle beasts learn to count, all right, but more important, they learn, once again, that being strong is not the same as being smart. Witty illustrations.

TY'S ONE-MAN BAND [565]

Written by Mildred Pitts Walter
Illustrated by Margot Tomes
Cloth: Four Winds
Paper: Scholastic
Published: 1979; reprinted 1987

A little boy named Andro tells about the hot summer evening a peg-legged man came into town. He was a one-man band and he brought music and dancing into the night and then, while everyone was distracted, slipped away. It is a magical story, and the subtle full-color illustrations capture the heat and shadows of summer nights. *The Little Band* tells a similar story of enchantment for younger children.

[565]

THE UGLY DUCKLING [566]

Written by Hans Christian Andersen
Illustrated by Robert Van Nutt
Cloth: Knopf
Published: 1986   Prizes: New York Times Best Illustrated Book

A muted version of the story of the duckling who turns into a swan, with illustrations that focus close up on the cygnet and the other creatures. This edition can be purchased with an audio tape or as a book alone. There are other interesting retellings, illustrated by Thomas Locker, whose style is very painterly; Monica Laimbgruber, who does richly colored, fine pen-and-ink drawings; and Lorinda Bryan Cauley, whose work typically has a sweet and old-fashioned air.

UNDER THE SUNDAY TREE [567]

Written by Eloise Greenfield
Illustrated by Amos Ferguson
Cloth: Harper & Row/HarperCollins
Paper: Harper Trophy
Published: 1989

An American poet has elaborated on some of the brilliantly colorful primitive-style paintings of a Bahamian artist. It's a delightful collaboration.

UP NORTH IN WINTER [568]

Written by Deborah Hartley
Illustrated by Lydia Dabcovich
Cloth: Dutton
Published: 1986

Grandpa Ole missed the last train home one bitter-cold night a long time ago. He had to walk, and encountered what he thought was a frozen fox, which he picked up and used as a scarf as he trudged home. The surprise ending is startling and funny.

THE VELVETEEN RABBIT [569]

Written by Margery Williams
Illustrated by William Nicholson
Cloth: Doubleday
Paper: Zephyr
Published: 1926

The slightly syrupy tale of the toy that so loved its boy that it did, ultimately, become real was a modest standard title until a surge of popularity with college students and younger adults gave it visibility in the late 1970s and early 1980s. Through carelessness, the copyright was allowed to expire, and presto, a half-dozen other editions appeared, including those illustrated by Michael Hague, David Jorgensen, and Tien Ho. This is the original and most affecting edition and comes plain or in a fancy slipcase.

VERY LAST FIRST TIME [570]

Written by Jan Andrews
Illustrated by Ian Wallace
Cloth: McElderry
Published: 1986

A memorable picture book about Eva, an Inuit girl, and her first trip under the sea ice to gather mussels for her family to eat for a winter meal. Eerie and exciting.

THE VILLAGE OF ROUND AND SQUARE HOUSES [571]

Written and illustrated by Ann Grifalconi
Cloth: Little, Brown
Published: 1986   **Prizes: Caldecott Honor**

There is a reason that in one small East African village the men live in square houses and the women live in round ones. A fascinating story, with mysterious full-color illustrations.

[548]

A VISIT TO THE
SESAME STREET LIBRARY   [572]

Written by Deborah Hautzig
Illustrated by Joe Mathieu
Paper: Random House
Published: 1986

Big Bird visits the public library and discovers some of the things there are to do there. This inexpensive paperback could lead a child to corners he or she might miss on an early library visit.

A VISIT TO THE
SESAME STREET HOSPITAL   [573]

Written by Deborah Hautzig
Illustrated by Joe Mathieu
Paper: Random House
Published: 1985

One of the best of the Sesame Street guidebooks. Grover, Ernie, Bert, and Grover's mother go to visit the hospital in preparation for Grover's tonsillectomy. Lots of detail and reassurance for preschoolers and older children as well. The full-color illustrations are interesting without being obtrusive.

A VISIT TO WILLIAM BLAKE'S INN:
POEMS FOR INNOCENT AND
EXPERIENCED TRAVELERS   [574]

Written by Nancy Willard
Illustrated by Alice and Martin Provensen
Cloth: HBJ
Paper: Voyager
Published: 1981

Prizes: Newbery Medal
Caldecott Honor

A collection of intriguing poems inspired by William Blake's "Songs of Innocence" and "Songs of Experience," with stylized, witty illustrations capturing a mysterious sense of nineteenth-century London. While this is a book meant for older children and adults, younger children who are used to listening to poetry may well be interested.

WALK TOGETHER CHILDREN: BLACK AMERICAN SPIRITUALS   [575]

Written and illustrated by Ashley Bryan
Cloth: Atheneum
Paper: Aladdin
Published: 1974

This richly illustrated collection of spirituals includes songs that are generally familiar and some that are less so. There is a companion volume, *I'm Going to Sing*. Wonderful for bedtime singing.

[578]

THE WAY TO START A DAY   [576]

Written by Byrd Baylor
Illustrated by Peter Parnall
Cloth: Scribner's
Paper: Aladdin
Published: 1978   **Prizes: Caldecott Honor**

A lyrical evocation of the simple fact that all over the world, in many different cultures and throughout history, people have welcomed the sun. A morning book!

A WEEKEND IN THE COUNTRY   [577]

Written and illustrated by Lee Lorenz
Cloth: Prentice Hall
Published: 1985

Two dear friends are cordially, oh so cordially, invited to come spend a summer weekend in the country, but it turns out there is no way to get there. Each indirect route is filled with hazards and pitfalls. It's an old joke told in high-style cartoon fashion.

WENDELL   [578]

Written and illustrated by Eric Jon Nones
Cloth: Farrar, Straus & Giroux
Published: 1989

Wendell is a responsible tortoiseshell cat who lives in a suburban 1950s household drawn in sepia tones, except for the small, full-color creatures only Wendell (and the reader) can see, who do impish mischief

[578]

such as cracking plates and hiding eyeglasses. It's just one funny idea, but it's a good one, and older children, who may even find the settings amusing, enjoy the double vision as much as preschoolers.

WHATEVER HAPPENED TO THE DINOSAURS? [579]

Written and illustrated by Bernard Most
Cloth: HBJ
Paper: Voyager
Published: 1978

Some possible, and some impossible, answers to a very commonly asked question. The illustrations putting the great lizards in improbable settings—like pirate ships and large cities—are bright and amusing. The companion title is *If the Dinosaurs Came Back.*

WHEN THE DARK COMES DANCING: A BEDTIME POETRY BOOK [580]

Written by Nancy Larrick
Illustrated by John Wallner
Cloth: Philomel
Published: 1983

This collection of lullabies and poems particularly suitable for reading aloud was chosen by a distinguished anthologist and is charmingly illustrated. The selections are short and easily memorized.

WHEN WE WERE VERY YOUNG [581]

[582]

Written by A. A. Milne
Illustrated by Ernest H. Shepard
Cloth: Dutton
Paper: Dell Yearling
Published: 1924

A collection of verse for young children that has been considered classic for generations, full of fantasy and vignettes to remember for a lifetime. Household pets, kings and queens, games, illness, pirates, and prayers—and lilting, sometimes silly rhymes. The line drawings are models of illustration balancing the sometimes fey poems. *Now We Are Six* is the companion volume.

WHERE THE BUFFALOES BEGIN [582]

Written by Olaf Baker
Illustrated by Stephen Gammell
Cloth: Frederick Warne
Paper: Puffin
Published: 1981

Prizes: Caldecott Honor
New York Times Best Illustrated Book

This is a subtly illustrated retelling of the American Indian legend of Little Wolf, the boy who led the stampeding buffaloes away from his people.

WHERE THE RIVER BEGINS [583]

Written and illustrated by Thomas Locker
Cloth: Dial
Paper: Pied Piper
Published: 1984

Prizes: New York Times Best Illustrated Book

The first of a series of lush story books featuring landscape paintings in the style of the Hudson River School of the nineteenth century. The story line, which is secondary to the spectacular illustrations, tells of two boys who hike with their grandfather to the river's source. Related titles include *The Mare on the Hill* and *Sailing with the Wind*.

[582]

WHITE DYNAMITE AND
CURLY KIDD [584]

Written by Bill Martin Jr. and John Archambault
Illustrated by Ted Rand
Cloth: Henry Holt
Published: 1986

A grand account of White Dynamite, a mean old bull, and Curly Kidd, the toughest rodeo rider around. Designed for reading aloud.

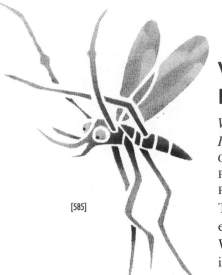

[585]

WHY MOSQUITOES BUZZ IN PEOPLE'S
EARS: A WEST AFRICAN TALE [585]

Written by Verna Aardema
Illustrated by Leo and Diane Dillon
Cloth: Dial
Paper: Pied Piper
Published: 1975   Prizes: Caldecott Medal

This is an eccentric and wonderful story based on an odd chain of events. Mosquito tells a lie that ultimately results in the sun's not rising. When the animals, led by lion, figure out just what happened, mosquito is punished. A fine read-aloud text is supported by stylized illustrations.

THE WILD SWANS [586]

Written by Hans Christian Andersen
Illustrated by Susan Jeffers
Cloth: Dial
Paper: Pied Piper
Published: 1981

A contemporary illustrator with a distinctive style featuring large, luminous faces has done a series of Andersen tales. In addition to this version of the familiar and haunting story of the flock of swans, she has done "Thumbelina" and "The Snow Queen." (The text adaptations of these selections are by Amy Ehrlich.) Another lovely edition of "The Wild Swans" is illustrated by Angela Barrett.

WILL I HAVE A FRIEND? [587]

Written by Miriam Cohen
Illustrated by Lillian Hoban
Cloth: Macmillan
Paper: Aladdin
Published: 1967

[588]

The first of three books dealing with some perfectly reasonable fears and anxieties about kindergarten. The answer to the title question, happily, is yes. Paul makes friends with Jim on the very first day. In *The New Teacher*, they cope with a midyear replacement, and in *Best Friends*, they cope with an emergency.

THE WINTER WREN [588]

Written and illustrated by Brock Cole
Cloth: Farrar, Straus & Giroux
Paper: Sunburst
Published: 1984

Simon, a simple boy, and his little sister, Meg, hear that Spring is asleep at Winter's farm. When they get there and Meg disappears, a winter wren intercedes. The story has the tone and richness of a fable, and the watercolor illustrations catch winter's dark grayness and the sweet tones of spring.

WORSE THAN WILLY! [589]

Written and illustrated by James Stevenson
Cloth: Greenwillow
Published: 1984

This is one of the many raucous, improbable, impossible, and soothing stories Grandpa tells Louie and Mary Ann about the childhood he shared with Uncle Wainwright. The layout is half story book, half cartoon. This one, about sibling rivalry, has Grandpa captured by pirates and an octopus and rescued by Wainey. Some other titles in the series include *Could Be Worse, That Dreadful Day,* and *What's Under My Bed?* They are wonderful, and fun even after the formula is familiar.

THE YEAR OF THE PERFECT CHRISTMAS TREE: AN APPALACHIAN STORY [590]

Written by Gloria Houston
Illustrated by Barbara Cooney
Cloth: Dial
Paper: Pied Piper
Published: 1988

It's 1918 in the mountains of North Carolina, and the custom in the village is for one family to select and donate the Christmas tree each year. In the spring, Ruthie and her father choose a perfect balsam high on a rocky crag. Then Father goes off to World War I. Still, on Christmas Eve the tree is in the church and Ruthie plays the angel. The winning illustrations perfectly match the tone of the story, which comes from the author's family.

YERTLE THE TURTLE AND OTHER STORIES [591]

Written and illustrated by Dr. Seuss
Cloth: Random House
Published: 1958

Dr. Seuss from his classic period: three modern fables with improbable characters, illustrations, and story lines all in verse—but with very real morals.

YOU READ TO ME, I'LL READ TO YOU [592]

Written by John Ciardi
Illustrated by Edward Gorey
Cloth: Lippincott/HarperCollins
Paper: Harper Trophy
Published: 1962; reprinted 1981

A collection of thirty-five poems, mostly lighthearted, organized for a child and an adult to read out loud alternately and together. The illustrations are appropriately amusing, too.

Early Reading Books

These well-illustrated books are designed for children who are learning to read and making the transition into "chapter books." Some of them are a particular pleasure to read aloud to younger children.

A, MY NAME IS ALICE   [593]

Written by Jane E. Bayer
Illustrated by Steven Kellogg
Cloth: Dial
Paper: Pied Piper
Published: 1984

An assortment of animals jump rope and bounce balls to those familiar rhymes that pass from generation to generation, with only minor and gradual changes.

AMANDA PIG AND HER
BIG BROTHER OLIVER   [594]

Written by Jean Van Leeuwen
Illustrated by Ann Schweninger
Cloth: Dial (Easy to Read)
Paper: Pied Piper
Published: 1982

One of the finest early-reader series is also particularly astute about sibling rivalry and sibling strength and affection. It features a family of plausible pigs and their endearing children in a range of domestic adventures that will resonate in the lives of most young readers. These books are a pleasure to read to children until they can read them to each other. Titles include *Tales of Oliver Pig, More Tales of Oliver Pig,* and *More Tales of Amanda Pig*.

[594]

AMELIA BEDELIA [595]

Written by Peggy Parish
Illustrated by Fritz Seibel
Cloth: Harper & Row/HarperCollins
Paper: Harper Trophy
Published: 1963

The eleven Amelia Bedelia books have been published in two series by Harper & Row and Greenwillow with no diminution in their wacky charm and appeal. The literal-minded housekeeper was first hired by Mr. and Mrs. Rogers more than a quarter of a century ago, when social class in this country was less of an issue, but she remains beloved by beginning readers. She goes on "dressing" chickens, "separating" the eggs, and earnestly misunderstanding. Happily, she always puts "a little of this" and "a little of that" together and bakes her way into job security. Other titles are *Come Back, Amelia Bedelia; Good Work, Amelia Bedelia; Amelia Bedelia and the Baby; Amelia Bedelia Goes Camping;* and *Merry Christmas, Amelia Bedelia.*

[594]

AND THEN WHAT HAPPENED, PAUL REVERE? [596]

Written by Jean Fritz
Illustrated by Margot Tomes
Cloth: Coward
Paper: Coward
Published: 1973

A biography of Paul Revere for young readers that is good-natured and accessible as well as being accurate and good history. The prizewinning author has written a veritable history course of lighthearted but provocative biographies for children. Other fine titles include *Can't You Make Them Behave, King George?; Why Don't You Get a Horse, Sam Adams?;* and *What's the Big Idea, Ben Franklin?* There is a boxed set of six biographies of figures in the American Revolution available in both hardcover and paperback.

ARE YOU MY MOTHER? [597]

Written and illustrated by P. D. Eastman
Cloth: Random House (Beginner Books)
Published: 1960

In this classic beginning reader, a baby bird falls from the nest and tries to find his mother. The simple text is augmented by bright pictures.

ARTHUR'S HONEY BEAR [598]

Written and illustrated by Lillian Hoban
Cloth: Harper (I Can Read)/HarperCollins
Paper: HarperCollins (I Can Read)
Published: 1974

Arthur the chimpanzee and his little sister, Violet, are two favorite siblings in the world of early-reader books. Their relationship and adventures are plausible and entertaining. The other titles include *Arthur's Prize Reader*, *Arthur's Pen Pal* (which has a good antisexist surprise in the plot), *Arthur's Christmas Cookies*, and *Arthur's Funny Money*.

"B" IS FOR BETSY [599]

Written and illustrated by Carolyn Haywood
Cloth: HBJ
Paper: Odyssey
Published: 1939

This is the first of a series of easy-to-read and perennially popular chapter books that follow Betsy from first to fourth grade in an idyllic town. Other titles include *Back to School with Betsy*, *Betsy and the Boys*, and *Betsy and Billy*.

A BEAR CALLED PADDINGTON [600]

Written by Michael Bond
Illustrated by Peggy Fortnum
Cloth: Houghton Mifflin
Paper: Dell Yearling
Published: 1960

The lovable bear from darkest Peru found by Mr. and Mrs. Brown in London's Paddington Station makes his debut here. There are ten

[600]

books in the original series and nearly half a dozen others, plus all sorts of franchise paraphernalia and merchandise to be found everywhere. The original stories are still delightfully funny and hard, but challenging as early readers. The same author created Olga De Polga, a very imaginative guinea pig, who appears in three books.

BEST ENEMIES   [601]

Written by Kathleen Leverich
Illustrated by Susan Condie Lamb
Cloth: Greenwillow
Paper: Bullseye
Published: 1989

Felicity Doll was probably born a menace. Certainly by the time she enters the second grade and does her best to make Priscilla Robin's life a nightmare, she is. Felicity is like a snake in lavender ruffles, and these four short, funny stories capture her at her memorable worst—snitching, bullying, teasing, shaking her curls, and fussing. And Priscilla? She stands up for herself very nicely, thank you. Their adventures continue in *Best Enemies Again*.

BETSY-TACY   [602]

Written by Maud Hart Lovelace
Illustrated by Lois Lenski
Cloth: Harper & Row/HarperCollins
Paper: Harper Trophy
Published: 1940

The Betsy-Tacy series, set in Deep Valley, Minnesota, around the turn of the century, follows three girls, Betsy (WASP), Tacy (Irish), and Tib (German), from the time they are five on through high school, college, and marriage. It is a model of an enduring and appealing kind of series fiction in which the text increases in complexity with each book and the characters are fully developed as they grow up. The girls' concerns and adventures are more than plausible—they ring true even now. The first six titles are the childhood sequence and are available in a boxed paperback edition. They include *Betsy-Tacy and Tib, Betsy and Tacy Go Over the Big Hill, Betsy and Tacy Go Downtown, Heaven to Betsy,* and *Betsy in Spite of Herself.* The illustrations in the first books are by Lois Lenski, in the later books, by Vera Neville. Both are appropriate choices.

[603]

THE CAT IN THE HAT [603]

Written and illustrated by Dr. Seuss
Cloth: Random House (Beginner Books)
Published: 1956

The one—not the only, but certainly the original—contemporary beginning reader. (It makes no difference that it is over thirty years old.) One rainy afternoon, when Mother is out and there is nothing to do, that Cat in the Hat comes to visit, and mayhem ensues. It continues in *The Cat in the Hat Comes Back.*

[603]

CAT'S CRADLE, OWL'S EYES: A BOOK OF STRING GAMES [604]

Written by Camilla Gryski
Illustrated by Tom Sankey
Paper: Mulberry
Published: 1984

A collection of forty string games, with clear instructions and fine photographs, beginning, of course, with cat's cradle. If you think about it, string games are more than fun, they are an introduction to math as well. If you get hooked on string, there is a sequel, *Many Stars, and More String Games.*

THE CHALK BOX KID [605]

Written by Clyde Robert Bulla
Illustrated by Thomas B. Allen
Paper: Random House (Step into Reading)
Published: 1987

Since Gregory's family's fortunes are on the decline, they have moved into a new house, and the lonely boy searches for a place to play. He makes a secret garden in a surprising way. This story is one title in the Stepping Stone series of paperback originals for readers who are between early-reading books and real chapter books. Other titles include *Next Spring an Oriole, Lily and the Runaway Baby,* and *Julian's Glorious Summer.*

COMMANDER TOAD IN SPACE [606]

Written by Jane Yolen
Illustrated by Bruce Degen
Cloth: Coward
Paper: Coward
Published: 1980

This is the first in a series of ridiculously funny early-reader texts that spin wildly off *Star Wars*, a movie the current generation of beginning readers may know only from videos. Which goes to prove that you didn't have to be there to enjoy this set of jokes. Other titles include *Commander Toad and the Planet of the Grapes, Commander Toad and the Intergalactic Spy, Commander Toad and the Dis-Asteroid,* and *Commander Toad and the Space Pirates.*

DANNY AND THE DINOSAUR [607]

Written and illustrated by Syd Hoff
Cloth: Harper (I Can Read)/HarperCollins
Paper: HarperCollins (I Can Read)
Published: 1958

A museum dinosaur spends a perfectly wonderful day wandering around the city with Danny. There is a Spanish-language edition of this perennial favorite in print as well. The author also created *Sammy the Seal* and *Chester the Horse* in the early-reader series.

DID YOU CARRY THE FLAG TODAY, CHARLEY? [608]

Written by Rebecca Caudill
Illustrated by Nancy Grossman
Cloth: Henry Holt
Paper: Henry Holt
Published: 1966

At Charley's school in Appalachia, you don't get to carry the flag unless you learn to behave. Mischievous Charley wins the honor in the end.

DIGGING UP DINOSAURS [609]

Written and illustrated by Aliki
Cloth: Harper & Row/HarperCollins
Paper: Harper Trophy
Published: 1981

All right, dinosaur fans, just how did those bones get from the ground into the museums? This book provides serious answers in a light-hearted and informative way sure to please young scientists.

DINNIEABBIESISTER-R-R [610]

Written by Riki Levinson
Illustrated by Helen Cogancherry
Cloth: Bradbury
Published: 1987

A gentle story of life in a Jewish family in Brooklyn in the 1930s. It is slightly longer than an early reader but set out in fourteen short chapters, which are indeed easy to read.

DINOSAURS ARE DIFFERENT [611]

Written and illustrated by Aliki
Cloth: Harper & Row/HarperCollins
Paper: HarperCollins
Published: 1985

The differences among the giant creatures is explained in simple text and clear illustrations in this dinosaur book—for example, how to tell the meat eaters from the vegetarians. Essential for the fanatics, interesting to the merely curious.

[611]

SCOLOSAURUS
20 feet long
6,000 pounds

FISH FACE [612]

Written by Patricia Reilly Giff
Illustrated by Blanche Sims
Cloth: Delacorte
Paper: Dell Yearling
Published: 1984

This is one of the twelve titles in "The Kids in the Polk Street School" series, which follows the adventures of the children in Ms. Rooney's

room, especially Emily Arrow and Richard "Beast" Best, throughout the year. Here, Emily Arrow discovers that the girl who sits next to her, Dawn Tiffanie Bosco, is a thief. The illustrations are cheerful. The series is very popular with beginning readers. Some of the other titles are *The Beast in Ms. Rooney's Room*, *The Valentine Star*, *Snaggle Doodles*, and *Say Cheese*.

FOX AND HIS FRIENDS   [613]

Written by Edward Marshall
Illustrated by James Marshall
Cloth: Dial (Easy to Read)
Paper: Pied Piper
Published: 1982

Fox, an eager fellow, and his assorted friends appear in a funny series, whose other titles include *Fox at School*, *Fox in Love*, *Fox on Wheels*, and *Fox All Week*.

FROG AND TOAD TOGETHER   [614]

Written and illustrated by Arnold Lobel
Cloth: Harper (I Can Read)/HarperCollins
Paper: Harper Trophy (I Can Read)
Published: 1972   Prizes: Newbery Honor

There are four books about those amiable friends Frog and Toad and their modest but utterly engrossing adventures and activities—everything from planting a garden and dreaming of grandeur to getting the house clean or flying a kite. The language is pleasing, the illustrations amusing. *Days with Frog and Toad*, *Frog and Toad Are Friends*, and *Frog and Toad All Year* are the other titles. Younger children love hearing them, beginning readers pore over them, and adults remember them with abiding affection.

[614]

GIVE US A GREAT BIG SMILE, ROSY COLE   [615]

Written and illustrated by Sheila Greenwald
Cloth: Little, Brown/Joy Street
Paper: Pocket
Published: 1981

This easy-to-read chapter book about Rosy Cole, who is growing up middle-class in New York City with ordinary problems and quandaries, is the first in a series. *Rosy Cole's Great American Guilt Club* takes a sharp look at fad fashions, family budgets, and the consequences of lying.

GREEN EGGS AND HAM   [616]

Written and illustrated by Dr. Seuss
Cloth: Random House (Beginner Books)
Published: 1960

One of the fine Seuss early readers, with a limited vocabulary and a narrator who keeps insisting, "I do not like them, Sam I am," until he tastes those eggs.

THE GREEN LION OF ZION STREET   [617]

Written by Julia Fields
Illustrated by Jerry Pinkney
Cloth: McElderry
Published: 1988

A short, quirky poem about a group of children waiting for the school bus on a foggy morning. They decide to walk through the park and over a bridge, where a lion crouches. Mysterious, thrilling, pleasing to

[614]

215

read aloud and ponder. The illustrations concentrate on the children, so the reader has to peer through the fog and imagine the challenges they face.

GROVER LEARNS TO READ   [618]

Written by Dan Elliott
Illustrated by Norman Chartier
Cloth: Random House (Beginner Books)
Published: 1985

Grover is worried that if he learns to read, his mother won't read to him anymore, so he decides not to learn now. Of course he does, but the story has a nice twist and is reassuring to many children, who are afraid of the same thing.

GUYS FROM SPACE   [619]

Written and illustrated by Daniel Pinkwater
Cloth: Macmillan
Published: 1989

The boy who tells this story was properly brought up and knows that you don't go off with anybody without your parents' permission—even if they're guys from space. His mother, who is busy weaving, gives permission. The spacemen and their guest have a nifty trip, and the boy is home in time for supper.

HUGH PINE   [620]

Written by Janwillem Van de Wetering
Illustrated by Lynn Munsinger
Cloth: Houghton Mifflin
Paper: Bantam
Published: 1980

The first of a delightful trio of short books about a very wise porcupine in the Maine woods who learns to dress in boots, coat, and hat and dispenses advice. In *Hugh Pine and the Good Place* he just has to get away from all his responsibilities, and in *Hugh Pine and Something Else,* he gets to the big city. Good for reading aloud to younger children and as an early chapter-book series.

I AM *NOT* GOING TO
GET UP TODAY! [621]

Written by Dr. Seuss
Illustrated by James Stevenson
Cloth: Random House (Beginner Books)
Published: 1987

The narrator of this funny Seussian verse is a lad who firmly insists that he is not getting up today no matter what happens—send neighbors, bands, even the United States Marines. The illustrations are suitably manic.

IN A DARK, DARK ROOM [622]

Written by Alvin Schwartz
Illustrated by Dirk Zimmer
Cloth: Harper (I Can Read)/HarperCollins
Paper: Harper Trophy
Published: 1984

A nicely nasty collection of mysterious stories, based on traditional folktales but written for the beginning reader.

IT'S ME, HIPPO! [623]

Written by Mike Thaler
Illustrated by Maxie Chambliss
Cloth: Harper (I Can Read)/HarperCollins
Published: 1983

A lighthearted early reader about Hippo and his jungle friends, who disagree about most things—like what constitutes a home, art, and games. But they all love Hippo. A sequel is *Hippo Lemonade*. Preschoolers like to listen to these stories, too.

JANE MARTIN, DOG DETECTIVE [624]

Written by Eve Bunting
Illustrated by Amy Schwartz
Cloth: HBJ
Paper: Voyager
Published: 1984

For a fee of just twenty-five cents a day Jane Martin finds missing dogs. Three short, easy-to-read detective stories with whimsical illustrations.

KEEP THE LIGHTS BURNING, ABBIE [625]

Written by Peter and Connie Roop
Illustrated by Peter E. Hanson
Cloth: Carolrhoda
Paper: Carolrhoda
Published: 1985

An easy-to-read and well-illustrated version of the true story of Abbie Burgess, a little girl who kept the lighthouse lamps burning when a storm hit the coast of Maine in 1856 and her father, the lighthouse keeper, was ashore. There is a story-book version of the same incident told in *The Lighthouse Keeper's Daughter*.

THE KID NEXT DOOR AND OTHER HEADACHES: STORIES ABOUT ADAM JOSHUA [626]

[627]

Written by Janice Lee Smith
Illustrated by Dick Gackenbach
Cloth: Harper & Row/HarperCollins
Paper: Harper Trophy
Published: 1984

Adam Joshua and Nelson are best friends and next-door neighbors; and they play and battle as best friends do. Their finest hour is coping with a visit from Nelson's truly horrid cousin Cynthia. Funny, realistic stories. There are four titles, including *The Kid Next Door & Other Headaches: More Stories About Adam Joshua; It's Not Easy Being George; The Show-and-Tell War;* and *The Turkey's Side of it*.

[627]

LITTLE BEAR [627]

Written by Else Holmelund Minarik
Illustrated by Maurice Sendak
Cloth: HarperCollins
Paper: HarperCollins (I Can Read)
Published: 1957

One of the first and very finest series of early-reader books features Little Bear and his considerate friends, including Hen, Duck, Cat, his doting parents in their Victorian dress, and eventually his friend Emily and her doll Lucy. The use of a controlled vocabulary does not inhibit the stories, which appeal to toddlers and preschoolers almost as much as to beginning readers. The other titles are *Little Bear's Friend, Father Bear Comes Home, Little Bear's Visit,* and *A Kiss for Little Bear,* in which the various animals deliver the kiss Grandma sends Little Bear in return for a picture.

LITTLE BROTHER OF THE WILDERNESS: THE STORY OF JOHNNY APPLESEED [628]

Written by Meridel Le Sueur
Illustrated by Suzy Sansom
Cloth: Holy Cow! Press
Published: 1947

[627]

John Chapman, who really did walk from Massachusetts to Indiana in the early nineteenth century planting apple seeds, is a heroic figure of the frontier. For contemporary children, who seem to consume gallons of apple juice daily, his achievement is both wonderful and genuinely relevant to their lives. This story of Johnny Appleseed is beautifully written and very easy to read—indeed, although tentative readers can manage it alone, it asks to be read aloud. Among the other accounts of

his life and deeds available, Stephen Kellogg's has a typically energetic quality, and Kathy Jakobsen did primitive-style illustrations incorporating quilt motifs to accompany a verse version by Reeve Lindbergh. Le Sueur's prose, however, is matchless.

LITTLE HOUSE IN THE BIG WOODS   [629]

Written by Laura Ingalls Wilder
Illustrated by Garth Williams
Cloth: Harper & Row/HarperCollins
Paper: Harper Trophy
Published: 1932

The Little House books follow the Ingalls family as they move west from Wisconsin into Indian lands and finally settle in the Dakota territory. The stories begin in the 1870s, when Laura, the central character, is not quite five, and continue through her girlhood and adolescence to her marriage to Almanzo Wilder, a young settler. His boyhood in New York State is described in *Farmer Boy*. The prose becomes more sophisticated as Laura grows up. The details of pioneer life are vivid and exact, and the books are thrilling in their artless didacticism and portrayal of close and rewarding family life. There is an endlessly replaying television series very loosely based on the books, but with none of their charm. The other titles include *Little House on the Prairie, On the Banks of Plum Creek, By the Shores of Silver Lake, The Long Winter, Little Town on the Prairie,* and *Those Happy Golden Years*. There is a boxed paperback edition of nine titles. *The Little House Cookbook: Frontier Foods from Laura Ingalls Wilder's Classic Stories* is a good cookbook for children, drawing on the recipes that occur so naturally in the stories.

LITTLE WITCH'S BIG NIGHT   [630]

Written by Deborah Hautzig
Illustrated by Marc Brown
Paper: Random House (Step into Reading)
Published: 1985

Little Witch has been so good she is punished and has to stay at home on Halloween. She takes three friends—a pirate, an astronaut, and a devil—riding on her broomstick. In *Little Witch's Birthday*, her friends manage to come to her birthday party.

LOTTA ON TROUBLEMAKER STREET [631]

Written by Astrid Lindgren
Illustrated by Julie Brinkloe
Cloth: Macmillan
Paper: Aladdin
Published: 1984

Lotta, who is five, wakes up cranky, and things get worse from there in this short novel. By the author of *Pippi Longstocking,* and in the same rebellious spirit. There are other stories about Lotta.

LULU GOES TO WITCH SCHOOL [632]

Written by Jane O'Connor
Illustrated by Emily Arnold McCully
Cloth: Harper (I Can Read)/HarperCollins
Paper: HarperCollins (I Can Read)
Published: 1987

This Lulu, who starred in *Lulu and the Witch Baby,* has moved on to witch school and she just loves it. She loves Miss Slime, her teacher, her cubby with the bat picture, the lizard tarts at snack time, and flying lessons. Eventually, she even makes friends with Sandy Witch. Light-hearted fun.

MORRIS AND BORIS, THREE STORIES [633]

Written and illustrated by Bernard Wiseman
Cloth: Dodd, Mead
Paper: Scholastic
Published: 1974

Morris the Moose and Boris the Bear are friends and their early-reader adventures are consistently funny. The other titles in the series include *Halloween with Morris and Boris, Morris Has a Cold,* and *Morris Tells Boris Mother Moose Stories and Rhymes.*

MOUSE TALES [634]

Written and illustrated by Arnold Lobel
Cloth: Harper (I Can Read)/HarperCollins
Paper: Harper Trophy (I Can Read)
Published: 1972

Papa Mouse promises his boys one story each before bedtime. There are seven, all short, some funny, some wise, and all wonderful. There are a talking wishing well, a tall and a short mouse, a flood, and more. Engrossing for a beginning reader. *Mouse Soup* is a sequel of sorts.

MR. POPPER'S PENGUINS [635]

Written by Richard and Florence Atwater
Illustrated by Robert Lawson
Cloth: Little, Brown
Paper: Dell Yearling
Published: 1938   Prizes: Newbery Honor

After more than half a century, readers are still enchanted by the classic tale of Mr. Popper, a kindly housepainter in a town called Stillwater, who loved penguins. It's about how his family coped with the gift of one, Captain Cook, who was joined by another, Greta, and begat a small flock of penguins. The illustrations capture the humor of both penguins and the story. The essential curiosity of the penguins and Mr. Popper's goodwill are something children remember all their lives.

[636]

MY FATHER'S DRAGON [636]

Written by Ruth Stiles Gannett
Illustrated by Ruth Chrisman Gannett
Cloth: Random House
Paper: Knopf
Published: 1948   Prizes: Newbery Honor

The narrator's father, Elmer Elevator, sets out to rescue a baby dragon
from the Wild Island. He uses his wits and imagination and only a few
props. The illustrations, especially the endpaper maps, are enchanting.
Good early chapter book for reading aloud or reading alone. There is
a boxed paperback set that includes two other dragon titles, *Elmer and
the Dragon* and *The Dragons of Blueland*.

NATE THE GREAT [637]

Written by Marjorie Weinman Sharmat
Illustrated by Marc Simont
Cloth: Coward (a Break-of-Day Book)
Paper: Dell Young Yearling
Published: 1972

Nate the Great is the neighborhood detective, a serious sleuth only
three feet high. The hat's a little big, the sentences are short, the de-
tecting pretty easy. Lots and lots of fun for beginning readers. Other
titles include *Nate the Great and the Fishy Prize*, *Nate the Great and the
Snowy Trail*, and *Nate the Great and the Missing Key*.

[637]

NO MORE MONSTERS FOR ME [638]

Written by Peggy Parrish
Illustrated by Marc Simont
Cloth: Harper (I Can Read)/HarperCollins
Paper: HarperCollins (I Can Read)
Published: 1981

Minneapolis Simpkin is quite desperate to have a pet, and her mother
didn't say she couldn't have a monster. So she brings home a baby one
and then tries to keep it hidden. A fine, farcical early reader. The
single-child/single-parent household is a given.

NO ONE IS GOING TO NASHVILLE   [639]

Written by Mavis Jukes
Illustrated by Lloyd Bloom
Paper: Knopf
Published: 1983

An unusually well written, easy-to-read book about how new families evolve, in this case a "weekend family"—stepmother, father, and child, and a stray dog.

OLD MOTHER WEST WIND   [640]

Written by Thornton W. Burgess
Illustrated by Harrison Cady
Cloth: Little, Brown
Paper: Little, Brown
Published: 1910

This delightful collection of short, easy-to-read stories about Reddy Fox, Peter Rabbit, Danny Meadow Mouse, and the other creatures of the meadow and woods has been a favorite for generations and with good reason. The type is large and clear, the illustrations, old-fashioned and simple. Good for reading aloud to younger children, too.

[640]

OWL AT HOME   [641]

Written and illustrated by Arnold Lobel
Cloth: HarperCollins
Paper: HarperCollins (I Can Read)
Published: 1975

A fine set of stories about Owl, a rather stay-at-home fellow, who lets winter come in to visit with chilling results, makes tear-water tea, and finds a friend in the moon. A splendid early reader, good for reading aloud to lap listeners.

PIPPI LONGSTOCKING [642]

Written by Astrid Lingren
Illustrated by Louis S. Glanzman
Cloth: Viking
Paper: Puffin
Published: 1950

Pippi is a scamp, a mischief maker, and a very nice little girl all in one. She lives all alone in a little house at the edge of the village. Her manners, housekeeping methods, and everything else about her are unconventional. The translation from the Swedish is slightly awkward and clumsy to read aloud, but listeners invariably want another chapter, please, or reread the books for themselves. Other Pippi books include *Pippi Goes on Board, Pippi on the Run,* and *Pippi in the South Seas.*

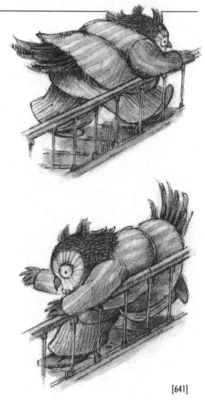

[641]

RAMONA THE PEST [643]

Written by Beverly Cleary
Cloth: Morrow Junior Books
Paper: Avon
Published: 1952–1984

Ramona is a national treasure and an institution. This series of novels about the Quimby family and their neighbors, written over a thirty-year period but bringing Ramona only to the third grade, is a mine of information about loving, ordinary day-to-day family life, told with increasing skill and laced with irresistible humor. Read one, read 'em all, learn to love Ramona, Beezus, and the rest. Enjoy kindergarten and the early grades again. It's not all sunshine, but it all rings true. These books may be slightly difficult to read alone at first, but if you begin them as read-aloud books, they will surely be reread independently for years to come. The illustrations by Louis Darling in the early books, and Allen Tiegreen in the later ones, are a perfect fit. Some of the best titles are *Henry and Beezus, Beezus and Ramona, Ramona the Brave,* and *Ramona Quimby, Age 8.*

RHYMES AND VERSES: COLLECTED POEMS FOR YOUNG PEOPLE [644]

Written by Walter de la Mare
Illustrated by Elinore Blaisdell
Cloth: Henry Holt
Paper: Owlet
Published: 1947

This pretty edition of poetry includes many familiar and half-known verses as well as unfamiliar ones. These are very pleasing to read aloud with younger children and to give to independent readers who enjoy poetry.

RICHARD KENNEDY: COLLECTED STORIES [645]

Written by Richard Kennedy
Illustrated by Marcia Sewall
Cloth: Harper & Row/HarperCollins
Published: 1987

Sixteen tales that were originally published separately as picture and story books work very well as a large volume of relatively easy reading chapters and are accompanied by fourteen new illustrations. The stories are mostly a little bit fantastic, like the one about a porcelain man glued together from a broken vase.

SAM THE MINUTEMAN [646]

Written by Nathaniel Benchley
Illustrated by Arnold Lobel
Cloth: Harper (I Can Read)/HarperCollins
Paper: HarperCollins (I Can Read)
Published: 1969

Here is one little boy's version of the beginnings of the American Revolution. The remarkably well written story is both accurate and clear and makes a number of sophisticated points about the causes of the revolution in ways young children can absorb. The companion volume is *George the Drummer Boy*, about a British drummer boy.

SEVEN TALES BY H. C. ANDERSEN: TRANSLATED FROM THE DANISH [647]

Written by Eva Le Gallienne
Illustrated by Maurice Sendak
Cloth: HarperCollins
Published: 1959; reissued 1990

A bouquet of well-loved stories has been set out here in medieval style, with pretty, decorative borders and costumes. You think you know them, but you may be surprised. In this spare translation, devoid of any sweetening as in Disney versions, the tales are thrilling . . . and also quite chilling. Included are "The Fir Tree," "The Princess and the Pea," "The Steadfast Tin Soldier," and "The Ugly Duckling."

THE SHRINKING OF TREEHORN [648]

Written by Florence Parry Heide
Illustrated by Edward Gorey
Cloth: Holiday
Paper: Dell Yearling
Published: 1971   **Prizes: New York Times Best Illustrated Book**

This is the first of three wistfully comic tales about Treehorn, the sort of boy who is ignored by others, even his parents and teachers. He is actually fading away and they don't notice. The morbid and hilarious illustrations are by a master. The paperback edition *The Adventures of Treehorn* includes *Treehorn's Treasure*. There is also *Treehorn's Wish*.

[648]

SOMETHING SLEEPING IN THE HALL [649]

Written and illustrated by Karla Kuskin
Cloth: Harper (I Can Read)/HarperCollins
Published: 1985

A collection of twenty-eight short, mostly funny poems about pets that a beginning reader can enjoy independently. The line-drawing illustrations are spare and whimsical.

THE STORIES JULIAN TELLS [650]

Written by Ann Cameron
Illustrated by Ann Strugnell
Cloth: Knopf
Paper: Knopf
Published: 1981

In this chapter book for beginning readers—six stories about Julian and his modest, cheerful middle-class black family, including his engaging little brother, Huey—there is an appealing everydayness—losing a tooth, ordering a cat from a catalog. The sequel is *More Stories Julian Tells*.

[649]

STORIES TO SOLVE: FOLKTALES FROM AROUND THE WORLD   [651]

Written by George Shannon
Paper: Beech Tree
Published: 1985

Oh, so clever, these fourteen very short folktales that pose problems, twisty problems. Two fathers and two sons went fishing . . . What did the bride say to persuade her mother-in-law that she hadn't eaten all the chickpeas? Witty illustrations add to the fun. The temptation is to devour them like peanuts. Better still to read aloud one or two at a time and savor the wit. There is also *More Stories to Solve*.

SUGARING TIME   [652]

Written by Kathryn Lasky
Illustrated by Christopher G. Knight
Cloth: Macmillan
Paper: Aladdin
Published: 1983

This excellent collaborative effort in photojournalism tells about the Lacey family in Vermont and how they make maple syrup. *Cranberries* does a plainer job of describing another New England crop.

SURPRISES   [653]

Written by Lee Bennett Hopkins
Illustrated by Megan Lloyd
Cloth: Harper & Row/HarperCollins
Paper: Harper Trophy
Published: 1984

An anthology of thirty-eight easy-to-read and surprising poems, with inviting illustrations. *More Surprises* is a companion book.

TIKTA'LIKTAK: AN ESKIMO LEGEND   [654]

Written and illustrated by James Houston
Cloth: HBJ
Paper: Voyager
Published: 1965

The adventures of a young hunter, which include surviving terrible weather, encountering a polar bear, and struggling to get home.

[649]

TURTLE IN JULY   [655]

Written by Marilyn Singer
Illustrated by Jerry Pinkney
Cloth: Macmillan
Published: 1989   Prizes: New York Times Best Illustrated Book

In this volume, a series of nature poems celebrating the seasons have been illustrated with exquisite watercolors of different wildlife species. There are four poems, one for each season, celebrating, of all overlooked creatures, the bullhead, the bottom-loving catfish.

UNCLE ELEPHANT   [656]

Written and illustrated by Arnold Lobel
Cloth: Harper (I Can Read)/HarperCollins
Paper: HarperCollins (I Can Read)
Published: 1981

A little elephant who thinks his parents have been lost at sea is rescued by an elderly uncle. The book addresses separation anxieties carefully, so even adults may find themselves teary.

A VERY YOUNG DANCER   [657]

Written and illustrated by Jill Krementz
Paper: Dell Yearling
Published: 1976

Part of the "Very Young" series, this is a lavishly illustrated photo essay about a ten-year-old girl's experience playing Marie under the direction of George Balanchine in his New York City Ballet production of "The Nutcracker." The photographs of Mr. Balanchine have certain historic value, and this book is much loved, particularly by aspiring young ballerinas. The production, of course, continues. Other titles in the series are about gymnasts, circus riders, skaters, and horseback riders.

WAKE UP, SUN [658]

Written by David L. Harrison
Illustrated by Hans Wilhelm
Paper: Random House
Published: 1986

This entertaining early reader is about a silly dog who wakes up in the middle of the night, can't find the sun, and then wakes up his friends to help him find it.

WHITE BIRD [659]

Written by Clyde Robert Bulla
Illustrated by Donald Cook
Paper: Random House (Stepping Stone)
Published: 1966; 1990

A long time ago, at the beginning of the nineteenth century, in a valley in Tennessee, a lonely and suspicious hermit, Luke, raised a foundling he called John Thomas. The boy trained a white bird, his only friend. When the bird was stolen from him, John Thomas disobeyed Luke and went to town. Although the story is short and easy to read, its poignance resonates and is affecting to much older children, too.

THE WHITE STALLION [660]

Written by Elizabeth Shub
Illustrated by Rachel Isadora
Cloth: Greenwillow
Paper: Bantam
Published: 1982

As her family heads across Texas in a Conestoga wagon, Gretchen falls asleep tied onto the back of an old mare. She awakens in the midst of a band of wild horses. It's a thrilling story, beautifully illustrated.

The books in this section are part of
the rich treasure chest of childhood—
adventures, fairy stories, folktales, chapter
books, series—books to listen to, read, reread, and
then reread again for the pleasure of knowing what is
going to happen next. The appropriate age range for listening
to these stories is very wide. Preschoolers can follow some of them;
many teenagers comfortably read others. A number of the titles
were once considered appropriate for adolescent readers
only. For good or ill, our children grow up too soon
these days, and in a world made small by television
and the electronic media, a parent should use
judgment about what individual children
know and understand. The annotations
make such distinctions clear.

ABEL'S ISLAND [661]

Written and illustrated by William Steig
Cloth: Farrar, Straus & Giroux
Paper: Sunburst
Published: 1976   Prizes: Newbery Honor

Abelard Hassam di Chirico Flint, an artist and mouse, is swept away in a rainstorm and is stranded for a year on an island in the middle of a river. Splendid Steig for independent readers or reading aloud.

AN ACTOR'S LIFE FOR ME [662]

Written by Lillian Gish
Illustrated by Patricia Henderson Lincoln
Cloth: Viking
Published: 1987

Here's an engaging memoir of life in the American theater at the turn of the century, before there were movies, let alone television or VCRs, as told by an actress whose later work may be familiar to some readers. It is a fascinating story well told, with particularly insightful and appealing illustrations.

THE ADVENTURES OF DOCTOR DOLITTLE [663]

Written and illustrated by Hugh Lofting
Cloth: Delacorte
Paper: Yearling
Published: 1920; reissued 1988   Prizes: Newbery Medal

The adventures of the good doctor from Puddleby-on-the-Marsh who understood the languages of animals have come back into print. The socially objectionable passages have been removed, with the help of Lofting's son, without really diminishing the charm of the stories in the least. Young Tommy Stubbins, Polynesia the Parrot, Dab-Dab the duck, and the Pushmipulu are as charming as you remember them. Half a dozen individual titles are available.

THE ADVENTURES OF PINOCCHIO [664]

Written by Carlo Collodi
Illustrated by Attilo Mussino
Cloth: Macmillan
Published: 1925

This enchanting edition of the classic story of the little wooden puppet who wants to become a real boy first appeared in Italy in 1911 and in the United States in 1925. Happily, it is available again. The large, open format that sets off both the stylish illustrations and the gracefully displayed text make it easy to read aloud. The original was written for serialization, so the narrative is somewhat jerky, but if you are reading it at bedtime, you may not notice that at all. There are numerous other editions. The contemporary Italian artist Roberto Innocenti has illustrated a good translation of the full text by E. Harden, with astonishing grim, gray realistic illustrations that are his signature style. An adaptation by Marianna Mayer illustrated by Gerald McDermott is also quite good. Most of the others are mediocre. Children weaned on the Disney version, which is quite wonderful in its own right indeed (some, including Maurice Sendak, claim better), should be warned that the book is much harsher and more sinister.

[664]

AFTERNOON OF THE ELVES [665]

Written by Janet Taylor Lisle
Cloth: Orchard Books
Paper: Scholastic
Published: 1989   **Prizes: Newbery Honor**

Sara-Kate, an odd child no one likes, is befriended by Hilary, the very conventional fourth-grader who lives next door. Soon it is Hilary who is drawn into Sara-Kate's magical world—the miniature village behind her house that the girl claims was built by elves. The novel addresses many of the questions of loyalty, friendship, and privacy that concern middle-grade children.

ALAN AND NAOMI   [666]

Written by Myron Levoy
Cloth: Harper & Row/HarperCollins
Paper: Harper Trophy
Published: 1977

Naomi is a refugee child from Paris who moves into Alan Silverman's New York City apartment building during World War II. She seems very peculiar, so he avoids her at first, but a genuine friendship ensues in the honestly told story.

ALL-OF-A-KIND FAMILY   [667]

Written by Sidney Taylor
Illustrated by Helen John
Paper: Yearling
Published: 1951

There are five books in the well-loved series about a close-knit Jewish family living on New York City's Lower East Side in the early part of this century. The five daughters are high-spirited and make their own good times. And their little brother turns out to be a charmer. Who can forget the library lady? The other titles include *All-Of-A-Kind Family Downtown, All-Of A Kind Family Uptown,* then *Ella of All-Of-A-Kind Family* and *More All-Of-A-Kind Family.* These are read-aloud favorites of lower-grade listeners.

AMY'S EYES   [668]

Written by Richard Kennedy
Illustrated by Richard Egielski
Cloth: Harper & Row/HarperCollins
Paper: Harper Trophy
Published: 1985

This big, rollicking fantasy adventure begins in an orphanage. Amy pines away for her sailor doll, who turns into a real captain; then she herself turns into a doll, and off they go with a crew of animals, seeking more than gold.

[664]

ANASTASIA KRUPNIK   [669]

Written by Lois Lowry
Illustrated by Diane de Groat
Cloth: Houghton Mifflin
Paper: Yearling
Published: 1979

The heroine's name marks the beginning of an affectionate, comic series about the Krupnik family and Anastasia in particular. She is growing up bright and articulate in a contemporary Boston suburb. The other members of the family, especially her little brother, Sam, are vividly portrayed, too. The series begins in the fourth grade, and by the fifth book, Anastasia is in junior high school. Other titles include *Anastasia at Your Service; Anastasia, Ask Your Analyst; Anastasia on Her Own;* and *Anastasia and Her Chosen Career.*

. . . AND NOW MIGUEL   [670]

Written by Joseph Krumgold
Illustrated by Jean Charlot
Cloth: Harper & Row/HarperCollins
Paper: Harper Trophy
Published: 1953   **Prizes: Newbery Medal**

Miguel Chaven, a twelve-year-old boy, lives with his family of sheep-herders in the Sangre de Cristo Mountains in New Mexico. He tells how he wishes to accompany the men and the sheep to their summer pasture, a journey that is both a rite of passage and a symbol of belonging to the community. This book has passed the test of time and remains engrossing.

THE ANIMAL FAMILY   [671]

Written by Randall Jarrell
Illustrated by Maurice Sendak
Cloth: Pantheon
Paper: Knopf   **Prizes: Newbery Honor**
Published: 1965   **New York Times Best Illustrated Book**

This is a facsimile of the handsome original edition of the distinguished American poet's memorable fantasy about a solitary hunter who mirac-

[669]

[671]

ulously acquires a family, including a mermaid, a bear, a lynx and, finally, a boy. Extraordinary writing and fine, restrained decorations. Splendid for reading aloud again and again.

ANNE FRANK: THE DIARY OF A YOUNG GIRL HIDING FROM THE NAZIS [672]

Written by Anne Frank
Cloth: Doubleday
Paper: Pocket
Published: 1947

The diary of the thirteen-year-old Jewish girl, hidden in an attic during the Nazi occupation of Holland, remains a powerful and poignant book. The universally appealing aspects—the simple problems of adolescence and Anne's family relationships as well as her optimism—are in shocking contrast to the terror of her situation. And, of course, there

was no happy ending. Children often read this to themselves, but it needs to be discussed, often at length and sometimes in the middle of the night. The introduction to the hardcover edition is by Eleanor Roosevelt, who may also require some introduction for contemporary readers.

ANNE OF GREEN GABLES   [673]

Written by L. M. Montgomery
Illustrated by Jody Lee
Cloth: Grosset & Dunlop
Paper: Bantam
Published: 1908

Anne Shirley, the red-haired heroine of the perennially popular girls' series, moves to Canada's Prince Edward Island at the turn of the century. As the story begins, she is eleven and full of talk and troubles. She sorts out her relationship with her initially uneasy foster parents, Matthew and Merilla Cuthbert. In later installments she goes to college, returns to the island to teach, and eventually marries. The other titles include *Anne of Avonlea, Anne of the Island, Anne of Windy Poplars, Anne's House of Dreams,* and *Anne of Ingleside.*

ANNO'S COUNTING HOUSE   [674]

Written and illustrated by Mitsumasa Anno
Cloth: Philomel
Published: 1982

The world-renowned Japanese artist is a splendid teacher. He has embarked on a dazzling set of picture books that teach mathematical theory and logic. This one deals with numbers, addition, subtraction, number sets, and game theory. *Anno's Hat Tricks* is about binary logic; *Anno's Mysterious Multiplying Jar* is about factorials; *Socrates and the Three Little Pigs* is about combinational analysis; and *Anno's Math Games* and *More Math Games* are an introduction to mathematics. These remarkable books are not to be handed out lightly. They are rich, delicious, and difficult. However beautiful to look at, they can be daunting to those with math aversion (adults as well as children). Equally, if you enjoy working with bright children, they are a wonderful way to do mathematics at home for the pure fun of it.

ARE YOU THERE, GOD? IT'S ME, MARGARET. [675]

Written by Judy Blume
Cloth: Bradbury
Paper: Dell Yearling
Published: 1970

Almost twelve, both longing for and fearing adolescence, Margaret, who chats with God on a regular basis about her worries, is a heroine most children identify with, at least for a minute, as they move along the path toward growing up. Controversial when they were first published, the Blume books are part of the rites of passage for many, if not most, American children. Some of the other most popular titles are *Then Again, Maybe I Won't; Otherwise Known as Sheila the Great;* and *Tiger Eyes. Are You There, God?* is also available in Spanish.

AROUND THE WORLD IN EIGHTY DAYS [676]

Written by Jules Verne
Illustrated by Barry Moser
Cloth: Morrow Junior Books
Published: 1873; 1989

The story of how Phileas Fogg accepted a daring wager—to circumnavigate the globe in a ludicrously short period of time—was first published in 1873. In this elegant, well-translated new edition, he and his faithful manservant, Passepartout, race on boldly, pursued by Detective Fix. There are sixteen illustrations.

ARTHUR, FOR THE VERY FIRST TIME [677]

Written by Patricia MacLachlan
Illustrated by Lloyd Bloom
Cloth: Harper & Row/HarperCollins
Paper: Harper Trophy
Published: 1980

It is a transitional summer for Arthur, a fussy ten-year-old boy who is spending time at his eccentric aunt and uncle's farm while his mother awaits a new baby at home. A charmingly illustrated and well-written story of self-discovery and assertion.

ASK ANOTHER QUESTION: THE STORY AND MEANING OF PASSOVER [678]

Written by Miriam Chaikin
Illustrated by Marvin Friedman
Cloth: Clarion
Paper: Clarion
Published: 1985

A welcoming explanation of the story, symbols, and rituals of Passover, full of nuggets of information and points for conversation. It is one of a series of books on the Jewish holidays, including *Light Another Candle*, for Hanukkah; *Make Noise, Make Merry*, for Purim; and *Shake a Palm Branch*, for Sukkot. These books are useful for the family reference shelf and can be read aloud or excerpted for younger children.

BADGER ON THE BARGE: AND OTHER STORIES [679]

Written by Janni Howker
Cloth: Greenwillow
Paper: Puffin
Published: 1985

The five deeply affecting short stories, all set in England, in this fine collection all involve lonely young people who come into contact with elderly strangers. Beautifully written.

THE BAGTHORPE SAGA [680]

Written by Helen Cresswell
Cloth: Macmillan
Paper: Puffin
Published: 1977

The Bagthorpes, an eccentric British family, are fiercely competitive, terribly clever, and slightly nutty. They inhabit a six-part series of mad-cap novels: *Ordinary Jack, Absolute Zero, Bagthorpes Unlimited, Bagthorpes v. the World, Bagthorpes Abroad,* and *Bagthorpes Haunted.*

BALLET SHOES   [681]

Written by Noel Streatfeild
Cloth: Random House
Paper: Dell Yearling
Published: 1937

This is the first in an internationally popular series of books for girls. It tells the story of the three Fossil girls, adopted by an ever-traveling professor, who has sent them to be raised in London and trained for the stage. They are plucky and determined and beguilingly British. Similarly appealing other families and their adventures are told in *Movie Shoes, Dancing Shoes, Skating Shoes, Theatre Shoes,* and other titles.

BASEBALL IN APRIL   [682]

Written by Gary Soto
Cloth: HBJ
Paper: Odyssey
Published: 1990

These short stories, set in Mexican-American neighborhoods in California, are about youngsters caught in the dilemma of transformation. They are becoming both American by popular culture and adult experiences, and yet their community is still Mexican. A bittersweet air of resignation pervades.

THE BAT-POET   [683]

Written by Randall Jarrell
Illustrated by Maurice Sendak
Cloth: Macmillan
Paper: Macmillan
Published: 1964   **Prizes: New York Times Best Illustrated Book**

A little brown bat cannot sleep during the day—he keeps waking up and looking at the world. This collaboration between a fine poet and a fine artist is properly considered a classic.

BE EVER HOPEFUL, HANNALEE   [684]

Written by Patricia Beatty
Cloth: Morrow Junior Books
Published: 1989

Hannalee Reed is the heroine of an earlier historical novel, *Turn Homeward, Hannalee,* which follows the girl through much of the Civil War.

This book, which can be read as a sequel or independently, begins as the family returns to the devastated city of Atlanta in the summer of 1865. Unusually ambitious and well researched.

THE BEARS' HOUSE   [685]

Written by Marilyn Sachs
Cloth: Dutton
Published: 1971

Fran Ellen is a nine-year-old who has a great many real problems with her family and in school. Her greatest pleasure is in visiting the classroom doll house, the Bears' House, which she loves. This is a beautifully written short novel about struggle and maturation and a steady favorite among middle-grade readers. The sequel is *Fran Ellen's House*.

BEAUTY: A RETELLING OF THE STORY OF BEAUTY AND THE BEAST   [686]

Written by Robin McKinley
Cloth: Harper & Row/HarperCollins
Paper: Pocket
Published: 1978

Here is a first-person fantasy novel that retells the fairy tale with great style and is particularly appealing to upper-grade readers.

BEHIND THE ATTIC WALL   [687]

Written by Sylvia Cassedy
Cloth: Harper & Row/HarperCollins
Paper: Avon/Camelot
Published: 1983

This satisfying novel is in a classic tradition. As it begins, twelve-year-old Maggie, who has been shunted from school to school, pale, unhappy, and unwanted, is sent off to Uncle Morris and the two great-aunts. They don't seem like prizes, and the house, Adelphi Hills Academy, really is creepy, with strange sounds. Ghosts. Very satisfying.

BEN AND ME   [688]

Written and illustrated by Robert Lawson
Cloth: Little, Brown
Paper: Little, Brown
Published: 1939

This is one of a series of confidential biographies of historical figures as narrated by a pet or animal with inside information and a light-hearted view of history, in this case Benjamin Franklin as seen by a mouse. Other titles include *Mr. Revere and I* and *Captain Kidd's Cat.* Generations of middle-grade schoolchildren have adored these.

THE BEST CHRISTMAS
PAGEANT EVER   [689]

Written by Barbara Robinson
Illustrated by Judith Gwyn Brown
Cloth: Harper & Row/HarperCollins
Paper: Harper Trophy
Published: 1972

What is the true meaning of Christmas? When the ramshackle, chaotic, impossible Herdman children are cast in the annual Christmas pageant, some important lessons are learned all around the community. This could have been treacle, but it's told so deftly it has become a classic. Good to read aloud.

THE BFG   [690]

Written by Roald Dahl
Illustrated by Quentin Blake
Cloth: Farrar, Straus & Giroux
Paper: Puffin
Published: 1982

Here is the story of the Big Friendly Giant who kidnapped Sophie, an eight-year-old orphan, and took her to Giantland. It was the author's favorite and for many adults is the most appealing of his books. The wordplay of the gentle giant as he bottles dreams and protects Sophie from the nine giants who eat children is dazzling. The absurdly funny plot turns and turns again, and eventually, with the help of the queen of England herself, is resolved. As in all Dahl books, there is a proper ending. Splendid.

BIG RED [691]

Written by Jim Kjelgaard
Illustrated by Bob Kuhn
Cloth: Holiday
Paper: Bantam
Published: 1945

An enduring and appealing dog-and-boy story, in this case a champion Irish setter and a trapper's son. The sequels are *Irish Red* and *Outlaw Red.*

[692]

BILL PEET: AN AUTOBIOGRAPHY [692]

Written and illustrated by Bill Peet
Cloth: Houghton Mifflin
Published: 1989   Prizes: Caldecott Honor

Bill Peet's first memories are of World War I. He came of age in the Midwest in the 1920s and during the Great Depression drove to California, where he became a top writer and illustrator for Walt Disney, all before he began a career as a successful children's book writer. His plainly written but lavishly illustrated memoir is enthralling. He is unsparing of himself and the difficulties he faced, and generous to others, including Disney. The drawings, which fill half or more of most pages, seem to race along.

BLACK BEAUTY [693]

Written by Anna Sewell
Illustrated by Fritz Eichenberg
Cloth: Grosset & Dunlop
Paper: Grosset & Dunlop
Published: 1877; reissued 1945

There are many abridged editions of the best-known horse story of all. This is the full text of the story of the beautiful black animal who is traded into many adventures and ultimately rescued. A handsome modern edition illustrated by Charles Keeping also has a complete text.

BLACK BEAUTY   [694]

Written by Anna Sewell; adapted by Robin McKinley
Illustrated by Susan Jeffers
Cloth: Random House
Published: 1986

[692]

An award-winning contemporary novelist, Robin McKinley, has adapted the ultimate horse story in somewhat simplified language. The lush illustrations fairly gallop across the page. This version works well for younger readers.

THE BLACK CAULDRON   [695]

Written by Lloyd Alexander
Cloth: Henry Holt
Paper: Dell Yearling
Published: 1965   Prizes: Newbery Honor

This is the best-known volume of a favorite fantasy quintet about the imaginary land of Prydain, which has some basis in Welsh legend and traditional mythology. In this volume, a council of warriors face villainy. The first book is *The Book of Three,* and the others are *The Castle of Llyr, Taran Wanderer,* and *The High King.* The last title won the Newbery Medal in 1968.

THE BLACK PEARL   [696]

Written by Scott O'Dell
Cloth: Houghton Mifflin
Paper: Dell Yearling
Published: 1967   Prizes: Newbery Honor

This is a thrilling adventure story set off the Baja California coast, about a village of pearl divers, rivalry, and a giant manta guarding a huge black pearl.

THE BLACK STALLION   [697]

Written by Walter Farley
Cloth: Random House
Paper: Knopf
Published: 1941

One of the all-time favorite animal series—there are nineteen tales about that mighty champion the black stallion and his various relations. Titles include *The Black Stallion and Flame, The Black Stallion Challenged!*, and *The Black Stallion's Sulky Colt*.

BLOWFISH LIVE IN THE SEA   [698]

Written by Paula Fox
Cloth: Bradbury
Paper: Aladdin
Published: 1970

His stepsister is the narrator of this novel about eighteen-year-old Ben Felix, an unhappy, erratic boy trying to come to terms with himself and his real father.

BLUE WILLOW   [699]

Written by Doris Gates
Illustrated by Paul Lantz
Cloth: Viking
Paper: Puffin
Published: 1940

This story of migrant workers in California is over half a century old but remains fresh and affecting. Janey, who is an only child, longs to live in a house and have an orderly life. As it is, the only possession she and her parents have of value or beauty is a blue-willow plate.

[702]

THE BOOK OF ADAM TO MOSES   [700]

Written by Lore Segal
Illustrated by Leonard Baskin
Cloth: Knopf
Paper: Schocken
Published: 1986

Here is a graceful modern rendition of the first five books of the Bible in language that is also close to the original Hebrew. It is an achievement of both scholarship and art. The illustrations are dark and serious.

A BOOK OF AMERICANS   [701]

Written by Rosemary and Stephen Vincent Benét
Illustrated by Charles Child
Cloth: Henry Holt
Paper: Henry Holt
Published: 1933; reissued 1986

A collection of fifty-six poems about historic Americans, both lesser and well known, written with style and wit more than half a century ago and reissued for new generations to enjoy. There are presidents and plain folk inventoried, and even a few villains here. Perfect for reading aloud. The woodcut illustrations are dramatic.

[702]

THE BORROWERS   [702]

Written by Mary Norton
Illustrated by Beth and Joe Krush
Cloth: HBJ
Paper: Odyssey
Published: 1953   Prizes: Carnegie Medal

This is the first volume of a series of grand novels about Pod, Homily, and Arrietty, a family of little people who lived under the kitchen floor in a quiet house some time not so very long ago. The idea of these little people often appeals to children who otherwise have no taste for whimsy. The fine line illustrations certainly add to their charm. Other titles include *The Borrowers Afield, The Borrowers Afloat, The Borrowers Aloft,* and *The Borrowers Avenged.* A boxed paperback edition is available.

THE BRAVE LITTLE TOASTER   [703]

Written by Thomas M. Disch
Illustrated by Karen Schmidt
Cloth: Doubleday
Published: 1986

Five domestic appliances—a vacuum cleaner, a tensor lamp, an electric blanket, a clock radio, and a toaster—have been left at a cabin in the woods. Thinking they have been abandoned, they set off to find their master. The toaster is the leader. This is the kind of fantasy that requires a sure hand. The author, who writes science fiction for adults, has one. Well done.

BRIDGE TO TERABITHIA   [704]

Written by Katherine Paterson
Illustrated by Donna Diamond
Cloth: T. Y. Crowell/HarperCollins
Paper: Harper Trophy
Published: 1977   **Prizes: Newbery Medal**

This is an astonishingly powerful novel about an improbable friendship between Jess, a poor local boy, and Leslie, the willful, brilliantly imaginative girl who moves into a house nearby. They establish a secret hiding place they call Terabithia and develop a rich friendship that is severed when Leslie is accidentally killed. There are only a few novels for children about death and they are generally unsatisfactory. This one succeeds brilliantly and speaks to the resolution of grief among the living. But because the writing is so fine and persuasive, the impact on readers of all ages is deep. This is a six-Kleenex late-night-talk-time story, and worth the effort.

BROTHERS OF THE HEART   [705]

Written by Joan Blos
Cloth: Scribner's
Paper: Aladdin
Published: 1985

A historical novel set in the far north in the mid-nineteenth century, during a bitter-cold winter. Shem, a boy from an Ohio family, who moved to Michigan and later on was hired as clerk to a fur-trading expedition, is found in an isolated cabin by an elderly Ottowan Indian woman. Their relationship becomes the core of the story.

BUNNICULA: A RABBIT TALE OF MYSTERY [706]

Written by Deborah and James Howe
Illustrated by Alan Daniel
Cloth: Atheneum
Paper: Avon
Published: 1979

Is Bunnicula really a vegetarian vampire bunny? Harold, the Monroe family's dog and the narrator of this comic novel, thinks so. This is the first of a funny trilogy featuring Harold, Chester the dog, and Howie the dachshund puppy. Middle-grade readers find them very entertaining. *The Celery Stalks at Midnight* is followed by *Nightly Nightmare*.

CADDIE WOODLAWN [707]

Written by Carol Ryrie Brink
Illustrated by Trina Schart Hyman
Cloth: Macmillan
Paper: Aladdin
Published: 1935   Prizes: Newbery Medal

This popular novel about pioneer life in Wisconsin in the 1860s, reillustrated in 1973, is still convincing and compelling reading.

CALL IT COURAGE [708]

Written and illustrated by Armstrong Sperry
Cloth: Macmillan
Paper: Macmillan
Published: 1939   Prizes: Newbery Medal

Set in the South Pacific, this is a timelessly interesting adventure story about Mafatu, the son of the Great Chief of Hikueru, who conquers his fear of the sea.

CANYON WINTER   [709]

Written by Walt Morey
Cloth: Dutton
Published: 1972

Pete, a fifteen-year-old boy, is stranded in a canyon after a plane crash. He finds his way to the cabin of Omar, a solitary old man, and spends the whole winter with him. There is an underlying theme of conservation and a concern for ecology and nature. Among Morey's other popular boys-and-nature books are *The Lemon Meringue Dog, Sandy and the Rock Star,* and *The Year of the Black Pony.*

THE CAT WHO WENT TO HEAVEN   [710]

Written by Elizabeth Coatsworth
Cloth: Macmillan
Paper: Aladdin
Published: 1930   **Prizes: Newbery Medal**

This short novel tells of a starving young artist in long-ago Japan, his faithful servant, a white cat, and a rare commission. And there is a Buddhist miracle. Religious values are subtly conveyed within the story.

CATHEDRAL: THE STORY OF ITS CONSTRUCTION   [711]

Written and illustrated by David Macaulay
Cloth: Houghton Mifflin
Paper: Houghton Mifflin   **Prizes: New York Times Best Illustrated Book**
Published: 1977   **Caldecott Honor**

A remarkable re-creation of the building of a French Gothic cathedral. The illustrations are pen-and-ink; the text is utterly clear. If you are mesmerized by this explanation, then look for *Castle* and *Pyramid* or the brilliant fantasy *Unbuilding.*

[711]

THE CHANGES   [712]

Written by Peter Dickinson
Cloth: Delacorte
Paper: Dell Yearling
Published: 1970

A splendid trilogy of early novels by a distinguished British author who writes for both adults and younger readers has been collectively reissued as *The Changes*. It includes *The Devil's Children, Heartsease,* and *The Weathermonger.* As the series begins, there has been a revolt in Britain and twelve-year-old Nicola Gore is alone in London, which is now a deserted city. The society advances into a kind of superstitious medievalism. Readers who ordinarily don't like fantasy or science fiction get caught up in these.

CHARLIE AND THE CHOCOLATE FACTORY [713]

Written by Roald Dahl
Illustrated by Joseph Schindelman
Cloth: Knopf
Paper: Penguin
Published: 1963

The story of how poor but honest Charlie Bucket came to visit Willie Wonka's fantastic and marvelous chocolate factory in the company of a memorable band of truly obnoxious children (all of whom get their just desserts, ha, ha) is one of the deserved, and certainly the most delicious, modern classics. There is an adaptation in play form available in paperback from Penguin, and a sequel, *Charlie and the Great Glass Elevator*.

CHARLOTTE'S WEB [714]

Written by E. B. White
Illustrated by Garth Williams
Cloth: Harper & Row/HarperCollins
Paper: Harper Trophy
Published: 1952   **Prizes: Newbery Honor**

Wilbur, an innocent and amiable pig, is saved from slaughter by a true friend and a fine writer, Charlotte, the gray spider in the barnyard door. The language, the subplots, the details (especially the science and nature observations), and the moral seem more insightful and rewarding with each reading. The feature-length cartoon is not a travesty and does not usually dissuade children from actually listening to, or reading, the book. As Charlotte herself wrote, "Terrific."

[714]

CHEAPER BY THE DOZEN [715]

Written by Ernestine Carey and Frank B. Gilbreth
Paper: Bantam
Published: 1948

This memoir of growing up in the Gilbreth family with twelve children and dozens of ideas and adventures is lighthearted and entertaining, as is the sequel, *Belles on Their Toes*.

THE CHILDREN OF
GREEN KNOWE   [716]

Written by Lucy Boston
Illustrated by Peter Boston
Cloth: HBJ
Paper: Odyssey
Published: 1954

A lonely little boy called Tolly is sent to stay with his ancient great-grandmother, who lives in an eccentric house in England called Green Knowe. It has belonged to the family for hundreds of years. Tolly finds the toys and possessions of other children who lived and played there, and gradually he finds that the seventeenth-century siblings, Toby, Linnet, and Alexander, still do. Totally mysterious and magical, the writing in these elegant novels is superb. The series includes *Treasure of Green Knowe, The River at Green Knowe,* and *A Stranger at Green Knowe,* which won the Carnegie Medal. The best way to begin is to read aloud in dark December so you reach the memorable Christmas scenes at the appropriate time.

[714]

THE CHILDREN'S HOMER: THE ADVENTURES OF ODYSSEUS AND THE TALE OF TROY [717]

Written by Padraic Colum
Illustrated by Willy Pogany
Paper: Macmillan
Published: 1918

This is a splendid use of paperback publishing—making available to new readers the beautifully illustrated 1918 edition of Homer told by the distinguished Irish poet. The prose is brilliant, and the fine line drawings are fairly breathtaking. The companion volume, *The Golden Fleece: And the Heroes Who Lived Before Achilles,* which tells many Greek myths within the framework of the story of Jason and the Argonauts, is also again in print.

[718]

A CHILD'S CHRISTMAS IN WALES [718]

Written by Dylan Thomas
Illustrated by Trina Schart Hyman
Cloth: Holiday
Published: 1985

The Welsh poet's evocative memoir of Christmas early in this century is full of snow, cats, aunties, and boyish adventure. This is a fine edition with affectionate watercolor illustrations (the cats in the snow are especially appealing), nicely sized to hold in small hands. There is another beautifully drawn version, illustrated by the British artist Edward Ardizzone.

CHIMNEY SWEEPS: YESTERDAY AND TODAY [719]

Written by James Cross Giblin
Illustrated by Margot Tomes
Cloth: T. Y. Crowell/HarperCollins
Paper: Harper Trophy
Published: 1982

An entertaining and well-illustrated history of an old and colorful profession, full of folklore and stories going back to the fifteenth century.

CHOCOLATE FEVER [720]

Written by Robert Kimmel Smith
Illustrated by Gioia Fiammenghi
Paper: Dell Yearling
Published: 1978

Henry Green ate so much of the yummy stuff he caught chocolate fever. How was he cured? Read and find out. Funny enough to read aloud to middle-grade listeners.

THE CHOCOLATE TOUCH [721]

Written by Patrick Skene Catling
Illustrated by Margot Apple
Paper: Bantam
Published: 1979

Chocoholics beware! Imagine the Midas story, only the object of lust has turned from gold to rich, dark, chocolaty brown. Here it is, and now imagine what happens to John when everything he touches turns to . . . chocolate. Funny, and sweetly moral.

[718]

A CHRISTMAS CAROL [722]

Written by Charles Dickens
Illustrated by Trina Schart Hyman
Cloth: Holiday
Published: 1983

Bless us one and all. Here's a setting of the familiar text set off with decorated initials and six color-plates by a well-known contemporary artist. There are many other good, legible (important if you are reading out loud) editions available, including those illustrated by Michael Foreman, Roberto Innocenti, and Lisbeth Zwerger.

[719]

THE CHRONICLES OF NARNIA [723]

Written by C. S. Lewis
Illustrated by Pauline Baynes
Cloth: Macmillan
Paper: Collier
Published: 1950

This seven-volume allegorical Christian fantasy has steadily gained worldwide popularity since it was first published in the 1950s. In the beginning Aslan, the white lion, freed Narnia from the spell of the White Witch, but that was just the beginning. These tales are very good for reading aloud. The titles are *The Lion, the Witch, and the Wardrobe; Prince Caspian; The Voyage of the "Dawn Treader"; The Silver Chair; The Horse and His Boy; The Magician's Nephew;* and *The Last Battle.*

CITY: A STORY OF ROMAN PLANNING AND CONSTRUCTION [724]

Written and illustrated by David Macaulay
Cloth: Houghton Mifflin
Paper: Houghton Mifflin
Published: 1974

The planning and construction of an imaginary Roman city is set forth in clear pen-and-ink illustrations and a lucid text. The idea of rational city planning is explicit.

CLEVER GRETCHEN AND OTHER FORGOTTEN FOLKTALES [725]

Written by Alison Lurie
Illustrated by Margot Tomes
Cloth: T. Y. Crowell/HarperCollins
Published: 1980

A good selection of fourteen stories with active heroines—young women who are doers and clever thinkers, whether they are princesses or commoners. There is a refreshing tartness to both the text and the illustrations.

COLOUR FAIRY BOOKS [726]

Written by Andrew Lang
Paper: Dover
Published: 1889; reissued 1978

These are facsimiles of the famed colour fairy books—Blue, Green, Pink, Red, and Yellow—in their original, 1889/90/92 editions. They are a trove of lore and provide nearly endless hours of delight for older readers who like fairy tales.

COME SING, JIMMY JO [727]

Written by Katherine Paterson
Cloth: Lodestar
Paper: Avon
Published: 1985

A fine novel about an eleven-year-old boy who has been content to live in the mountains with his grandmother. When he joins the family bluegrass troupe, he confronts not only family problems but also the realities of fame. This is an interesting inside look at the peculiar, invasive dynamic of modern celebrity that children can begin to understand.

COMMODORE PERRY IN THE LAND OF THE SHOGUN [728]

Written by Rhoda Blumberg
Cloth: Lothrop, Lee & Shepard
Published: 1985   Prizes: Newbery Honor

The story of the American expedition to Japan led by Commodore Matthew Perry in 1853. Not only is the text well written, but the large-format book is unusually well designed, with reproductions of Japanese illustrations of the period.

COUSINS [729]

Written by Virginia Hamilton
Cloth: Philomel
Published: 1990

Cammy didn't get along with her practically perfect cousin Patty Ann, but she holds herself responsible for the freak accident that takes place in this short, accessible novel. Cammy and her Gram—who may be old and frail, but is sharp and wise—are vivid characters.

COWBOYS OF THE WILD WEST   [730]

Written by Russell Friedman
Cloth: Clarion
Published: 1985
Terrific period photographs enliven this introduction to the trail drivers of the later nineteenth century, the most romantic of American heroes. *Children of the Wild West* is a companion book.

CRACKER JACKSON   [731]

Written by Betsy Byars
Cloth: Viking
Paper: Puffin
Published: 1985
In this compellingly plausible novel, twelve-year-old Cracker realizes that Alma, his former baby-sitter, is being beaten by her husband. It isn't his problem, but it is.

THE CRICKET IN TIMES SQUARE   [732]

Written by George Selden
Illustrated by Garth Williams
Cloth: Farrar, Straus & Giroux
Paper: Dell Yearling
Published: 1960
The first of a fine series of heart-warming adventures involving Harry the cat, Tucker the mouse, Chester the musical cricket, and their friends in the Times Square newsstand. Other titles include *Tucker's Countryside, Chester Cricket's New Home, Harry Cat's Pet Puppy,* and the prequel *Harry Kitten and Tucker Mouse.*

CUSTARD AND COMPANY   [733]

Written by Ogden Nash
Illustrated by Quentin Blake
Cloth: Little, Brown
Paper: Little, Brown
Published: 1980

This is a hilarious collection of eighty poems, including, of course, "Custard the Dragon," that "realio, trulio cowardly dragon," written by the popular American poet and illustrated by a distinguished British artist.

DADDY-LONG-LEGS   [734]

Written by Jean Webster
Paper: Bantam
Published: 1912

Today's young readers may be infinitely more sophisticated, but this remains a timeless, romantic favorite. Miraculously, a mysterious benefactor sends seventeen-year-old Jerusha, an orphan, to college. Her only obligation is to write him progress reports.

DANNY THE CHAMPION OF THE WORLD   [735]

Written by Roald Dahl
Illustrated by Jill Bennett
Cloth: Knopf
Paper: Puffin
Published: 1975

In the Dahl canon, the story of Danny and his dad, living happily in a gypsy caravan parked behind a filling station in rural England and masterfully poaching pheasants, is possibly the sunniest and most purely humorous. Dad's technique for trapping pheasants is wonderfully ingenious and must be encountered, not described. Great fun to read out loud.

THE DARK IS RISING [736]

Written by Susan Cooper
Illustrated by Alan Cober
Cloth: McElderry
Paper: Aladdin
Published: 1973   Prizes: Newbery Honor

The second of five in a thrilling cycle of fantasy novels—including *Over Sea, Under Stone; Greenwitch; The Grey King;* and *Silver on the Tree*—that deal with Will Stanton, his siblings, the ancient sleepers, a crystal sword, and good and, of course, evil.

DEAR MR. HENSHAW [737]

Written by Beverly Cleary
Illustrated by Paul O. Zelinsky
Cloth: Morrow Junior Books
Paper: Dell Yearling
Published: 1983   Prizes: Newbery Medal

A fine novel about that painful issue—divorce. Leigh Botts, who is not only the new kid in school but also adjusting to his parents' divorce, follows a class assignment and writes to his favorite author.

THE DEVIL IN VIENNA [738]

Written by Doris Orgel
Cloth: Dial
Paper: Puffin
Published: 1978

An affecting autobiographical novel told in diary form of a Jewish girl in Vienna and her friend, the daughter of a Nazi, during the Anschluss.

THE DEVIL'S STORYBOOK [739]

Written and illustrated by Natalie Babbitt
Cloth: Farrar, Straus & Giroux
Paper: Sunburst
Published: 1974

The devil seen in these ten stories is a clever joker who, when restless, comes to earth and plays dirty tricks on unsuspecting types. He returns, spry and inventive as ever, in *The Devil's Other Storybook*. There is interesting moral fiction hidden in the supple prose.

DINOSAURS WALKED HERE: AND OTHER STORIES FOSSILS TELL   [740]

Written by Patricia Lauber
Cloth: Bradbury
Published: 1987

If you are past entry-level cute-and-funny books about dinosaurs, this well-written photo essay is a particularly good discussion of fossil formation and the fossil record.

DIRT BIKE RACER   [741]

Written by Matt Christopher
Illustrated by Barry Bomzer
Cloth: Little, Brown
Paper: Little, Brown
Published: 1979

This is an action-filled boys' book by a popular writer whose other stories mostly deal with team sports. Typically, a strong character with an obsession works his way through a problem . . . just watch his dust.

[739]

DOES GOD HAVE A BIG TOE? [742]

Written by Marc Gellman
Illustrated by Oscar de Mejo
Cloth: Harper & Row/HarperCollins
Published: 1989   Prizes: New York Times Best Illustrated Book

Here are twenty fables involving familiar characters and stories from the Bible but pushed and twisted into familiar and contemporary concerns. What about the fish swimming in the Red Sea when the waters were parted? How did God name things? How did Noah feel when one of his friends demanded to be let on the ark? The writing manages to be both respectful and lighthearted; the primitive-style illustrations are slightly wacky and quite fine.

A DOG ON BARKHAM STREET [743]

Written by Mary Stolz
Illustrated by Leonard Shortall
Cloth: Harper & Row/HarperCollins
Paper: Harper Trophy
Published: 1960

Edward wants a dog and he wants to be free of Martin Hastings, the bully who lives next door. *The Bully of Barkham Street* reveals Martin's problems clearly. There is also *The Explorer of Barkham Street*. These are good books about preadolescent boys and favorite first books for independent reading.

THE DOG WHO WOULDN'T BE [744]

Written by Farley Mowat
Illustrated by Paul Galdone
Cloth: Little, Brown
Paper: Bantam
Published: 1957

Here is a classic of canine adventure fiction by a distinguished Canadian writer.

THE DOLL'S HOUSE [745]

Written by Rumer Godden
Paper: Puffin
Published: 1948

The story of Charlotte and Emily's great-grandmother's doll house, restored after World War II for the dolls who think of themselves as the Plantagenet family, is skillfully written. The story is about Tottie, the brave farthing doll, and the villainess is Marchpane, too beautiful to be played with, only to be admired. A grand girls' book.

DOMINIC [746]

Written and illustrated by William Steig
Cloth: Farrar, Straus & Giroux
Paper: Sunburst
Published: 1972

Dominic is a hero and a multitalented gent, as well as being a dog. He sets out to see the world and tests his many talents to wide acclaim.

DRAGONWINGS [747]

Written by Laurence Yep
Cloth: Harper & Row/HarperCollins
Paper: Harper Trophy
Published: 1975   Prizes: Newbery Honor

The setting is San Francisco in the first years of the century. A Chinese immigrant father and son build a flying machine shortly after the Wright brothers build theirs. The immigrant perspective on the turbulent period and place is particularly interesting.

THE EGYPT GAME [748]

Written by Zilpha Keatley Snyder
Illustrated by Alton Raible
Cloth: Macmillan
Paper: Dell Yearling
Published: 1967   Prizes: Newbery Honor

April and Melanie are eleven years old and best friends in a small town in California. They are deeply interested in ancient Egypt, and the game they invent leads them into real-life criminal investigation. Inventive plotting. Great fun for middle-grade readers.

EIGHTY-EIGHT STEPS TO SEPTEMBER   [749]

Written by Jan Marino
Cloth: Little, Brown
Paper: Avon
Published: 1989

The setting is Boston in the summer of 1948, and the subject is death within the immediate family. Amy Martin's thirteen-year-old brother is dying of leukemia. Amy's denial and anger and fear are captured poignantly, and by the end of the book, she is accepting the new condition of her family's life.

EINSTEIN ANDERSON, SCIENCE SLEUTH   [750]

Written by Seymour Simon
Illustrated by Fred Winkowski
Paper: Puffin
Published: 1980

This is the first in a series of lighthearted adventures by a fine science writer for children. Adam "Einstein" Anderson, boy detective, applies scientific principles to everyday problems. Other titles include *Einstein Anderson Shocks His Friends, Einstein Anderson Makes Up for Lost Time, Einstein Anderson Tells a Comet's Tale, Einstein Anderson Goes to Bat, Einstein Anderson Lights Up the Sky,* and *Einstein Anderson Sees Through the Invisible Man.*

ENCYCLOPEDIA BROWN   [751]

Written by Donald J. Sobol
Illustrated by Leonard Shortall
Cloth: Lodestar/Morrow
Paper: Bantam
Published: 1963

Idaville's chief of police, Mr. Brown, nicknamed his son Leroy "Encyclopedia" because of all the facts he knows and his methodical way of observing and using his mind. Thus was a hero born. There are several dozen books available from several publishers in hard and soft cover. Most of the books consist of ten cases the boy detective solves. Some of the titles are *Encyclopedia Brown: Boy Detective*, *Encyclopedia Brown and the Case of the Midnight Visitor*, and *Encyclopedia Brown Finds the Clues*. In addition, there is the *Encyclopedia Brown Wacky-But-True* series about animals, crimes, spies, sports, and weird and wonderful facts.

THE ENORMOUS EGG [752]

Written by Oliver Butterworth
Illustrated by Louis Darling
Cloth: Little, Brown
Paper: Dell Yearling
Published: 1956

Life was just going along, until one of Nate Twitchell's hens laid an egg the size of a melon and then hatched a . . . think prehistoric favorite. Great fun to read aloud.

EVERY LIVING THING [753]

Written by Cynthia Rylant
Illustrated by S. D. Schindler
Cloth: Bradbury
Published: 1985

The well-written short stories in this collection are about people whose lives are affected by animals ranging from a stray puppy and other household pets to a nesting robin.

THE EYES OF THE AMARYLLIS [754]

Written by Natalie Babbitt
Cloth: Farrar, Straus & Giroux
Paper: Sunburst
Published: 1977

A fine novel about Geneva Reade's grandmother, who lives in a cabin by the sea and has been struggling for over thirty years to get a message from the depths.

THE FINDING   [755]

Written by Nina Bawden
Cloth: Lothrop, Lee & Shepard
Paper: Dell
Published: 1985

Alex is eleven and adopted and unexpectedly has an inheritance that prompts him to run away from home. A short, effective novel from a British writer.

FIVE CHILDREN AND IT   [756]

Written by E. Nesbit
Paper: Scholastic/Apple
Published: 1902

Long ago, in the mid-nineteenth century, five English children on a summer holiday were digging in the sand of a gravel pit, just digging for fun, when they encountered it, a mysterious creature with the power to grant wishes. The two other books about Cyril, Anthea, Robert, Jane, and the baby are *The Phoenix and the Carpet* and *The Story of the Amulet.* It is often hard to persuade children to begin reading "classic" titles, like this older fantasy and adventure novel. But if you begin them as bedtime read-aloud books, they often prove irresistible.

THE FLEDGLING   [757]

Written by Jane Langton
Cloth: Harper & Row/HarperCollins
Paper: Harper Trophy
Published: 1980   Prizes: Newbery Honor

A fine fantasy, set at Walden Pond, about a girl named Georgie who longs to fly. She meets a mysterious Canada goose, and her dream comes true. Her cousins, Eleanor and Eddie, are prominent in the fantasies *The Astonishing Stereoscope* and *The Diamond in the Window.*

THE FLUNKING OF
JOSHUA T. BATES   [758]

Written by Susan Richards Shreve
Illustrated by Diane de Groat
Cloth: Knopf
Paper: Scholastic
Published: 1984

Sometimes children, especially boys, are held back in school even if
they are smart. To his dismay, Joshua T. Bates was supposed to repeat
the whole third grade, but he was lucky enough to have a very sympathetic teacher. Although a touch bibliotherapeutic, this may be helpful to read with some children who have school troubles.

FOUR DOLLS: IMPUNITY JANE,
THE FAIRY DOLL, HOLLY,
CANDY FLOSS   [759]

Written by Rumer Godden
Illustrated by Pauline Baynes
Cloth: Greenwillow
Paper: Dell Yearling
Published: 1984

A quartet of well-known and -loved doll stories in one volume. Each
story involves faith, longing, goodwill, and a good heart. *The Story of
Holly and Ivy* (available separately in paperback, with illustrations by
Barbara Cooney) is also one of the all-time Christmas tearjerkers.

THE FOX STEALS HOME   [760]

Written by Matt Christopher
Illustrated by Larry Johnson
Cloth: Little, Brown
Paper: Little, Brown
Published: 1978

This book happens to be about baseball, but it is also about coping with
divorce. The author specializes in persuasive stories about boys, sports,
and personal challenge. Other titles signal the sports: *Jackrabbit Goalie,*

Johnny No Hit, The Kid Who Only Hit Homers, and *The Dog That Called the Signals.* Four autumn sports titles are in paperback: *Tough to Tackle, Ice Magic, Touchdown for Tommy,* and *Soccer Halfback.*

FRANKLIN DELANO ROOSEVELT   [761]

Written by Russell Freedman
Cloth: Clarion
Published: 1990

The thirty-second president of the United States, the first president fully recorded on film and sound, was probably the most complex and interesting American political leader in the twentieth century. He is a historical figure to today's young readers, who may hear of him only through grandparents or great-grandparents. This handsomely illustrated biography has a soundly researched, gracefully written introduction.

FREAKY FRIDAY   [762]

Written by Mary Rogers
Cloth: Harper & Row/HarperCollins
Paper: Harper Trophy
Published: 1972

Imagine that you are Annabel Andrews, a thirteen-year-old girl, and you wake up one Friday—in your mother's body. It's a funny premise, told with great style and conviction. In *A Billion for Boris,* the upstairs neighbor has a get-rich-quick scheme for exploiting his television set that shows everything one day in advance. In *Summer Switch,* Annabel's twelve-year-old brother, Ben, trades bodies with his father. These books remain fresh, appealing, and popular.

FREDDY AND THE PERILOUS ADVENTURE   [763]

Written by Walter R. Brooks
Illustrated by Kurt Wiese
Paper: Knopf
Published: 1942

The delightful porcine detective Freddy, who first charmed readers half a century ago, is back in a paperback reissue of eight titles, including *Freddy Goes Camping, Freddy Goes to Florida,* and *Freddy the Politician.* On the Beans' farm, where many animals speak English, the political maxims are cooperate and organize. There's Felix the cat and Mrs. Wiggins the cow as well. Some adults remember with joy the interpretation of R.S.V.P.—Refreshments Served Very Promptly. Although these are long chapter books, they are popular with younger independent readers. They are very funny, and read aloud splendidly.

FROM THE MIXED-UP FILES OF MRS. BASIL E. FRANKWEILER   [764]

Written and illustrated by E. L. Konigsburg
Cloth: Atheneum
Paper: Aladdin
Published: 1967   **Prizes: Newbery Medal**

Living inside the Metropolitan Museum of Art in New York City turns out to have some unexpected problems for Claudia and Jamie, who try it. It's part of Claudia's scheme to escape from the suburbs. The children are smart, but Mrs. Frankweiler, the rich old lady whose files reveal all, is the really clever one. A prized comic novel.

GAFFER SAMPSON'S LUCK   [765]

Written by Jill Paton Walsh
Illustrated by Brock Cole
Cloth: Farrar, Straus & Giroux
Paper: Sunburst
Published: 1984

James Lang's family has moved to the Fens, the flatland portion of England, where he is befriended by, and in turn befriends, an elderly eccentric, Gaffer Sampson. The fine nature writing, about the Fens themselves and the flooding of the marshes, becomes an integral part of the exciting plot as James searches for the "luck" Gaffer buried some seventy years earlier.

A GATHERING OF DAYS: A NEW ENGLAND GIRL'S JOURNAL, 1830–32 [766]

Written by Joan Blos
Cloth: Scribner's
Paper: Aladdin
Published: 1979   Prizes: Newbery Medal

A haunting work of historical fiction, this novel takes the form of a New Hampshire farm girl's diary written in the 1830s, full of the stuff of everyday life. It is both evocative and poignant.

THE GATHERING ROOM [767]

Written by Colby Rodowsky
Cloth: Farrar, Straus & Giroux
Paper: Sunburst
Published: 1981

This remarkable novel is set in a graveyard. Mudge's parents cannot cope with the world and become caretakers there, and Mudge has grown up happily in this unusual environment. An aunt wants to bring the family back into the more conventional world.

THE GENIE OF SUTTON PLACE [768]

Written by George Selden
Cloth: Farrar, Straus & Giroux
Paper: Sunburst
Published: 1973

In his father's archaeological notebooks, Tim finds an ancient spell for calling up a genie, which he thinks he needs because his aunt is insisting that he give up his dog, Sam. The genie turns out to be trapped in a museum nearby. Delightful fantasy for those who would like a little more magic in their lives.

GENTLE BEN [769]

Written by Walt Morey
Illustrated by John Schoenherr
Cloth: Dutton
Paper: Puffin
Published: 1965

A boy and a bear in Alaska long ago—that is, before statehood: friendship and adventure popular for decades, especially with middle-grade boy readers.

GETTING SOMETHING ON MAGGIE MARMELSTEIN [770]

Written by Marjorie Weinman Sharmat
Illustrated by Ben Shecter
Cloth: Harper & Row/HarperCollins
Paper: HarperCollins
Published: 1971

The first of a series of books for middle-grade readers about Maggie Marmelstein and her friend Thad Smith. In this one, he is determined to keep her from learning his secret. There are also *Maggie Marmelstein for President; Sincerely Yours, Maggie Marmelstein;* and *Mysteriously Yours, Maggie Marmelstein.*

GIDEON AHOY [771]

Written by William Mayne
Cloth: Delacorte
Paper: Dell Yearling
Published: 1989

As a result of an accident at the age of three, Gideon, now seventeen, is both deaf and brain-damaged. He lives at home, and his story is told from the perspective of his loving younger sister, Eva. The routines of his care are detailed with affection, and the family joy at his getting and holding a job ring true. Both the plotting and the writing are convincing, and when, after enduring suffering and trials, Gideon regains his hearing, the reader, too, rejoices.

A GIRL CALLED AL   [772]

Written by Constance C. Greene
Illustrated by Byron Barton
Cloth: Viking
Paper: Puffin
Published: 1969

The first of a series of books about Al(exandra)—bright, fat, noncon-formist, and vulnerable. The other titles include *I Know You, Al; Your Old Pal, Al; Al(exandra) the Great;* and *Just Plain Al.* Good fiction about real-life growing up.

THE GIRL WHO CRIED FLOWERS AND OTHER TALES   [773]

Written by Jane Yolen
Illustrated by David Palladini
Cloth: T. Y. Crowell/HarperCollins
Paper: Schocken
Published: 1974   Prizes: New York Times Best Illustrated Book

A beautifully illustrated collection of five original stories in the folkloric manner. Themes of love and melancholy, eternally appealing to young romantics, especially girls, run through them.

THE GOLD CADILLAC   [774]

Written by Mildred Taylor
Illustrated by Michael Hays
Cloth: Dial
Paper: Bantam
Published: 1987

A short, easy-to-read, but very powerful story about a black family living in Ohio in 1950. 'lois's daddy buys a gold Cadillac and tries to take the family home to Mississippi. The proud, loving family and the shock of their harsh encounter with institutionalized racism are skill-fully described in a book that stands as fiction and history and is suitable for early-grade children.

THE GOLDEN KEY   [775]

Written by George MacDonald
Illustrated by Maurice Sendak
Cloth: Farrar, Straus & Giroux
Paper: Sunburst
Published: 1967
This is a fine illustrated edition of one of the classic Victorian fairy tales. Sendak also illustrated MacDonald's *The Light Princess*. These are titles contemporary children don't pick up, but often listen to and then read.

THE GREAT BRAIN   [776]

Written by John Fitzgerald
Illustrated by Mercer Mayer
Cloth: Dial
Paper: Dell Yearling
Published: 1967
The first of a series of good-natured books, based on the author's memories of growing up in Utah at the beginning of this century, in awe of his older brother, who was called the Great Brain. Other titles include *The Great Brain at the Academy, The Great Brain Does It Again, The Great Brain Reforms,* and *The Return of the Great Brain.* They are especially appealing to boys.

THE GREAT GILLY HOPKINS   [777]

Written by Katherine Paterson
Cloth: T. Y. Crowell/HarperCollins
Paper: Harper Trophy
Published: 1978

Prizes: Newbery Honor
National Book Award

Gilly Hopkins is a tough, angry girl who has been shunted from foster home to foster home and is determined not to fit in at this new house of misfits and eccentrics: fat Trotter, little William Ernest, and old Mr. Randolph, who is blind. But she does. It's a fine novel that deals sensitively with issues of racism and class as well as the more obvious problems the plot presents, but it is more likely to draw young readers because of the story itself and Gilly's strong, absolutely believable voice —especially her "creative cursing."

GROWING UP AMISH   [778]

Written by Richard Ammon
Cloth: Atheneum
Published: 1989

This account of the daily life of a girl named Anna and her Amish family on a farm in Pennsylvania addresses both the myths and the realities of the Anabaptist sect, most popularly known for their traditional dress and conscientious objection to military service. The text is unusually thoughtful, and the photographs are well chosen.

HALF MAGIC   [779]

Written by Edward Eager
Illustrated by N. M. Bodecker
Cloth: HBJ
Paper: Odyssey
Published: 1954

Four children double-wish on an ancient coin and—presto!—their dull summer turns into a series of splendid, exciting adventures. Other titles by Edward Eager include *Magic or Not?* and *Magic by the Lake.* Good for reading aloud, too.

HANDLES   [780]

Written by Jan Mark
Cloth: Atheneum
Published: 1985   Prizes: Carnegie Medal

A fine British novel (complete with glossary) about Erica Timperley, a girl whose real passion in life is motorcycles. She's sent to a country village on holiday and stumbles into a motorcycle repair shop and a glorious summer of adventure and self-discovery.

HARRIET THE SPY   [781]

Written and illustrated by Louise Fitzhugh
Cloth: Harper & Row/HarperCollins
Paper: Harper Trophy
Published: 1964

This justly acclaimed modern classic is about Harriet, a clever little girl who wants to be a writer, so she watches and takes notes about everything she sees and hears. Which is fine until her notebooks fall into the wrong hands.

HARRY'S MAD [782]

Written by Dick King-Smith
Illustrated by Jill Bennet
Cloth: Crown
Paper: Dell
Published: 1987

An American relative he never knew has left young Harry his African gray parrot named Madison, or Mad. The bird proves a tremendous asset to the British family and speaks both British and American, indeed full sentences of both. Very funny.

HAZEL RYE [783]

Written by Vera and Bill Cleaver
Cloth: Lippincott/HarperCollins
Paper: Harper Trophy
Published: 1983

Hazel is an admirable heroine, an eleven-year-old who is determined to make money. When she lets a poor family live and work on restoring an orange grove on some property she owns, Hazel's character undergoes a metamorphosis.

THE HEADLESS CUPID [784]

Written by Zilpha Keatley Snyder
Illustrated by Alton Raible
Cloth: Atheneum
Paper: Dell Yearling
Published: 1971   Prizes: Newbery Honor

There are several comic novels about the Stanley family. In this one, the children's new stepsister believes in the occult. In *Blair's Nightmare*, they are joined by a very large dog, two escaped convicts, and a school bully. In *The Famous Stanley Kidnapping Case*, they go to Italy. Entertaining reading.

HEAR THE WIND BLOW: AMERICAN FOLK SONGS RETOLD   [785]

Written by Scott R. Sanders
Illustrated by Ponder Goembel
Cloth: Bradbury
Published: 1985

The author proposes stories that explain, with imagination and wit, the origins of twenty well-known American folk songs, such as "Yankee Doodle."

HENRY HUGGINS   [786]

Written by Beverly Cleary
Illustrated by Louis Darling
Cloth: Morrow Junior Books
Paper: Avon
Published: 1950

Because Henry Huggins lives on Klickitat Street, he is sometimes lost in the shadow of his neighbors the Quimbys—Beezus and Ramona. But Henry is a champion himself, the kind of boy you would like to have for a neighbor. On his own he first appears in third grade, adopting, or being adopted by, his splendid mutt, Ribsy. Their adventures continue in *Henry and Ribsy* and *Henry and the Clubhouse*.

THE HERO AND THE CROWN   [787]

Written by Robin McKinley
Cloth: Greenwillow
Paper: Berkley
Published: 1984   Prizes: Newbery Medal

The prizewinning sequel to *The Blue Sword*, a high fantasy involving the adventures of the Damarian king's daughter, Aerin. A favorite with fantasy fans.

HIROSHIMA NO PIKA [788]

Written and illustrated by Toshi Maruki
Cloth: Lothrop, Lee & Shepard
Published: 1982

This beautifully illustrated but disturbing story about the atomic bomb details a family's experiences in Hiroshima at the time the bomb was dropped. Though it is a story book in format, it should not be offered to any child to read alone. It requires adult support and discussion. It is not for the very young, either, and is best read with children in the middle and upper grades.

HITTY: HER FIRST HUNDRED YEARS [789]

Written by Rachel Field
Illustrated by Dorothy P. Lathrop
Cloth: Macmillan
Published: 1929   Prizes: Newbery Medal

Hitty is a doll who was carved out of a piece of white ash wood one winter in Maine nearly two hundred years ago. She belonged to Phoebe Prible, who took her everywhere. It's an old-fashioned historical novel with charm.

THE HOBBIT [790]

Written by J. R. R. Tolkein
Illustrated by Michael Hague
Cloth: Houghton Mifflin
Paper: Ballantine
Published: 1937

The background volume to the "Lord of the Rings" trilogy tells the story of Bilbo Baggins and the Hobbits. It can be read to or by younger children, who may not be ready to absorb the other novels, which are richer and more complex.

HOLIDAY TALES OF
SHOLOM ALEICHEM [791]

Written by Sholom Aleichem
Illustrated by Thomas diGrazia
Cloth: Scribner's
Paper: Aladdin
Published: 1979

From the pen of the best-known Yiddish storyteller comes a collection of seven stories about Passover, Hanukkah, and other religious holidays as celebrated by the Jews in the shtetl called Kasrilevka.

HOMESICK: MY OWN STORY [792]

Written by Jean Fritz
Illustrated by Margot Tomes
Cloth: Putnam
Paper: Dell Yearling
Published: 1982

Prizes: American Book Award
Newbery Honor

A historian who writes for children, Jean Fritz was born and raised in China. Here she remembers that world and what it was like in the mid-1920s to be "homesick" for the United States, giving a vivid picture of life where she actually was. Her return to China, after the book was published in 1982, is described in *China Homecoming*.

THE HOSPITAL BOOK [793]

Written by James Howe
Illustrated by Mal Warshaw
Cloth: Crown
Published: 1981

Here is a detailed introduction to both routine and unusual hospital procedures for older children. It is illustrated with black-and-white photographs showing everything from the insertion of intravenous tubes to special oxygen tanks. The text is straightforward and very informative.

THE HOUSE OF DIES DREAR   [794]

Written by Virginia Hamilton
Cloth: Macmillan
Paper: Collier
Published: 1968

This lushly written novel tells about a contemporary black family who buy the house in Ohio in which, a century earlier, Dies Drear and two slaves he had been hiding were murdered. (The house was a stop on the Underground Railroad.) At its simplest level this is an entertaining mystery, yet it can be read as a parable. In the sequel, *The Mystery of Drear House*, the Small family deals with hidden treasure.

THE HOUSE WITH A CLOCK
IN ITS WALLS   [795]

Written by John Bellairs
Illustrated by Edward Gorey
Cloth: Dial
Paper: Dell Yearling
Published: 1973

The first of a dozen mysteries about a boy and his uncle, who is a kind of wizard, illustrated by an artist whose style is, in itself, mysterious. One of the most popular mystery series for children, it's clanic in form, reasonably well written, and reasonably scary. The other titles include *The Figure in the Shadows* and *The Letter, the Witch, and the Ring*.

HOW IT FEELS TO BE ADOPTED   [796]

Written and illustrated by Jill Krementz
Paper: Knopf
Published: 1982

A group of adopted children discuss many of their special feelings and interests in first-person accounts. The nineteen youngsters from eight to sixteen whose pictures are shown with their stories speak frankly and look directly at the camera. This reassuringly low-key book is of special interest to children, family, and friends of adoptive families.

HOW IT FEELS TO FIGHT
FOR YOUR LIFE   [797]

Written and illustrated by Jill Krementz
Cloth: Little, Brown
Paper: Pocket
Published: 1989

These stories are told by a group of children between seven and eighteen years old who are coping with different forms of chronic and acute diseases and disabilities. They are brave and candid, both aware and accepting of their conditions. Their accounts may help others facing similar problems and may help blessedly ordinary children become aware of the courage and dignity of others they encounter.

HOW IT FEELS WHEN A
PARENT DIES   [798]

Written and illustrated by Jill Krementz
Paper: Knopf
Published: 1981

Some eighteen children of different ages and backgrounds talk about the death of a parent—how it felt, how it feels. Their health and well-being in the photographs is subtle reinforcement of the implicit message that life goes on.

HOW IT FEELS WHEN PARENTS
DIVORCE   [799]

Written and illustrated by Jill Krementz
Paper: Knopf
Published: 1984

A group of nineteen boys and girls from eight to sixteen years old talk about their widely varying experience of divorce in their own families.

[802]

HOW TO EAT FRIED WORMS [800]

Written by Thomas Rockwell
Illustrated by Emily McCully
Cloth: Franklin Watts
Paper: Dell Yearling
Published: 1973

Billy accepted the bet, and now he has to eat fifteen worms in fifteen days. The story moves along pell-mell, in short, boisterous chapters, as Billy comes up with some pretty inventive ways to get the wigglers down. Will he succeed? This is a book that holds the attention of even the most restless listeners and readers.

HOW WAS I BORN? A PHOTOGRAPHIC STORY OF REPRODUCTION AND BIRTH FOR CHILDREN [801]

Written by Lennart Nilsson
Cloth: Delacorte
Published: 1975

Some of the famous photographs of fetal development by the photographer of the adult book *A Child Is Born* are used in this explanation of conception and birth.

THE HUNDRED DRESSES [802]

Written by Eleanor Estes
Illustrated by Louis Slobodkin
Cloth: HBJ
Paper: Voyager
Published: 1944

Prizes: Newbery Honor

The story of Wanda Petronski, the little Polish girl whose classmates did not believe she had a hundred dresses, has been a classic for several generations, teaching quiet, painful lessons of tolerance and dignity. The pale, delicate illustrations are memorable, too. The writing is simple enough for younger readers to manage independently and powerful enough so they never forget it.

[802]

I, JUAN DE PAREJA [803]

Written by Elizabeth Borton De Trevino
Cloth: Farrar, Straus & Giroux
Paper: Sunburst
Published: 1965   **Prizes: Newbery Medal**

This compelling historical novel takes the form of the autobiography of Juan de Pareja, the son of a black African woman and a white Spaniard, who was willed to the Spanish artist Velázquez. Their lifelong relationship evolved toward equality and friendship. Challenging but worth it.

IN THE BEGINNING: CREATION STORIES FROM AROUND THE WORLD [804]

Written by Virginia Hamilton
Illustrated by Barry Moser
Cloth: HBJ
Paper: HBJ
Published: 1988

Here are twenty-five creation myths from nearly every continent, richly told in singing language. A lot of cultural conventions adults know are turned upside down—for example, in a Melanesian story, "In the beginning, there was light. It never dimmed, this light over darkness." People are never too young or too old to listen to myths—to hear how other people explain what we think we know. The mysterious illustrations enhance the charms of this collection. Read aloud.

IN THE YEAR OF THE BOAR AND JACKIE ROBINSON [805]

Written by Bette Bao Lord
Illustrated by Marc Simont
Cloth: Harper & Row/HarperCollins
Paper: Harper Trophy
Published: 1984

Shirley Temple Wong arrives in Brooklyn able to speak only two words of English. She works her way into the American dream via the classic route—baseball—turning into a fan and a player the same season

Jackie Robinson joined the Dodgers. It is an old-fashioned middle-grade story, told humorously and well. The illustrations are both stylish and witty.

INCOGNITO MOSQUITO, PRIVATE INSECTIVE [806]

Written by E. A. Hass
Illustrated by Don Madden
Paper: Knopf
Published: 1985
The world's greatest "insective" stars in a series of short, pun-infested books in which the crimes he sleuths are less serious than those he launches against the language. Hilarious. The companion titles include *Incognito Mosquito Flies Again!* Readers have to be old enough to pun.

THE INCREDIBLE JOURNEY [807]

Written by Sheila Burnford
Illustrated by Carl Burger
Paper: Bantam
Published: 1961
This immensely popular story tells about three loyal house pets, Tao, a Siamese cat, Bodger, a bull terrier, and Luash, a Labrador retriever, who follow "their" family, a kind man, through many an adventure across 250 miles of Canada to their new home.

INDIAN CHIEFS [808]

Written by Russell Freedman
Cloth: Holiday
Published: 1987
Here is a good introduction to six of the great American Indian chiefs who led their people against the encroaching pioneers—Red Cloud, Santana, Quanah Parker, Washakie, Joseph, and Sitting Bull—illustrated with memorable historic photographs.

THE INDIAN IN THE CUPBOARD   [809]

Written by Lynne Reid Banks
Illustrated by Brock Cole
Cloth: Doubleday
Paper: Avon
Published: 1981

Omri, a boy living near London, is given an old bathroom cupboard as an odd sort of birthday present. The key his mother digs up to unlock it has magical powers, so that when Omri puts one of his toys, a miniature plastic Indian, in the cupboard and locks the door, the figure is brought to life. Little Bear, a warrior from another civilization, with his bow and arrow, and others who travel through the cupboard into the modern world teach Omri and his friend Patrick a great deal. The adventure story is exciting, sometimes thrilling. Young readers, like Omri himself, brood about taking responsibility for and interfering in other people's lives. The sequel, *The Return of the Indian,* in which Omri's friends are caught up in war, is equally rewarding; the third book, *The Secret of the Indian,* is less so. Terrific for reading aloud with middle-grade children, especially boys.

ISLAND OF THE BLUE DOLPHINS   [810]

Written by Scott O'Dell
Illustrated by Milton Johnson
Cloth: Houghton Mifflin
Paper: Dell Yearling
Published: 1960   Prizes: Newbery Medal

A memorable adventure and coming-of-age novel about Karana, an Indian girl who spends eighteen years alone on a rocky island off the coast of California in the early nineteenth century. It is based on the true experiences of "The Lost Woman of San Nicolas." *Zia* is the sequel. A popular title with older-grade schoolchildren of both sexes. A commemorative hardcover edition, also published by Houghton Mifflin, came out in 1990, with new illustrations.

IT'S LIKE THIS, CAT   [811]

Written by Emily Cheney Neville
Cloth: Harper & Row/HarperCollins
Paper: Harper Trophy
Published: 1963   **Prizes: Newbery Medal**

This dandy coming-of-age novel tells about Dave, who is fourteen and
lives near Gramercy Park in New York City. He has family troubles,
acquires a cat, and is launched into adventures in the neighborhood.
The absence of drugs as a fact of life gives the story an old-fashioned
quality, but Dave's relationship with his parents rings true.

JACOB TWO-TWO
AND THE DINOSAUR   [812]

Written by Mordecai Richler
Illustrated by Norman Eyolfson
Cloth: Knopf
Paper: Bantam
Published: 1987

Jacob Two-Two (who always says things twice) is brought a tiny green
lizard for a pet. Dippy turns into a dinosaur who eventually has the
whole Canadian government on his tail, as it were. Hilarious farce, with
political commentary.

JAMES AND THE GIANT PEACH   [813]

Written by Roald Dahl
Illustrated by Nancy Ekholm Burkert
Cloth: Knopf
Paper: Penguin
Published: 1961

A Dahl fantasy about how James escapes from dreary life with his two
aunts by developing a giant peach. This is one of those scary, wonderful
books, best read aloud the first time. Quite, er, delicious.

A JAR OF DREAMS [814]

Written by Yoshiko Uchida
Cloth: McElderry
Paper: Aladdin
Published: 1981

This is the first of three novels about Rinko, a Japanese-American girl growing up in Berkeley, California, in the 1930s. The extended family, the conflicting cultural influences, and the warmth of the characters are appealing. The other titles are *The Best Bad Things* and *The Happiest Ending*.

JELLY BELLY [815]

Written by Robert Kimmel Smith
Illustrated by Bob Jones
Cloth: Delacorte
Paper: Dell Yearling
Published: 1981

The kids tease Ned because he's so fat and they call him Jelly Belly, so his family sends him off to diet camp. His bunk mate turns out to be a cheater, but Ned learns a lot over that summer about life as well as diet. This is good fiction for upper-grade readers, not just bibliotherapy.

JIM ON THE CORNER [816]

Written by Eleanor Farjeon
Illustrated by Edward Ardizzone
Paper: Knopf/Bullseye
Published: 1958

Nearly eighty now, old Jim, who was once a sailor, sits on his box on the corner and watches the street life go by. He tells a little boy called Derry wonderful tales of his days at sea, under the sea, and with sea serpents. Magical stories in the spirit of *Little Tim*, and illustrated by Edward Ardizzone in the same spirit.

JOHNNY TREMAIN   [817]

Written by Esther Forbes
Cloth: Houghton Mifflin
Paper: Dell
Published: 1943   **Prizes: Newbery Medal**

It's 1775 in Boston, and after a tragic accident in the silversmith's shop, the young apprentice becomes involved in political activity leading to the American Revolution. A popular favorite for generations, in book and film form.

JOURNEY TO AMERICA   [818]

Written by Sonia Levitin
Illustrated by Charles Robinson
Cloth: Atheneum
Published: 1970

This is the compelling fictionalized story of how one Jewish family fled from Hitler's Germany and managed to get to Switzerland and eventually to the United States. *Silver Days* is the sequel, describing life in this country.

JULIA AND THE HAND OF GOD   [819]

Written by Eleanor Cameron
Illustrated by Gail Owens
Cloth: Dutton
Paper: Puffin
Published: 1977

In the first of three old-fashioned girls' novels, Julia is growing up in Berkeley, California, during World War I, in the custody of her aunt and grandmother. The two other titles are *That Julia Redfern* and *Julia's Magic*. For middle-grade readers who liked *Betsy-Tacy*.

JULIE OF THE WOLVES   [820]

Written by Jean Craighead George
Illustrated by John Schoenherr
Cloth: Harper & Row/HarperCollins
Paper: HarperCollins
Published: 1972   Prizes: Newbery Medal

The memorable and very exciting story of Julie, a thirteen-year-old Eskimo girl. She gets lost on the tundra and is protected by a wolf pack. Another book by the same author, *Water Sky,* also deals with the Eskimos.

JUMP! THE ADVENTURES OF BRER RABBIT   [821]

Written by Van Dyke Parks and Malcolm Jones
Illustrated by M. Barry Moser
Cloth: HBJ
Published: 1986   Prizes: New York Times Best Illustrated Book

A cheerful retelling of the Uncle Remus stories by a Southern composer and writer, with truly memorable watercolor illustrations by a distinguished artist best known for his lavish wood-cut illustrations. The just-as-good sequels are *Jump Again!* and *Jump on Over.*

THE JUNGLE BOOK   [822]

Written by Rudyard Kipling
Illustrated by Michael Foreman
Cloth: Viking
Paper: Puffin
Published: 1896

Here are the thrilling stories of Mowgli, the man cub raised in the jungle, and other creatures, including Bashira and Shere Khan. As with the *Just So Stories,* these perfect-for-bedtime tales deserve to be read aloud the first time if only for the pleasure of watching children hear the language. There are many editions with lavish illustrations, and there are paperback editions of the second volume as well.

[821]

THE JUNIPER TREE [823]

Written by Jacob and Wilhelm Grimm
Illustrated by Maurice Sendak
Cloth: Farrar, Straus & Giroux
Paper: Sunburst
Published: 1973   **Prizes: New York Times Best Illustrated Book**

This two-volume set of twenty-seven stories by the brothers Grimm was translated with scrupulous care and tact by Lore Segal and Randall Jarrell and illustrated with equal grace by Maurice Sendak. It's a labor of love that shows no age. The stories are by turn heartbreaking and terrifying, gentle and sharp, poignant and funny. If you want one edition of Grimm, to read or to read aloud, this is the most satisfying one available.

JUST SO STORIES [824]

Written by Rudyard Kipling
Illustrated by Michael Foreman
Cloth: Viking
Paper: Puffin
Published: 1902

Listen, O Best Beloved, to the wondrous tales of animals—the little elephant child, the whale, the leopard, the cat, and others. Listen carefully, for these stories should be heard first and read independently later. They are among the greatest short fictions for children in the language and fairly roll off the reader's tongue. There are many picture-book editions of individual stories; some recent ones are packaged with audio or video tapes as well. This 1987 edition, illustrated by a distinguished British artist, is appealing and comprehensive.

KATIE JOHN   [825]

Written by Mary Calhoun
Illustrated by Paul Frame
Cloth: Harper & Row/HarperCollins
Paper: Harper Trophy
Published: 1960

This series of novels, mostly for middle-grade girl readers, is about Katie John. They follow the heroine from the age of ten, when the lonely child moves into a big old house, on into junior high school, when she discovers that romance isn't like the novels she reads. The other titles are *Depend on Katie John; Honestly, Katie John;* and *Katie John and Heathcliff.*

THE KID FROM TOMKINSVILLE   [826]

Written by John R. Tunis
Cloth: HBJ
Paper: Odyssey
Published: 1940

Several generations of sports fans have grown up with the series of splendid baseball novels known collectively as *Baseball Diamonds.* The others include *World Series, Keystone Kids,* and *Rookie of the Year.* The writing is always deft, and the action on the field is sensational and easy to follow even for non-fans.

KIDNAPPED: BEING THE MEMOIRS OF THE ADVENTURES OF DAVID BALFOUR IN THE YEAR 1751   [827]

Written by Robert Louis Stevenson
Illustrated by N. C. Wyeth
Cloth: Scribner's
Published: 1982

One of the classic stories of adventure and self-realization, this novel is about a sixteen-year-old orphan boy who becomes involved with the Scottish highlanders fighting British rule. This reissue of the handsome old edition is a favorite, but there are others available in both hard and soft cover. The sequel is *David Balfour.*

KING MATT THE FIRST   [828]

Written by Janusz Korczak
Cloth: Farrar, Straus & Giroux
Paper: Sunburst
Published: 1985

This fable, first published in 1923 in Poland, is widely known in Europe but relatively recently available in the United States. It tells the utopian tale of young Matt, who becomes king on his father's death and undertakes the dramatic reform of sending adults to school and allowing children to run the country. Exciting fiction.

THE KING'S FIFTH   [829]

Written by Scott O'Dell
Illustrated by Samuel Bryant
Cloth: Houghton Mifflin
Paper: Dell
Published: 1966   Prizes: Newbery Honor

A brisk historical novel about Esteban, a seventeen-year-old mapmaker in the Spanish colonies in the seventeenth century. He is charged with murder and withholding the king's gold.

KITTY IN THE MIDDLE   [830]

Written by Judy Delton
Cloth: Houghton Mifflin
Published: 1979

The first in a series of books about a girl growing up in the 1940s in a Roman Catholic family in the Midwest. Other titles, which carry her into high school, include *Kitty in the Summer* and *Kitty in the High School*.

KNEEKNOCK RISE   [831]

Written and illustrated by Natalie Babbitt
Cloth: Farrar, Straus & Giroux
Paper: Sunburst
Published: 1970   Prizes: Newbery Honor

Villagers in Instep think that Kneeknock Rise (which is really little more than a hill) has mysterious properties. They think a fearsome creature they call a Megrimum lives at the top of the rise and is the source of strange sounds on stormy nights. Fine and persuasive, a little bit funny and a great deal wise.

THE LAND I LOST: ADVENTURES OF A BOY IN VIETNAM   [832]

Written by Quang Nhuong Nhuong
Illustrated by Vo-Dinh Mai
Cloth: Harper & Row/HarperCollins
Paper: Harper Trophy
Published: 1982

This is the true story of the author's childhood in a Vietnamese hamlet, told with affectionate details about social customs and nature. This is one of the few easily obtainable books for children about Vietnam or Vietnamese culture.

THE LANDMARK HISTORY OF THE AMERICAN PEOPLE   [833]

Written by Daniel J. Boorstin
Cloth: Random House
Paper: Random House
Published: Vol. 1, Vol. 2, 1970; revised 1987

Here is a two-volume boxed reissue of an accessible celebratory history text for young readers. It is a good, serious birthday or occasion present for a middle- to upper-grade child who is already interested in history and has mastered, say, the Jean Fritz biographies or other, more narrowly focused titles. Other Landmark titles on specific aspects of American history are also available in paperback.

LASSIE, COME HOME   [834]

Written by Eric Knight
Paper: Dell Yearling
Published: 1940

One of the most enduring of all dog stories is set in the wilds of Yorkshire. It features the best collie ever.

THE LAST OF THE MOHICANS [835]

Written by James Fenimore Cooper
Illustrated by N. C. Wyeth
Cloth: Scribner's
Paper: Signet
Published: 1826

Let us not discuss the prose or politics of Cooper (both of which have been judged often and found wanting), but suspend judgment and just dive back into the second of the Leatherstocking Tales about that quintessential man of the frontier, Natty Bumppo. It's 1757 in the middle of the French and Indian War. The N. C. Wyeth edition is available in hardcover; other volumes of the tales, including *The Deerslayer*, are available in various paperback editions.

LEARNING TO SAY GOOD-BYE: WHEN A PARENT DIES [836]

Written by Eda LeShan
Illustrated by Paul Giavanopoulos
Cloth: Macmillan
Published: 1976

This book is written like a conversation with children about some of the feelings they might encounter if they had to deal with the death of a parent. The author has a compassionate but frank tone. Among her other thoughtful books about problems are *What Makes Me Feel This Way: Growing Up with Human Emotions; What's Going to Happen to Me: When Parents Separate or Divorce;* and *When Kids Drive Kids Crazy.*

THE LEMMING CONDITION [837]

Written by Alan Arkin
Illustrated by Joan Sandin
Cloth: Harper & Row/HarperCollins
Published: 1976

An allegory about Bubber, an un-lemminglike lemming, who persists in asking questions and considering the consequences. A good choice for philosophical young readers.

A LIGHT IN THE ATTIC   [838]

Written and illustrated by Shel Silverstein
Cloth: Harper & Row/HarperCollins
Published: 1981

By turns happy, sad, funny, and affecting, this is an immensely popular collection of poetry, verse, and illustration. It is idiosyncratic but maintains a firm moral stance and appeals to all ages.

LINCOLN: A PHOTOBIOGRAPHY   [839]

Written by Russell Freedman
Cloth: Clarion
Published: 1887   Prizes: Newbery Medal

This sympathetic and well-balanced biography of Abraham Lincoln, accessible for middle-grade readers, sets out his life and career without minimizing the complexity of many of the issues he addressed, including slavery. The subtitle, *A Photobiography,* underscores the fact that Lincoln was the first president whose life was recorded by the camera; however, the illustrations include documents and artifacts as well as photographs.

THE LITTLE PRINCE   [840]

Written and illustrated by Antoine de Saint-Exupéry
Cloth: HBJ
Paper: Harvest
Published: 1943

The mystical fairy-tale story book about a little prince who comes from another planet has been an adult cult title since it was first published, and is most often read in French classes or by adults.

A LITTLE PRINCESS   [841]

Written by Frances Hodgson Burnett
Illustrated by Tasha Tudor
Cloth: Lippincott/HarperCollins
Paper: Harper Trophy
Published: 1963

Sweet-natured Sara Crewe, left by her father in a British boarding school, falls onto hard times and is badly treated after her father's death overseas. She is, of course, virtuous and is rescued and brought back to high estate by a rich gentleman who was her father's friend. It is old-fashioned soap opera, charming on its own antiquated terms, and told confidently. For many years this was the only edition available in the United States. But, as with all the other Burnett novels, the copyright has expired and numerous editions in hard- and softcover have appeared. Avoid clumsy and unnecessary abridgments. A great favorite for reading aloud.

LITTLE WOMEN [842]

Written by Louisa May Alcott
Illustrated by Jessie Wilcox Smith
Cloth: Little, Brown
Paper: Penguin; Bantam; Signet
Published: 1868

The March girls—Meg, Jo, Beth, and Amy—and how they grew in Massachusetts during the Civil War. More than a century later, this is still one of the most affecting and powerful novels written for girls, although contemporary parents may wish to give some running commentary about the narrow definition of proper female roles. The sequels include *Jo's Boys* and *How They Turned Out* and, of course, *Little Men* and *Rose in Bloom*. Because the titles are in the public domain, there are many editions: watch for abridgments, and browse before you buy. Several of the paperback editions have interesting introductions by contemporary writers.

LOOK TO THE NIGHT SKY: AN INTRODUCTION TO STAR WATCHING [843]

Written by Seymour Simon
Illustrated by Jan Brett
Paper: Puffin
Published: 1977

A good introduction to star watching, which can turn into a lifetime's avocation.

LUCY BABBIDGE'S HOUSE   [844]

Written by Sylvia Cassedy
Cloth: Harper & Row/HarperCollins
Published: 1989

At the same time that Lucy Babbidge is Goosey-Loosey, the unkempt, unpopular girl at Norwood Hall School, she is loved and admired at home, even if the family is a little eccentric. Keep reading through the rich prose, because all is not as it seems; it's much more complicated, particularly the "family." Know that Lucy will survive and triumph, bring her fantasies to her own aid. Memorable novel.

M. C. HIGGINS, THE GREAT   [845]

Written by Virginia Hamilton
Cloth: Macmillan
Paper: Aladdin
Published: 1974   Prizes: Newbery Medal

In this remarkable novel about thirteen-year-old M. C. Higgins, the black boy helps care for the younger children and dreams of escape for himself and his family from poverty and the slow-moving slag heap left from the strip mine. He fantasizes unrealistic possibilities and then realizes some real opportunities. The author's language is rich and subtle, demanding and worthwhile.

MAGIC ELIZABETH   [846]

Written by Norma Kassirer
Illustrated by Joe Krush
Paper: Knopf/Bullseye
Published: 1966

Sally is sent to spend the end of the summer with gloomy old Aunt Sarah, in her gloomy old house. In the child's room is a painting from long ago of another girl named Sally and her doll, Elizabeth. Magically, modern-day Sally visits them, and Elizabeth ends up in the present.

THE MAID OF THE NORTH: FEMINIST FOLKTALES FROM AROUND THE WORLD   [847]

Written by Ethel Johnston Phelps
Illustrated by Lloyd Bloom
Cloth: Henry Holt
Paper: Henry Holt
Published: 1981

A good collection of stories from different cultures and historical periods that emphasize interesting and clever heroines. Good to read aloud or browse through.

[849]

MAN O'WAR   [848]

Written by Walter Farley
Paper: Random House
Published: 1962

Here is a novel based on the life of the great race horse, full of information about the racing world and the excitement of thoroughbreds.

MARY POPPINS: REVISED EDITION   [849]

Written by P. L. Travers
Illustrated by Mary Shepard
Cloth: HBJ
Paper: Dell Yearling
Published: 1962

This is the first in the perennially popular series of books about the British nanny with magical abilities who arrives at the Banks family home on Cherry Tree Lane with the east wind. Other titles in the series include *Mary Poppins Comes Back*, *Mary Poppins in the Park*, and *Mary Poppins Opens the Door*. "Revised Edition" refers to the unfortunate explicit racism of the original edition. The movie version is not true to the stories, which have elements of mysticism and make subtle references to classical texts.

THE MASTER PUPPETEER   [850]

Written by Katherine Paterson
Illustrated by Haru Wells
Cloth: T. Y. Crowell/HarperCollins
Paper: Harper Trophy
Published: 1976   **Prizes: National Book Award**

It is eighteenth-century Japan in this historical novel. Most of the story is set inside the Hanaza puppet theater in Osaka during a period of famine. Jiro, the son of a starving puppet maker, runs away from home and apprentices himself in the theater. It is an extraordinarily well written and compelling novel, filled with detail. Brace yourself for the chilling ending. The author has written two other novels set in Japan's historical periods—*Of Nightingales That Weep* and *The Sign of the Chrysanthemum*—as well as many fine books set in the United States.

MATILDA   [851]

Written by Roald Dahl
Illustrated by Quentin Blake
Cloth: Viking
Paper: Puffin
Published: 1988

Matilda is a frighteningly precocious child burdened by wretched, selfish, silly parents and a fiendish headmistress, Miss Turnbull. Happily, Matilda has a gift for creative naughtiness, a good friend in Lavender, a wonderful teacher in the enchanting Miss Honey and, best of all, an inspired creator in Roald Dahl, who makes it all, somehow, believable.

[851]

MEMO: TO MYSELF WHEN I HAVE A TEEN-AGE KID   [852]

Written by Carol Snyder
Cloth: Coward
Paper: Putnam
Published: 1983

Karen Berman, a suburban thirteen-year-old with cute younger siblings and a father who is the class mother, can't imagine that anyone has ever felt the way she does now (rotten) until her mother shows Karen the diary she had kept at the same age. For preadolescent angst.

MISHMASH [853]

[851]

Written by Molly Cone
Illustrated by Leonard Shortall
Cloth: Houghton Mifflin
Paper: Archway
Published: 1962

The first of a series of books about a boy named Pete, and his dog, Mishmash, growing up in a small town.

Here, Pete finds a home for his dog and gives his teacher a super present. Other titles include *Mishmash and the Big Fat Problem* and *Mishmash and the Robot*.

MISTY OF CHINCOTEAGUE [854]

Written by Marguerite Henry
Illustrated by Dennis Wesley
Cloth: Macmillan
Paper: Aladdin
Published: 1947

Is there a more romantic vision than the wild ponies galloping on the beach of Chincoteague Island? Generations of readers have doubted it, and the ever-popular series includes *Stormy: Misty's Foal* and *Sea Star: Orphan of Chincoteague*.

THE MOFFATS [855]

Written by Eleanor Estes
Illustrated by Louis Slobodkin
Cloth: HBJ
Paper: Yearling
Published: 1941

This is a classic growing-up series about a plain, loving family, set in long ago America, in this case the New England town of Cranbury. There are Sylvie, Joey, Janie, Rufus, and their mama. Other titles include *The Middle Moffat*, *Rufus M.*, and *The Moffats' Museum*.

MOM, THE WOLF MAN AND ME [856]

Written by Norma Klein
Cloth: Pantheon
Paper: Avon
Published: 1972

Brett's mother never has been married, and sometimes her boyfriends stay over. All and all, it may be an unusual family but one that likes it that way. Controversial when it first appeared, this remains a good novel.

MOSES' ARK [857]

Written by Alice Bach and J. Cheryl Exum
Illustrated by Leo and Diane Dillon
Cloth: Delacorte
Published: 1989

These thirteen Bible stories, based on modern translations, are rich in scholarly, often subtle detail. For example, the authors tell us that the word for *ark* occurs only twice in the Hebrew—referring to the ship Noah built and the basket Moses' mother made for the infant, and meaning vehicle of salvation. Most of the stories are familiar; some, like the fable of Jotham, are less well known. The somber illustrations are in black-and-white.

THE MOUSE AND THE MOTORCYCLE [858]

Written by Beverly Cleary
Illustrated by Louis Darling
Cloth: Morrow Junior Books
Paper: Avon
Published: 1965

The first of three engaging books about Ralph, a mouse, who is given a toy motorcycle and finds it is the vehicle of his dreams. In *Runaway Ralph*, the generation gap intrudes, and in *Ralph S. Mouse* (illustrated by Paul O. Zelinsky), the hero goes to school.

MRS. ABERCORN AND THE BUNCE BOYS [859]

Written by Lisa Fosburgh
Illustrated by Julie Downing
Cloth: Four Winds
Published: 1986

Crochety, patrician, fascinating Mrs. Abercorn gets mixed up with Otis and Will Bunce, who are fatherless and adrift in their new home while their mother is at work. An appealing novel about adjustments and friendships across generations.

MRS. FRISBY AND THE RATS OF NIMH [860]

Written by Robert C. O'Brien
Illustrated by Zena Bernstein
Cloth: Atheneum
Paper: Aladdin
Published: 1971   Prizes: Newbery Medal

A prizewinning novel about Mrs. Frisby, a widowed mouse, and the rats of NIMH (National Institute of Mental Health), a well-educated group who are about to set up their own culture. The sequel is *Rasco and the Rats of NIMH,* completed by the author's daughter, Jane Conly.

MRS. PIGGLE-WIGGLE [861]

Written by Betty MacDonald
Illustrated by Hilary Knight
Cloth: Lippincott/HarperCollins
Paper: Harper Trophy
Published: 1957

These well-loved and easy-to-read books are a kind of catalog of childhood misbehavior and pranks, all cured by the delightful Mrs. Piggle-Wiggle. She is not a witch but a rare and perceptive old lady who never scolds but has some very clever ideas about how to handle children who aren't really naughty but are, for example, Never-Want-to-Go-to-Bedders or Tattle-Tales or Fraidy-Cats. The series includes *Hello, Mrs. Piggle-Wiggle; Mrs. Piggle-Wiggle's Farm;* and *Mrs. Piggle-Wiggle's Magic.* This is a boxed set of four titles.

MY BROTHER SAM IS DEAD   [862]

Written by James Lincoln Collier and Christopher Collier
Cloth: Four Winds
Paper: Scholastic
Published: 1974

The Revolutionary War has come to the Tory town of Redding, Connecticut, and this remarkably rich novel details how it affects the Meekers, a nonpartisan family. One of the most sophisticated and powerful historical novels ever written for young readers.

MY FRIEND THE VAMPIRE   [863]

Written by Angela Sommer-Bodenburg
Illustrated by Amelie Glienke
Cloth: Dial
Paper: Dial/Minstrel
Published: 1984

Ruldolph the vampire lands on the windowsill of Tony's bedroom in the apartment house where he lives and makes friends with the normally terrified nine-year-old boy. Their comic adventures continue in *The Vampire Moves In* and *The Vampire Takes a Trip*. They go on a summer vacation in *The Vampire on the Farm*.

MY GRANDMOTHER'S STORIES:
A COLLECTION OF
JEWISH FOLKTALES   [864]

Written by Adele Geras
Illustrated by Jael Jordon
Cloth: Knopf
Published: 1990

A grandmother's stories, though they may seem to ramble, usually have a point. This Russian-Jewish grandmother chats to her granddaughter as they busy themselves in the kitchen. Her soundly moral stories may be vaguely familiar to adult readers as variations of folktales, but the very familiarity gives a tone of authenticity. The charming black-and-white illustrations fit nicely.

MY SIDE OF THE MOUNTAIN [865]

Written and illustrated by Jean Craighead George
Cloth: Dutton
Paper: Puffin
Published: 1959 **Prizes: Newbery Medal**

The author, a distinguished nature writer, skillfully blends themes of nature, courage, curiosity, and independence in this novel about Sam Gribly, who built himself a tree house in the Catskill Mountains north of New York City. The details and technical illustrations have charmed and thrilled generations. The sequel, published thirty years later, is *On the Far Side of the Mountain,* and it has some exciting moments, too.

THE MYTHOLOGY OF
SOUTH AMERICA [866]

Written by John Bierhorst
Cloth: Morrow Junior Books
Paper: Quill
Published: 1988

Dividing the continent into seven mythological regions, the author, a dedicated scholar, has identified characteristic myths of the different areas and then retold them in clear, straightforward prose. As with any collection of myths, this one should not be read straight through but dipped in, sampled, and returned to again and again as themes and patterns are understood and appreciated. The two equally impressive companion volumes, also published as both adult and children's titles, are *The Mythology of North America* and *The Mythology of Mexico and Central America.*

NATIONAL VELVET [867]

Written by Enid Bagnold
Illustrated by Ted Lewin
Cloth: Morrow Junior Books
Paper: Avon
Published: 1935

The golden-anniversary edition of the story of Velvet Brown, her piebald horse, and their championship race has black-and-white as well as color illustrations. Children today may not know why their parents and grandparents think this book is about a grown-up actress named Elizabeth Taylor, but it's a terrific story nevertheless.

THE NIGHT JOURNEY   [868]

Written by Kathryn Lasky
Illustrated by Trina Schart Hyman
Cloth: Viking
Paper: Puffin
Published: 1981

Nana Sashie enjoys her afternoon visits with thirteen-year-old Rachel and eventually confides in her to tell the story of her Jewish family's escape from czarist Russia. Moving and well written. Good to read aloud.

NOBODY'S FAMILY IS GOING TO CHANGE   [869]

Written and illustrated by Louise Fitzhugh
Cloth: Farrar, Straus & Giroux
Paper: Sunburst
Published: 1974

In this compelling story about expectations, stereotypes, and family pressures, Emma wants to be a lawyer, but it is her brother Willie who feels the career pressure. Moreover, Willie wants to dance on the stage like Uncle Dipsey. The Sheridan family is black, but the problems are universal. The novel was the basis of the musical *The Tap Dance Kid.*

THE NOONDAY FRIENDS   [870]

Written by Mary Stolz
Illustrated by Louis S. Glanzman
Cloth: Harper & Row/HarperCollins
Paper: Harper Trophy
Published: 1965

A novel about school and family life in Greenwich Village as experienced by two eleven-year-old girls. Life was somewhat simpler in the olden days, but preadolescence remains a lot the same.

THE NOT-JUST-ANYBODY FAMILY   [871]

Written by Betsy Byars
Cloth: Delacorte
Paper: Dell Yearling
Published: 1986

The first of a trio of books about the Blossom family, beset by goodwill and bizarre mishaps. Mother is away on the rodeo circuit, Pap managed to get arrested for dumping 2147 soda cans, and Junior tried to fly and broke two legs. Adventures continue in *The Blossoms Meet the Vulture Lady* and *The Blossoms and the Green Phantom* and end with *A Blossom Promise*.

NOTHING'S FAIR IN FIFTH GRADE   [872]

Written by Barthe DeClements
Cloth: Viking
Paper: Puffin
Published: 1981

Early adolescence is funny, sad, awkward, and consistently interesting, no less so if you are like Elsie, the "fat girl" in her class. The follow-up story, about "Bad Helen," is *Sixth Grade Can Really Kill You*. Very popular series.

NUMBER THE STARS   [873]

Written by Lois Lowry
Cloth: Houghton Mifflin
Published: 1989   Prizes: Newbery Medal

The setting is Denmark in the fall of 1943 and the subject is the effort of Christian Danes to rescue Jews. The story is told from the perspective of Annmarie Johansen, whose best friend, Ellen Rosen, is Jewish. It is appropriate for middle-grade readers. Another novel, *Lisa's War*, by Carol Matas, for junior high school students, is on the same subject and addresses directly the enormity of the Nazi threat. If you are bringing up the Holocaust in discussions at home, also look for *Rescue: The Story of How Gentiles Saved Jews in the Holocaust*, by Milton Meltzer.

THE NUTCRACKER   [874]

Written by E. T. A. Hoffmann
Illustrated by Maurice Sendak
Cloth: Crown
Published: 1984   Prizes: New York Times Best Illustrated Book

Here is the ultimate *Nutcracker*. This text is the original story translated carefully by Ralph Manheim—far more complex than the familiar ballet versions such as the one George Balanchine choreographed for the New York City Ballet. The lavish illustrations derive from the Seattle Ballet's *Nutcracker,* which was designed by Maurice Sendak. A stunning and exciting book, it is much too complex for most youngsters going to the ballet for the very first time.

THE NUTCRACKER: A STORY AND A BALLET   [875]

Written by Ellen Switzer
Cloth: Atheneum
Published: 1985

Three stories in one: the author's version of E. T. A. Hoffmann's tale, a history of the ballet and, finally, the New York City Ballet version choreographed by George Balanchine, which is so well known to so many families. This fits rather neatly between the simple story book of the ballet and the Sendak version of the Hoffmann.

NUTTY FOR PRESIDENT   [876]

Written by Dean Hughes
Illustrated by Blanche Sims
Cloth: Atheneum
Paper: Bantam
Published: 1981

Nutty is a boy genius whose real name is William Bilks. Here he generally disrupts a student council election. Other titles in the popular series include *Nutty and the Case of the Mastermind, Nutty and the Case of the Ski-Slope Spy,* and *Nutty Can't Miss.*

OLYMPIC GAMES IN ANCIENT GREECE   [877]

Written by Shirley Glubok and Alfred Tamarin
Cloth: Harper & Row/HarperCollins
Published: 1976

This is a good introduction to the history of the Greek Olympics, full of details about events such as chariot races, which have disappeared, as well as running and jumping events, which are very evident in the modern games.

ONE-EYED CAT   [878]

Written by Paula Fox
Cloth: Bradbury
Paper: Dell Yearling
Published: 1984   Prizes: Newbery Honor

In this powerful novel about maturation, Ned, a rather isolated boy, has an invalid mother and a remote father. Ned believes he shot out the eye of a wildcat and must come to terms with the guilt he cannot express. The writing is both simple and eloquent, which increases the impact of the story.

ONION JOHN   [879]

Written by Joseph Krumgold
Illustrated by Symeon Shimin
Cloth: Harper & Row/HarperCollins
Paper: Harper Trophy
Published: 1959   Prizes: Newbery Medal

The story of a friendship between a twelve-year-old boy and an immigrant handyman that is misunderstood by well-intentioned townspeople. A didactic but well-written novel.

THE OUTLAWS OF SHERWOOD [880]

Written by Robin McKinley
Cloth: Greenwillow
Paper: Berkley
Published: 1988

Young readers today often arrive at the sequels to stories without knowing, let alone loving, the originals. Yet this imaginative and compelling novel about Robin Hood, his band of followers in the forest, and Maid Marian can be read alone or in sequence with library versions, comics, or movies. The tart, modern tone comes not least from Robin's temperamental personality and Marian's feisty independence.

THE OXFORD BOOK OF POETRY FOR CHILDREN [881]

Written by Edward Blishen
Illustrated by Brian Wildsmith
Cloth: Oxford Books
Paper: Bedrick
Published: 1986

An anthology of English poems for children, many of them, since there is a little of everything from Chaucer to Eliot, of course familiar to adults. Thoughtful introduction. *The Oxford Book of Story Poems* is very good for bedtime reading, too. The illustrations are exuberant.

[884]

PEEPING IN THE SHELL: A WHOOPING CRANE IS HATCHED [882]

Written by Faith McNulty
Illustrated by Irene Brady
Cloth: Harper & Row/HarperCollins
Published: 1986

At the center of this science book for middle-grade children is a thrilling description of the birth in captivity of a whooping crane. The larger text explains the plight of the whooping crane and the work of ornithologists, especially George Archibald, to help them survive.

THE PEOPLE COULD FLY: AMERICAN BLACK FOLKTALES   [883]

Written by Virginia Hamilton
Illustrated by Leo and Diane Dillon
Cloth: Knopf

Published: 1985   Prizes: New York Times Best Illustrated Book

Twenty-four black American folktales are retold here by a distinguished contemporary writer. There are animal stories, supernatural tales, and slave tales of freedom, all told in sharp, precise prose. The mystical illustrations are affecting.

PETER PAN   [884]

Written by J. M. Barrie
Illustrated by Jan Ormerod
Cloth: Viking
Paper: Puffin
Published: 1987

These are the well-known, albeit most from adaptation, adventures of the Darling children, the little lost boy Peter Pan, and the faithful fairy Tinker Bell. The language of the original, while formal, is not so difficult that it cannot be read at full length for an average middle-grade reader. There is no need for abridged-text editions, although there are some charming picture-book versions available for younger children. Until the copyright expired, the only full-length edition available had illustrations by Nora Unwin. A number of others have been published recently. This one has striking full-color plates, and Tinker Bell decorates nearly every text page. Incidentally, Barrie based the novel on his own play; the various Disney versions take liberties.

THE PHANTOM TOLLBOOTH   [885]

Written by Norton Juster
Illustrated by Jules Feiffer
Cloth: Random House
Paper: Knopf
Published: 1961

Milo drives his little car through what looks like a regular tollbooth, but it leads into enchanted lands of science, logic, and order as well as mystery and threat that surround the Mountains of Ignorance. A deserved classic. This brilliant story is perfectly illustrated in Feiffer's distinctive and timeless style. Great for reading aloud to middle-grade listeners.

PHILIP HALL LIKES ME.
I RECKON MAYBE.   [886]

Written by Bette Greene
Illustrated by Charles Lilly
Cloth: Dial
Paper: Dell Yearling
Published: 1974   **Prizes: Newbery Honor**

Beth is a bright, sassy eleven-year-old black girl living in rural Arkansas. She is the smartest girl in the class, and has a crush on the smartest boy in the class. The sequel is *Get On Out of Here, Philip Hall.*

[885]

THE PINBALLS   [887]

Written by Betsy Byars
Cloth: Harper & Row/HarperCollins
Paper: Harper Trophy
Published: 1977

Three children, unwanted and unconnected, one battered, one maimed, one lost, meet and join forces in a warm and caring foster home. Sounds awful, but in the hands of such a careful writer, it works and is actually rather inspiring.

PIPING DOWN THE VALLEYS WILD   [888]

Written by Nancy Larrick
Illustrated by Ellen Raskin
Cloth: Delacorte
Paper: Dell Yearling
Published: 1985

This is one of the most popular collections of poetry for younger children, and rightly so. The relatively short selections are varied and interesting and read aloud very well. The illustrations are apt.

POLLYANNA   [889]

Written by Jean Stratton Porter
Paper: Dell Yearling
Published: 1913

After years out of print, the story of the most relentlessly cheerful heroine in American literature, the inventor of the Glad Game, is available again. In fact it is easy to see why, in simpler days, she was such a popular heroine.

THE POWER OF LIGHT: EIGHT STORIES FOR HANUKKAH   [890]

Written by Isaac Bashevis Singer
Illustrated by Irene Lieblich
Cloth: Farrar, Straus & Giroux
Paper: Sunburst
Published: 1980

A collection of eight stories by the Nobel Prize-winning author to mark the eight nights of Hanukkah. The stories are set mostly in Poland in a time that seems very long ago. Very good for reading aloud.

A PROUD TASTE FOR SCARLET AND MINIVER   [891]

Written and illustrated by E. L. Konigsburg
Cloth: Atheneum
Paper: Aladdin
Published: 1973

A very witty and imaginative fictionalized biography of Eleanor of Aquitaine. The queen and others, including her mother-in-law and priest, are in heaven waiting for King Henry II to arrive. Good readers will find source material to answer their questions.

THE PUSHCART WAR   [892]

Written by Jean Merrill
Illustrated by Ronni Solbert
Cloth: Addison-Wesley
Paper: Dell Yearling
Published: 1964

This fictional account of a "war" between pushcart peddlers and truckers in New York City is told in a light and breezy way but raises serious political and social issues middle- and upper-grade students can address.

QUENTIN CORN   [893]

Written by Mary Stolz
Illustrated by Pamela Johnson
Cloth: David Godine
Published: 1985
A pig passes as a boy, with all manner of complications.

RABBIT HILL   [894]

Written and illustrated by Robert Lawson
Cloth: Viking
Paper: Puffin
Published: 1941   Prizes: Newbery Medal
Life among the creatures who live on Rabbit Hill is consistently enter-
taining. "New Folk" are coming to live in the Big House. This is a
popular favorite with middle-grade readers.

RABBLE STARKEY   [895]

Written by Lois Lowry
Cloth: Houghton Mifflin
Paper: Dell Yearling
Published: 1987
Her real name is Parable Ann, she's twelve and lives with her very
young mother and her grandmother in a small town in Appalachia.
Both smart and proud, she deals with the complexities of her life in a
determined and persuasive way.

THE RAINBOW PEOPLE   [896]

Written by Laurence Yep
Illustrated by David Wiesner
Cloth: Harper & Row/HarperCollins
Paper: Harper Trophy
Published: 1989
Chinese immigrants in the nineteenth and early twentieth centuries
told their children folktales reflecting the stories of their own youth,
spent mostly in a dozen provinces in China, but adapted to their new
circumstances in American Chinatowns. As part of a WPA project in
the 1930s, Jon Lee collected stories in Chinatown in Oakland, Califor-

nia. This collection is based on sixty-nine of those tales, all but one of which were set in China, and are retold here from a fascinating contemporary perspective. *Tales from Gold Mountain,* by Paul Yee, recounts eight stories heard in Vancouver's Chinatown and has stunning illustrations by Simon Ng.

THE RED PONY [897]

Written by John Steinbeck
Illustrated by Wesley Dennis
Cloth: Viking
Paper: Penguin
Published: 1937
A boy and his horse. A classic. Is there more to say?

THE RELUCTANT DRAGON [898]

Written by Kenneth Grahame
Illustrated by Ernest H. Shepard
Cloth: Holiday
Paper: Holiday
Published: 1938
In this timeless story with its perfect line-drawing illustrations, a little boy makes friends with a very peaceful dragon. It's a good fantasy, with implicit moral lessons. Other editions are available but are inadequate.

RISK N' ROSES [899]

Written by Jan Slepian
Cloth: Philomel
Published: 1990
Skip is a responsible eleven-year-old who becomes fascinated by a dynamic but wild girl named Jean Persico. Skip has special responsibilities for her older, retarded sister and an unusual relationship with old Kaminsky down the street, and both are threatened. The story moves fast and convincingly to a painful end. The author has written two other perceptive novels about outsider children.

ROLL OF THUNDER, HEAR MY CRY [900]

Written by Mildred Taylor
Cloth: Dial
Paper: Puffin
Published: 1976   Prizes: Newbery Medal

This bitter, memorable, and beautifully written story of a close-knit, poor black family in Mississippi during the Depression is drawn from stories from the author's family. Cassie Logan's story continues in *Let the Circle Be Unbroken* and *The Road to Memphis*, which brings her to the end of high school in Jackson at the beginning of World War II.

RONIA, THE ROBBER'S DAUGHTER [901]

Written by Astrid Lindgren
Paper: Puffin
Published: 1983

Brave and adventurous Ronia is the only child of Matt, the robber chief. They live deep in a forest. A rich and complex novel by the author of *Pippi Longstocking*, but for older readers.

ROOTABAGA STORIES: PART ONE [902]

Written by Carl Sandburg
Illustrated by Michael Hague
Cloth: HBJ
Paper: Odyssey
Published: 1936; 1988

The American poet and biographer also wrote glorious nonsense and stories for his own daughters. "The Potato Face Blind Man" still beguiles, and so does "The Two Skyscrapers Who Decided to Have a Child." This new edition is in a large, pleasing format, with period-style illustrations. Easy to read but better still to read aloud. The old edition, with illustrations by Maud and Miska Petersham, is still available in paperback.

ROUND BUILDINGS, SQUARE BUILDINGS & BUILDINGS THAT WIGGLE LIKE A FISH [903]

Written by Philip M. Isaacson
Cloth: Knopf
Paper: Knopf
Published: 1988

The author sees buildings as beautiful objects and as pieces of social and cultural history at the same time. His introduction to architecture, which is lavishly illustrated with full-color photographs of fascinating buildings from around the world, brims with enthusiasm and delight. He addresses the way buildings make people feel—as they look at them, walk through them, stay in them.

SAILING TO CYTHERA AND OTHER ANATOLE STORIES [904]

Written by Nancy Willard
Illustrated by David McPhail
Cloth: HBJ
Published: 1974

This is the first volume of a fantasy trilogy by an award-winning poet and novelist. Anatole, the hero, is a boy with unusual friends, and their adventures include sailing to a mythical kingdom, searching for a rare herb, and rescuing the victims of the wizard Arcimboldo. The other titles are *The Island of the Grass King: The Further Adventures of Anatole* and *Uncle Terrible: More Adventures of Anatole*.

SARAH, PLAIN AND TALL [905]

Written by Patricia MacLachlan
Cloth: Harper & Row/HarperCollins
Paper: Harper Trophy
Published: 1985   Prizes: Newbery Medal

In the sparest prose, Anna tells how her father placed an ad for a wife in an Eastern newspaper, and Sarah replied. Their mother died when Caleb was born, and the children want Sarah, who is "plain and tall" and comes from Maine with her cat, Seal, to stay with them and consider their proposal. A flawless piece of storytelling that touches on many aspects of longing, self-esteem, and raw family needs. Wonderful to read aloud, but have tissues handy.

SCARY STORIES TO TELL IN THE DARK: COLLECTED FROM AMERICAN FOLKLORE   [906]

Written by Alvin Schwartz
Illustrated by Stephen Gammell
Cloth: Lippincott/HarperCollins
Paper: HarperCollins
Published: 1981

Gather round and sit close by. Here's a dandy collection, including ghosts, folktales, and some modern scary stories. Ideal for campfires and reading aloud. The second volume is *More Scary Stories to Tell in the Dark.*

SCORPIONS   [907]

Written by Walter Dean Myers
Cloth: Harper & Row/HarperCollins
Paper: Harper Trophy
Published: 1988   Prizes: Newbery Honor

Jamal Hicks is twelve years old, lives in Harlem, and seems to be becoming the leader of the Scorpion street gang. There's pressure everywhere—at home, at school, and in the street. A grim, haunting novel that reflects real events and situations in American cities. A sunnier view is in *The Mouse Rap*—a summery novel about kids who find release in music, despite the wrenching details of their lives.

THE SECOND MRS. GIACONDA   [908]

Written by E. L. Konigsburg
Cloth: Atheneum
Paper: Aladdin
Published: 1975

A cleverly conceived and executed novel purporting to be the real story of the Mona Lisa, as told by Salai, Leonardo da Vinci's apprentice and valet. If you liked *A Proud Taste for Scarlet and Miniver,* try this. Illustrated with reproductions of works by da Vinci and others of the period.

THE SECRET GARDEN   [909]

Written by Frances Hodgson Burnett
Illustrated by Tasha Tudor
Cloth: Lippincott/HarperCollins
Paper: Harper Trophy
Published: 1912

One of the finest novels ever written for children, and one of the greatest novels about gardening and health, is the story of Mary Lennox, a spoiled orphan sent to live a solitary life on her guardian's estate on the Yorkshire moors. She encounters Dickon, a free-spirited country boy, Colin, the willful, ailing scion of the estate, and a secret walled garden. For many years this pretty edition was the only one available; however, the copyright on Burnett's work expired in 1987 and nearly a dozen illustrated editions appeared in both hard and soft cover. They all show essentially the same scenes in the same fashion, emphasizing the Victorian setting. Choose whichever version appeals, but do not choose one with an abridged text. Despite some bits of dialogue in dialect, the prose is not difficult. Rather, it is quite splendid as it carries Mary from her sallow self-absorption to radiant health. A thrilling book to read aloud. If you begin in late March, spring comes as you reach the garden.

[909]

SECRET OF THE ANDES   [910]

Written by Ann Nolan Clark
Illustrated by Jean Charlot
Cloth: Viking
Paper: Puffin
Published: 1952

Prizes: Newbery Medal

The exciting story of Cusi, an Inca boy living in a hidden valley in the mountains of Peru with Chuto, a llama herder, is a perennial favorite. It is an exciting introduction to another, remote, culture.

[909]

SEEING EARTH FROM SPACE   [911]

Written by Patricia Lauber
Cloth: Orchard Books
Published: 1990

In one sense this is a sophisticated picture book, a well-edited selection
of full-color photographs of earth taken from satellites, space shuttles,
and rockets. The individual photographs are stunning and worth por-
ing over for their details and for the cumulative information about the
earth and the ways humans continue to change it. The text is spare and
clear. It is of great interest to schoolchildren, who can detect features
and ask questions. Though not exactly a read-aloud book, it is certainly
one to talk about.

SEVEN KISSES IN A ROW   [912]

Written by Patricia MacLachlan
Illustrated by Maria Pia Marrella
Cloth: Harper & Row/HarperCollins
Paper: Harper Trophy
Published: 1983

Uncle Elliot and Aunt Evelyn come to take care of Emma and her older brother while their parents are away at a professional conference. The children must train the adults in the rituals and responsibilities of family life. Warm and funny.

THE SHADOWMAKER   [913]

Written by Ron Hansen
Illustrated by Margot Tomes
Cloth: Harper & Row/HarperCollins
Paper: Harper Trophy
Published: 1987

The Shadowmaker reaches town and convinces all the perfectly happy people that what they really need are new shadows. Drizzle and her brother, Soot, can't afford new shadows, but they learn the Shadowmaker's secret. There's great wit and style in both story and illustrations. Very good for reading aloud with younger siblings.

SING DOWN THE MOON   [914]

Written by Scott O'Dell
Cloth: Houghton Mifflin
Paper: Dell Yearling
Published: 1970   **Prizes: Newbery Honor**

A historical novel about Bright Morning, a fifteen-year-old Navaho girl whose tribe has been evicted from their homes. She tells about the forced march and her capture by Spanish slavers.

[913]

322

SIRENS AND SPIES   [915]

Written by Janet Taylor Lisle
Cloth: Bradbury
Paper: Aladdin
Published: 1985

[913]

It turns out that Elsie's beloved French violin teacher, Miss Fitch, was a collaborator with the Germans during World War II, and Elsie doesn't want to hear any more about it. But, of course, Miss Fitch has her own story to tell. A complex and moral novel.

THE SLAVE DANCER   [916]

Written by Paula Fox
Cloth: Bradbury
Paper: Dell
Published: 1973   **Prizes: Newbery Medal**

A stunning novel about a boy called Jessie Bollier, in which he recalls the summer of 1840, when he was press-ganged aboard a slave ship bound for Africa and played his flute while the slaves were exercised.

SMALL POEMS   [917]

Written by Valerie Worth
Illustrated by Natalie Babbitt
Cloth: Farrar, Straus & Giroux
Published: 1972

Here is a delightful series of small books of small poems, with small illustrations but great quantities of wit and style. The other titles, naturally, include *More Small Poems*, *Still More Small Poems*, and *Small Poems Again*. In paperback, there is a complete collection of *All the Small Poems*.

SMOKE AND ASHES: THE STORY OF THE HOLOCAUST   [918]

Written by Barbara Rogasky
Cloth: Holiday
Paper: Holiday
Published: 1988

Telling the story of the Nazi Holocaust to children and young adults is a formidable task and cannot be entrusted to a single book. This, however, is an unusually careful text, illustrated with powerful historic photographs. The author gives facts, asks tough questions, and discusses other crimes against masses of people in the twentieth century as well. Books such as this one deserve and indeed require discussion in the home. Parents and grandparents seeking out a book such as this one surely care enough to supervise the way it is read. In addition to *Anne Frank: The Diary of a Young Girl Hiding from the Nazis,* there are a number of novels for young readers dealing with aspects of the Holocaust across Europe and in the United States. *Rescue: The Story of How Gentiles Saved Jews in the Holocaust,* by Milton Meltzer, addresses a question children often raise.

THE SNOW QUEEN: TRANSLATED FROM THE DANISH   [919]

Written by Eva Le Gallienne
Illustrated by Arieh Zeldich
Cloth: Harper & Row/HarperCollins
Published: 1985

This elegant translation of the great work of Hans Christian Andersen, the haunting tale of friendship pursued against the coldest of hearts and in the deepest north, is nothing less than thrilling. There are many pretty editions, including those illustrated by Erroll Le Cain, Susan Jeffers, Angela Barrett, and Marcia Brown.

SOUNDER   [920]

Written by William H. Armstrong
Illustrated by James Barkley
Cloth: Harper & Row/HarperCollins
Paper: Harper Trophy
Published: 1969   Prizes: Newbery Medal

In this novel, set in the rural South in the late nineteenth century, a poor black sharecropper's family is struggling to get by. The father steals in order to feed his family and is arrested in front of them. His dog, Sounder, is wounded. Battered, the family does not fall. A related title, *Sour Land,* picks up the story when the son is an old man and helps three white children.

SOUP [921]

Written by Robert Newton Peck
Illustrated by Charles Gehm
Cloth: Knopf
Paper: Dell Yearling
Published: 1974

Soup, the author's childhood pal, stars in a popular series of novels. The setting is rural Vermont in the 1920s; the style is terse and funny. Other titles include *Soup on Ice, Soup on Wheels, Soup's Goat,* and *Soup and Me.*

STORIES FOR CHILDREN [922]

Written by Isaac Bashevis Singer
Cloth: Farrar, Straus & Giroux
Paper: Sunburst
Published: 1984

This splendid collection of short fiction, some never previously published in book form, is ostensibly for children but appropriate for all ages. The tales allow every reader to have a Polish-Jewish grandfather from whom to hear stories to think about at night.

THE STORY OF KING ARTHUR AND HIS KNIGHTS [923]

Written and illustrated by Howard Pyle
Cloth: Scribner's
Published: 1903

A four-volume retelling of the Arthurian legends begins with this book, which is fine, lushly illustrated, and in a large format that feels secure in the hand. The other titles are *The Story of Sir Lancelot & His Companions, The Story of the Champions of the Round Table,* and *The Story of the Grail & the Passing of Arthur.*

STRAWBERRY GIRL [924]

Written and illustrated by Lois Lenski
Cloth: Lippincott/HarperCollins
Paper: Dell Yearling
Published: 1945   Prizes: Newbery Medal

Birdie Boyer, a so-called Cracker girl, lived with her farming family in the rural Florida lake country half a century ago. The compelling and well-written novel tells of strawberry crops and neighborly strife.

A STRING IN THE HARP [925]

Written by Nancy Bond
Cloth: McElderry
Paper: Puffin
Published: 1976   Prizes: Newbery Honor

A dandy fantasy novel about three American children living in Wales and a harp-tuning key that transports a boy back to the sixth century and the life of the bard Taliesin.

STUART LITTLE [926]

Written by E. B. White
Illustrated by Garth Williams
Cloth: Harper & Row/HarperCollins
Paper: HarperCollins
Published: 1945

The Little family were surprised when their second son looked a great deal like a mouse. Stuart, a dignified chap, has some splendid adventures growing up, helping around the house, and exploring New York City. Eventually, he leaves his home and family to follow Margalo, a lovely wren who has flown north. This elegant fantasy is a prized example of fine writing.

[924]

THE SUMMER OF THE SWANS   [927]

Written by Betsy Byars
Illustrated by Ted CoConis
Cloth: Viking
Paper: Puffin
Published: 1970   **Prizes: Newbery Medal**

All on a summer's day, a fourteen-year-old deals with her conflicts about herself, her beloved but retarded younger brother, who is lost, and the attentions of a boy who offers to help. And in the end, she finds her wings. This is a compelling and powerful story for older-grade readers.

[928]

TALES OF A
FOURTH GRADE NOTHING   [928]

Written by Judy Blume
Illustrated by Roy Doty
Cloth: Dutton
Paper: Dell Yearling
Published: 1972

One of the early and brighter titles in the Blume canon, this is accessible and user-friendly fiction for middle-class children. Peter Hatcher, a nine-year-old, describes his life and problems with his little brother, the truly terrible two-year-old known as Fudge. In the sequels, *Superfudge* and *Fudge-A-Mania*, the boys and their friends are older but still full of mischievous and original ways of dealing with life.

THE TALES OF UNCLE REMUS:
THE ADVENTURES OF
BRER RABBIT   [929]

Written by Julius Lester
Illustrated by Jerry Pinkney
Cloth: Dial
Published: 1987

There are three slim, handsome volumes in this contemporary retelling of the Brer Rabbit stories by a distinguished black writer. They are sharp and colloquial and read aloud well. The watercolor illustrations, full of dappled light and sunshine, are sweeter than the tales. Two more collections are available: *More Tales of Uncle Remus* and *Further Tales of Uncle Remus*.

A TASTE OF BLACKBERRIES   [930]

Written by Doris Buchanan Smith
Illustrated by Charles Robinson
Cloth: T. Y. Crowell/HarperCollins
Paper: Harper Trophy
Published: 1973

In this short, thoughtful novel, a young boy describes his friendship with Jamie and Jamie's sudden death. This is not a substitute for parental support in real life; it is a good novel and not bibliotherapy.

THANK YOU, JACKIE ROBINSON   [931]

Written by Barbara Cohen
Illustrated by Richard Cuffari
Cloth: Lothrop, Lee & Shepard
Paper: Scholastic
Published: 1974

A poignant story tells about a young, fatherless white boy and an old black man who are passionate fans of the Brooklyn Dodgers and especially Jackie Robinson. Good deeds are done before the old man dies.

THIMBLE SUMMER   [932]

Written by Elizabeth Enright
Cloth: Henry Holt
Paper: Dell Yearling
Published: 1938   Prizes: Newbery Honor

This story of a little girl growing up on a farm in Wisconsin and learning to appreciate and love has period charm, particularly for avid girl readers, more than half a century later.

[929]

THE 13 CLOCKS [933]

Written by James Thurber
Illustrated by Marc Simont
Cloth: Donald I. Fine
Published: 1957

With the help of the one and only Golux, "not a mere device," the charming minstrel prince wins the hand of the lovely and warm Saralinda, ward of the cold, evil duke. You may remember the duke. He's the one who is always threatening to slit people from their "guggle to zatch." This fable of the fifties has aged well, as have the witty illustrations. The droll parable *The Wonderful O* has also been reissued.

TITUBA OF SALEM VILLAGE   [934]

Written by Ann Petry
Cloth: T. Y. Crowell/HarperCollins
Paper: Harper Trophy
Published: 1964

In this novel about Tituba, a slave from Barbados, she, along with her husband, is sold into the household of a Puritan minister and endures the hysteria of the Salem witchcraft trials. Vivid and frightening.

TO BE A SLAVE   [935]

Written by Julius Lester
Illustrated by Tom Feelings
Cloth: Dial
Paper: Scholastic
Published: 1968   Prizes: Newbery Honor

This landmark anthology of original material describing the experience of slavery is annotated with helpful commentary. An important and original book for older readers of all races.

TOM'S MIDNIGHT GARDEN   [936]

Written by Philippa Pearce
Illustrated by Susan Einzig
Cloth: Lippincott/HarperCollins
Paper: Dell Yearling
Published: 1958   Prizes: Carnegie Medal

A time-tripping novel, and a dandy one. In a magical garden, Tom can go back to meet a mysterious Victorian girl. This particular plot device works best when it combines realism with inherent, convincing fantasy, as it does here.

[937]

TOMI UNGERER'S HEIDI   [937]

Written by Johanna Spyri
Illustrated by Tomi Ungerer
Cloth: Delacorte
Published: 1880; 1990

The lavish illustrations are so much a part of this hardcover edition of the story of the Swiss orphan girl taken to live with her gruff and solitary grandfather, who lives in a simple cottage high on the Alm Mountain in the Swiss Alps, that the artist's name has gone into the title. No sooner is Heidi happily settled than it's off to Frankfurt and to the invalid Klara. There are many abridged editions, and a plain pocket-size paperback is available.

[937]

TREASURE ISLAND   [938]

Written by Robert Louis Stevenson
Illustrated by N. C. Wyeth
Cloth: Scribner's
Published: 1911

Here is a reissue of the elegant 1911 edition of that splendid adventure story dominated by Long John Silver, the pirate of all pirates. There are nearly a dozen other editions, some with illustrations, many abridged, but this one is peerless.

THE TRUMPET OF THE SWAN   [939]

Written by E. B. White
Illustrated by Edward Frascino
Cloth: Harper & Row/HarperCollins
Paper: Harper Trophy
Published: 1970

The third but not necessarily the least of E. B. White's classic books for children tells the story of Louis, a trumpeter swan born without a voice. The nature writing is splendid, the illustrations charming.

[937]

THE TRUMPETER OF KRAKOW   [940]

Written by Eric P. Kelly
Illustrated by Janina Domanska
Cloth: Macmillan
Paper: Aladdin
Published: 1928   Prizes: Newbery Medal

This exciting tale of a courageous boy and a precious jewel, set in Poland's most beautiful city, in the fifteenth century, was handsomely reillustrated in 1966.

TUCK EVERLASTING   [941]

Written by Natalie Babbitt
Cloth: Farrar, Straus & Giroux
Paper: Sunburst
Published: 1975

The best children's books address the most serious questions in life in ways that make them manageable to readers. The title of this novel is a clue to its rich contents. The Tuck family drank from a magical spring and has been blessed (or is it cursed?) with eternal life. They try to live very inconspicuously, but ten-year-old Winnie Foster discovers their secret. An enthralling fantasy that is good to read aloud with early- and middle-grade listeners.

UNDERGROUND   [942]

Written and illustrated by David Macaulay
Cloth: Houghton Mifflin
Paper: Houghton Mifflin
Published: 1976

Here is everything you really want to know about what happens underneath the pavement of a city street, told in clear pen-and-ink illustrations and spare, precise text. A book to study endlessly and enjoyably.

UP FROM JERICHO TEL   [943]

Written by E. L. Konigsburg
Cloth: Atheneum
Published: 1986

Two ambitious latchkey children, Jeanmarie and Malcolm, encounter an old and, it must be said, dead actress named Tallulah under a small hill called Jericho Tel. In inimitable style and sassy prose, Tallulah gives them some pointed lessons in how to succeed. Tart and sophisticated. If parents don't read aloud, they might read along with older-grade children.

UPON THE HEAD OF A GOAT: A CHILDHOOD IN HUNGARY, 1939–1944 [944]

Written by Aranka Siegal
Cloth: Farrar, Straus & Giroux
Paper: NAL
Published: 1981   Prizes: Newbery Honor

A remarkable autobiographical novel in which the author, as Piri Davidowitz, describes her Jewish childhood and the destruction of her family in World War II. The sequel, *Grace in the Wilderness: After the Liberation, 1945–1948,* carries her from the Bergen-Belsen concentration camp through quarantine in Sweden and on to embarkation for the United States. The two books are suitable companions to *Anne Frank.*

THE UPSTAIRS ROOM [945]

Written by Johanna Reiss
Cloth: T. Y. Crowell/HarperCollins
Paper: HarperCollins
Published: 1982   Prizes: Newbery Honor

This is an autobiographical novel about a Dutch-Jewish family during World War II. The narrator, the youngest of three sisters, tells how a peasant family, the Oostervelds, hid her and one sister for more than two years. *The Journey Back* tells what happened after the war.

VOLCANO: THE ERUPTION AND HEALING OF MOUNT ST. HELENS [946]

Written by Patricia Lauber
Cloth: Bradbury
Published: 1986   Prizes: Newbery Honor

A fine photo essay about the eruption of the Mount St. Helens volcano. The text and color photographs capture and explain with unusual clarity the healing abilities of nature in the years that followed.

WAR BOY: A COUNTRY CHILDHOOD   [947]

Written and illustrated by Michael Foreman
Cloth: Arcade
Published: 1990   Prizes: New York Times Best Illustrated Book

Michael Foreman grew up in Pakefield, "Britain's nearest town to Germany," during World War II. His memoir is remarkable for the laconic prose and the watercolor illustrations, which capture the war at home with spare beauty.

WATERSHIP DOWN   [948]

Written by Richard Adams
Cloth: Macmillan
Paper: Avon
Published: 1974   Prizes: Carnegie Medal

This band of maverick rabbits, with their rich culture and fully developed language, have become heroes to so many that the remarkable novel is considered a modern classic for both adults and children.

[947]

THE WAY THINGS WORK   [949]

Written and illustrated by David Macaulay
Cloth: Houghton Mifflin
Published: 1988

An enormous, imaginative, and witty exploration of the science of our lives. In it, the author/illustrator uses his drafting skill and a friendly mastodon to guide readers of every age through the processes of scientific invention from lever to laser. This is a family book, not to read from cover to cover, but to look at a few pages and poke around together. It's also a private browsing and study treasure. There is no need to proceed chronologically.

THE WESTING GAME   [950]

Written by Ellen Raskin
Cloth: Dutton
Paper: Avon/Puffin
Published: 1978   **Prizes: Newbery Medal**

A very sophisticated mystery novel for older readers in which sixteen heirs of an eccentric millionaire are assembled, organized, and given clues, which they believe will lead them to their inheritance.

[949]

WESTMARK   [951]

Written by Lloyd Alexander
Cloth: Dutton
Paper: Dell
Published: 1981

This first volume of an exciting trilogy is about Theo, a printer's apprentice who flees when his master is killed by the king's chief minister. The other titles are *The Kestrel* and *The Beggar Queen*.

WHAT I HEARD   [952]

Written by Mark Geller
Cloth: Harper & Row/HarperCollins
Published: 1987

After receiving a telephone of his own for his twelfth birthday, Michael gets into the habit of eavesdropping on other people's conversations. Then one day he overhears his father in a compromising call. This short novel for upper-grade readers is well told and plausibly resolved.

WHAT THE MAILMAN BROUGHT   [953]

Written by Carolyn Craven
Illustrated by Tomie dePaola
Cloth: Putnam
Published: 1988

William Beauregard has missed the first week of school and is about to miss the second because he is really sick. A box of paints arrives mysteriously and begins a kind of magical rest cure and a beguiling fantasy about the mailman's remarkable gifts.

[949]

THE WHEEL ON THE SCHOOL   [954]

Written by Meindert DeJong
Illustrated by Maurice Sendak
Cloth: Harper & Row/HarperCollins
Paper: Harper Trophy
Published: 1954   Prizes: Newbery Medal

All because Lina wondered why there were no storks in Shora, a tiny
Dutch village on the dikes, things began to happen. Six schoolchildren
set out to learn about the birds, but everyone becomes involved. The
rescue of two storks caught on a sandbar after a mighty storm and the
race against the turning of the powerful tide are so thrilling you have
to finish the chapter and continue to the end. This marvelous novel is
best read aloud today, but once begun, older children may choose to
finish or reread it themselves. A great deal of natural science about
storks and dikes and tides is conveyed effortlessly.

WHERE THE LILIES BLOOM   [955]

Written by Vera and Bill Cleaver
Illustrated by Jim Spanfeller
Cloth: Lippincott/HarperCollins
Paper: Harper Trophy
Published: 1969

Mary Call Luther, age fourteen, tells about her life in Appalachia and
her efforts to keep her family together after the death of her father, a
sharecropper. In *Trial Valley*, Mary Call's life is complicated by two
suitors and an abandoned child.

[957]

WHERE THE RED FERN GROWS   [956]

Written by Wilson Rawls
Cloth: Doubleday
Paper: Bantam
Published: 1961

A young boy in the Ozark Mountains during the Depression earns the
money to buy, and then trains, a fine pair of coon hounds—Old Dan
and Little Ann. It is a fine coming-of-age novel, with dreams and values
tested and justified. The book's enduring popularity among middle-
grade and older readers has been reinforced by a motion picture.

[957]

WHERE THE SIDEWALK ENDS: POEMS AND DRAWINGS [957]

Written and illustrated by Shel Silverstein
Cloth: Harper & Row/HarperCollins
Published: 1974

This wildly popular collection of poems and drawings for children and adults ranges from silly to sad and back again.

THE WHIPPING BOY [958]

Written by Sid Fleischman
Illustrated by Peter Sis
Cloth: Greenwillow
Paper: Troll
Published: 1986   **Prizes: Newbery Medal**

The theme is akin to that of the Prince and the Pauper, but done with a fine hand and a light heart. Jemmy is the whipping boy to Prince Brat, who deserves his name. The prince runs away, taking Jemmy with him, and their adventures with a motley bunch of silly and unsavory sorts teach them both good lessons. The black-and-white illustrations are deft and witty. Good for reading aloud.

THE WHITE STAG [959]

Written and illustrated by Kate Seredy
Cloth: Viking
Paper: Puffin
Published: 1938   **Prizes: Newbery Medal**

Here is the story of Attila and the migration of the Huns and Magyars from Asia to Europe. Bold and sweeping historical fiction of the timeless variety. The author has also written two novels set in early twentieth-century Hungary, *The Good Master* and *The Singing Tree*, that stand up well; they are available in paperback.

WIDER THAN THE SKY: POEMS TO GROW UP WITH   [960]

Written by Scott Elledge
Cloth: HarperCollins
Published: 1990

This unusually varied anthology of two hundred poems by British and American writers, mostly written for adults, is intended for older children who are independent readers. No illustrations at all, but helpful notes at the end. Splendid.

WILLIE BEA AND THE TIME THE MARTIANS LANDED   [961]

Written by Virginia Hamilton
Cloth: Greenwillow
Paper: Macmillan
Published: 1983

It is October 1938 in rural Ohio, and Willie Bea is getting ready for Halloween. The radio makes it sound as though the world is coming to an end. It is, of course, just Orson Welles's radio broadcast of "The War of the Worlds," a simple explanation that the grown-ups understand sooner than the child. The story is told sympathetically from the child's perspective.

THE WIND IN THE WILLOWS   [962]

[963]

Written by Kenneth Grahame
Illustrated by Ernest H. Shepard
Cloth: Scribner's
Published: 1908

The riverbank adventures of those fine fellows Rat, Mole, Toad, and Badger. The stories celebrate a golden time just before the modern world. (Was it ever really so golden?) Somehow, the 1933 edition, with Shepard's illustrations, captures the story so perfectly it seems pointless to consider others. However, the language is difficult, so younger readers may prefer to hear it rather than read it to themselves, and there are many abridged editions.

WINNIE-THE-POOH   [963]

Written by A. A. Milne
Illustrated by Ernest H. Shepard
Cloth: Dutton
Paper: Dell Yearling
Published: 1926

Winnie-the-Pooh is the bear of little brain who belongs to Christopher Robin, a proper English boy hero of not so very long ago. Their adventures in and around Pooh Corner, with Eeyore, Piglet, Tigger, and the rest of their friends, continue in *The House at Pooh Corner* and have been beloved for generations. They are small, whimsical adventures, but however charming the stories, some adults find the prose cloying. A fine early chapter book for reading aloud. The line drawings are enchanting.

[963]

WOLF STORY   [964]

Written by William McCleery
Illustrated by Warren Chappell
Cloth: Linnet Books/Shoestring Press
Published: 1947

In this charming tale, Michael, a bright and demanding five-year-old, orders his father to tell him a story about a hen the boy names Rainbow and Waldo, a rather foolish wolf. A very good early chapter book for bedtime reading aloud, with enough plot, humor, and recapitulation, and just enough black-and-white illustrations.

[963]

THE WONDERFUL WIZARD OF OZ [965]

Written by L. Frank Baum
Illustrated by W. W. Denslow
Cloth: Morrow Junior Books
Paper: Dover
Published: 1900

It is often called the original American fairy tale, and it certainly marked Kansas forever, because "there's no place like home." As a result of the film, it is hard to find a child who doesn't know the story, but as is often the case, the books are better. Much better. This is a facsimile of the handsome first edition. Most of the series—involving several writers and running to dozens of volumes—is available in large-format paperback from Dover and small paperback from Ballantine. Start with Dorothy, Toto, and that first trip to Oz, but don't miss Ozma or the Patchwork Girl. Grand for reading aloud to middle-grade and younger children.

A WRINKLE IN TIME [966]

Written by Madeleine L'Engle
Cloth: Farrar, Straus & Giroux
Paper: Dell Yearling
Published: 1962   Prizes: Newbery Medal

The first of the fine, and very popular, fantasy quartet of novels about the Murry family, especially Meg and Charles Wallace. In the first book they go on a dangerous mission in search of their scientist father. The other titles are *A Wind in the Door* and *A Swiftly Tilting Planet* (these three are available in a boxed edition) and *Many Waters*, which follows the twins, Sandy and Dennys, back into biblical times.

THE YEARLING [967]

Written by Marjorie Kinnan Rawlings
Illustrated by N. C. Wyeth
Cloth: Scribner's
Paper: Collier
Published: 1938   Prizes: Pulitzer

In the backwoods of Florida, a boy named Jody struggles to save the animals he loves, especially the yearling. The memorable N. C. Wyeth illustrations were rephotographed for the 1985 edition.

YOUNG FU OF THE
UPPER YANGTZE [968]

Written by Elizabeth Foreman Lewis
Illustrated by Ed Young
Cloth: Henry Holt
Published: 1932 Prizes: Newbery Medal
This 1973 edition of the 1932 Newbery Medal book is the story of life
in prerevolutionary China as seen by a coppersmith's apprentice and
has some enduring fascination as historical fiction.

ZLATEH THE GOAT AND
OTHER STORIES [969]

Written by Isaac Bashevis Singer
Illustrated by Maurice Sendak
Cloth: Harper & Row/HarperCollins
Paper: Harper Trophy Prizes: Newbery Honor
Published: 1966 New York Times Best Illustrated Book
Seven traditional Middle European folktales are told and illustrated by
modern masters with unusual poignancy in this fine collection. It ap-
peals to children and adults and is splendid to read aloud.

Young Adult Books

Τhis is a small selection of titles written for adolescent readers and principally concerned with coming of age, self-awareness, role models, and personal possibility. The serious-sounding fare is leavened with humor.

THE AMERICAN REVOLUTIONARIES: A HISTORY IN THEIR OWN WORDS 1750–1800 [970]

Written by Milton Meltzer
Cloth: Harper & Row/HarperCollins
Paper: T. Y. Crowell/HarperCollins
Published: 1987

This exemplary collection of excerpts from letters, diaries, journals, memoirs, and newspapers of the period gives a vivid sense of how the revolutionary era in this country felt to a wide range of people. Companion books are *The Jewish Americans: A History in Their Own Words, 1650–1950* and *The Black Americans: A History in Their Own Words, 1619–1983*.

ANNIE ON MY MIND [971]

Written by Nancy Garden
Cloth: Farrar, Straus & Giroux
Paper: Sunburst
Published: 1982

Here is an unusually strong and unsentimental novel that involves a lesbian relationship. Liza, the narrator, met Annie at the Metropolitan Museum of Art in New York City when they were in high school, before she had any understanding of her own sexuality.

ANTHONY BURNS: THE DEFEAT AND TRIUMPH OF A FUGITIVE SLAVE [972]

Written by Virginia Hamilton
Cloth: Knopf
Published: 1988

This is a novel about property, ownership, and law. Anthony Burns was raised a slave in Virginia. In 1854, when he was about twenty, he ran away to Massachusetts, was captured, and was tried under the Fugitive Slave Act. His incarceration and his master's suit were hotly debated and marked a turning point in the Northern antislavery move-

ment. The chapters of the novel alternate between objective and subjective chronicles—the "facts" and Burns's inner thoughts. A stunning achievement, this is a book to be discussed within families.

BAD MAN BALLAD   [973]

Written by Scott R. Sanders
Cloth: Bradbury
Published: 1986

In this exciting novel of search and adventure set during the War of 1812, a seventeen-year-old boy and an adventurous Philadelphia lawyer track a giant-like creature.

BEYOND THE DIVIDE   [974]

Written by Kathryn Lasky
Cloth: Macmillan
Paper: Dell Yearling
Published: 1983

This is a gripping pioneer story about Meribah and her father, who break with the Amish community and join a wagon train heading west for the gold rush.

BEYOND THE MYTH: THE STORY OF JOAN OF ARC   [975]

Written by Polly Schoyer Brooks
Cloth: Harper & Row/HarperCollins
Published: 1990

As the title says, the author has chosen to go beyond the romantic story of the maid of Domrémy and place the events of the real life of Joan of Arc in the social and political setting of fifteenth-century France. The illustrations, taken from contemporary manuscripts and other documents and maps are outstanding. The novel *Young Joan* addresses the early part of her life.

BOY: TALES OF CHILDHOOD [976]

Written by Roald Dahl
Cloth: Farrar, Straus & Giroux
Paper: Puffin
Published: 1984

The story of the author's childhood in Norway and (mostly) in England is filled with incidents as peculiar, sharp, funny, and sometimes awful as those in his stories. The memoir is illustrated with excerpts from schoolboy letters and photographs. The second volume, *Going Solo,* is for older readers and describes Dahl's experiences in Africa and as a pilot during World War II.

CAPTIVES OF TIME [977]

Written by Malcolm Bosse
Cloth: Delacorte
Paper: Dell Yearling
Published: 1987

After the death of their parents, Anne Valens and her mute brother live with their uncle Albrecht, who teaches Anne the valuable art and skill of clock making. This is an exciting although often violent novel set in medieval Europe that touches on many themes, including social breakdown and change and the rise of cities.

THE CAT ATE MY GYMSUIT [978]

Written by Paula Danziger
Cloth: Delacorte
Paper: Dell Yearling
Published: 1974

Marcy's view is that life is rotten: her social life, her weight, her parents—the usual. Then she encounters a remarkable teacher and things begin to change fast. Inside the humor is a lesson about social protest. The sequel is *There's a Bat in Bunk Five.*

CELINE   [979]

Written by Brock Cole
Cloth: Farrar, Straus & Giroux
Paper: Sunburst
Published: 1989

Celine is so bright and so self-aware, she's alarming. Her artist father has gone to Europe, leaving her with her young stepmother, school, and her baby-sitting responsibilities. The joy of Celine is her voice—smart but a little off-center, logical but not getting things quite right. She's a splendid teenager to keep in mind.

THE CHANGEOVER: A SUPERNATURAL ROMANCE   [980]

Written by Margaret Mahy
Cloth: McElderry
Paper: Scholastic
Published: 1984   **Prizes: Carnegie Medal**

A remarkably clever and stylishly written novel about witchcraft, family ties, and romance by the inventive New Zealand writer. When Laura's little brother becomes deathly ill, she realizes that the cause is witchcraft and that her only chance to save him is to "changeover" herself.

CHILD OF THE OWL   [981]

Written by Laurence Yep
Cloth: Harper & Row/HarperCollins
Paper: Harper Trophy
Published: 1977

This intriguing novel by the author of *Dragonwings* is also set in San Francisco's Chinatown, but it takes place in the 1960s, as teenage Casey searches for her roots and an understanding of her gambler father.

THE CHOCOLATE WAR   [982]

Written by Robert Cormier
Cloth: Pantheon
Paper: Dell
Published: 1974

One of the best contemporary young adult novels deals with power struggles and the misuse of power at a boys' boarding school in New England. The worthy sequel is *Beyond the Chocolate War*.

THE CONTENDER   [983]

Written by Robert Lipsyte
Cloth: Harper & Row/HarperCollins
Paper: Harper Trophy
Published: 1967

This fine novel about Alfred, a seventeen-year-old boy in Harlem, who almost accidentally begins training to be a professional fighter, does not seem dated. The issues—entrapment, education, escape, drugs—are ever-present in society. Engrossing sports writing, too.

DADDY'S GIRL   [984]

Written by J. D. Landis
Paper: Pocket
Published: 1984

Jennie, thirteen, the beloved only offspring of a "perfect marriage," sees her father passionately kissing a strange woman on a street corner. This novel develops the dramatic contemporary situation with sensitivity and also great wit. A raucous subplot involves Ms. Richter's Feminist Day School.

A DAY NO PIGS WOULD DIE   [985]

Written by Robert Newton Peck
Cloth: Knopf
Paper: Dell Yearling
Published: 1973

A thirteen-year-old Shaker boy living on a farm in Vermont is the central figure in this compelling novel as he takes on many of the

responsibilities of an adult. Graphic scenes of farm life, beginning with the opening chapter, offer a view of rural reality that may shock urban teens. The author wrote the popular, and lighter, Soup series for younger readers.

DINKY HOCKER SHOOTS SMACK!   [986]

Written by M. E. Kerr
Cloth: Harper & Row/HarperCollins
Paper: Harper Trophy
Published: 1972

Dinky doesn't use drugs, but she is fat and miserable and longs for attention. This novel from the wave of provocative young adult titles of the 1970s holds up very well. The adolescent issues are timeless, and the dialogue remains sharp and funny.

DOGSONG   [987]

Written by Gary Paulsen
Cloth: Bradbury
Paper: Puffin
Published: 1985   Prizes: Newbery Honor

An Eskimo boy sets out on a dogsled, turning his back on his modern village, and makes a journey of physical and spiritual self-discovery. Exciting reading for older-grade readers of both sexes. *Woodsong* is a first-person account of a challenging time in the woods. *Cookcamp* is about time nearly alone at a logging camp.

DREAMS INTO DEEDS: NINE WOMEN WHO DARED   [988]

Written by Linda Peavy and Ursula Smith
Cloth: Scribner's
Published: 1985

The companion volume to *Women Who Changed Things*, this is a collection of brisk biographical sketches of Jane Addams, Marian Anderson, Rachel Carson, Alice Hamilton, Mother Jones, Juliette Gordon Low, Margaret Mead, Elizabeth Cady Stanton, and Babe Didrikson. *American Women* is a narrative history covering over three hundred years of women's experiences.

FOREVER [989]

Written by Judy Blume
Cloth: Bradbury
Paper: Pocket
Published: 1975

A first sexual relationship, entered into in good faith but outgrown in the course of ordinary events, is described by an author who has earned the trust and faith of her readers.

FOREVER NINETEEN [990]

Written by Grigory Baklanov; translated by Antonia W. Bouis
Cloth: Harper & Row/HarperCollins
Published: 1989

The author, a Soviet journalist, was seventeen when the Nazis invaded his country. Of twenty boys in his high school class, he alone survived the war. This powerful autobiographical novel is his moving account of how teenagers quickly became officers as the number of casualties mounted. It is a moving tribute to those he remembers so well, and speaks clearly to contemporary American readers.

THE GIFT OF SARAH BARKER [991]

Written by Jane Yolen
Paper: Scholastic
Published: 1984

This is a wonderfully romantic novel set in a nineteenth-century Shaker community, rich with detail. It tells how Abel and Sarah are drawn to each other irresistibly in spite of the Shaker rules against sex or physical touching.

A GIRL FROM YAMHILL:
A MEMOIR [992]

Written by Beverly Cleary
Cloth: Morrow Junior Books
Published: 1988

Beverly Bunn, who grew up first on a farm in Yamhill, Oregon, and later in Portland during the 1920s, has written some of the most warm-

hearted stories of American childhood in the Ramona and Henry Huggins books. Her own story, though told lightly, has dark undertones that her fans in the years of their greatest enthusiasm for her work may not catch. Older children, loving her as they do, may find this memoir, which carries her through high school and departure for Southern California in the Great Depression, surprising. It is memorable and worth rereading.

THE GOATS   [993]

Written by Brock Cole
Cloth: Farrar, Straus & Giroux
Paper: Sunburst
Published: 1988

Two preadolescent misfits at summer camp are stripped of their clothes and left for the night on an island in the middle of a lake. Instead of going to pieces from fear and cold, they manage to escape, and spend a few days exploring their newfound strength and courage. The novel is wonderfully controlled and convincing and has quickly become a popular favorite, but not just for vacation reading.

GOING BACKWARDS   [994]

Written by Norma Klein
Cloth: Scholastic
Paper: Scholastic
Published: 1986

In this thoughtful domestic-problem novel, Charles's beloved Grandmother Gustel has Alzheimer's disease. The ending is arbitrary; however, the plot development and the descriptions of how the disease affects everyone in the family are particularly well done.

GOOD-BYE AND KEEP COLD   [995]

Written by Jenny Davis
Cloth: Orchard Books
Paper: Dell
Published: 1987

Edda, the heroine and narrator of this particularly well written first novel, set in the mountains of Kentucky, reconstructs her family life before and mostly after her father's death in a strip-mining accident when Edda was eight years old.

GRAVEN IMAGES: 3 STORIES   [996]

Written by Paul Fleischman
Illustrated by Andrew Glass
Cloth: Harper & Row/HarperCollins
Paper: Harper Trophy
Published: 1982

Here are three haunting stories about graven images—a sailor figure from a death ship, a weather vane figure of St. Crispin, and a statue commissioned by a ghost.

THE HAUNTING   [997]

Written by Margaret Mahy
Cloth: McElderry
Paper: Dell
Published: 1982   Prizes: Carnegie Medal

The New Zealand novelist is such a masterful storyteller that even people who actively dislike ghost stories read her books. Barney, a boy who is afraid to tell about the messages he receives from a dead relative, is the center of this prizewinning tale.

A HERO AIN'T NOTHIN'
BUT A SANDWICH   [998]

Written by Alice Childress
Cloth: Coward McCann
Published: 1973

This harrowing novel about Benjie, a thirteen-year-old black boy who is using heroin, is told from the perspectives of many of the people who know him. The ending is problematic but holds promise. Recognized at once when it was published, it remains one of the best of the socially aware young adult novels of the 1970s.

HOME BEFORE DARK   [999]

Written by Sue Ellen Bridgers
Cloth: Knopf
Paper: Bantam
Published: 1976

In broad outline, this is the story of a migrant-worker family settling down. The central character, Stella Mae Willis, is fourteen years old as the novel begins. Her father brings the family to live and work on the tobacco farm his younger brother has inherited.

I AM THE CHEESE   [1000]

Written by Robert Cormier
Cloth: Knopf
Paper: Dell Yearling
Published: 1977

This is a complex and suspenseful novel of psychological exploration. Adam Farmer describes his bicycle trip to see his father in Vermont, deals with a psychiatric interview, and confronts some memories. Very well written.

I WILL CALL IT GEORGIE'S BLUES   [1001]

Written by Suzanne Newton
Cloth: Viking
Paper: Puffin
Published: 1981

Despite the facade, the relationships inside the preacher's family are strained to the breaking point by the father's demand of perfection. The breaking point is reached.

IN SUMMER LIGHT   [1002]

Written by Zibby Oneal
Cloth: Viking
Paper: Bantam
Published: 1985

Kate Brewer's seventeenth summer is described in this insightful and romantic novel. Her father, a world-famous painter, dominates the family, which lives on a coastal island. Kate's unfinished paper on *The Tempest* helps carry the theme of Prospero through the novel.

JACK [1003]

Written by A. M. Homes
Cloth: Macmillan
Paper: Vintage
Published: 1990

The doggedly funny fifteen-year-old protagonist is a good guy caught in difficult circumstances. Jack is still grieving for the end of his parents' marriage when his father tells him that his roommate, Bob, is actually his lover. His friend Max's parents, whom Jack has perceived as the most stable adults in his world, turn out to be problematic, too.

JACOB HAVE I LOVED [1004]

Written by Katherine Paterson
Cloth: T. Y. Crowell/HarperCollins
Paper: Harper Trophy
Published: 1980   **Prizes: Newbery Medal**

Sara Louise, her relationship with her twin sister, adolescence and, incidentally, the Chesapeake Bay area are the heroine and themes of this well-written and thought-provoking novel.

KILLING MR. GRIFFIN [1005]

Written by Lois Duncan
Cloth: Little, Brown
Paper: Dell
Published: 1982

This gripping story takes a turn on the idea of best-laid plans going awry. The plan is to scare the teacher, but he suddenly dies of a heart attack.

KIM/KIMI [1006]

Written by Hadley Irwin
Cloth: McElderry
Paper: Puffin
Published: 1987

Kim is both Irish-American (mother's side) and Japanese-American (father's side), and to answer some questions about herself, she travels from Iowa, where she has grown up, to the California Japanese-American community her father came from. Absorbing.

THE LORD OF THE RINGS TRILOGY   [1007]

Written by J. R. R. Tolkein
Cloth: Houghton Mifflin
Paper: Houghton Mifflin
Published: 1954

The trilogy—*The Fellowship of the Ring, The Two Towers,* and *The Return of the King*—is a saga of good and evil, cast as the War of the Ring set in a mysterious Middle Earth. The writing is lush and fast-paced. There are many imitations of this formula and style, but none so riveting. It's a leap up in tone and complexity from *The Hobbit.*

THE MAGICAL ADVENTURES OF THE PRETTY PEARL   [1008]

Written by Virginia Hamilton
Cloth: Harper & Row/HarperCollins
Paper: Harper Trophy
Published: 1983

In an allegorical blending of folklore, fantasy, and history, this is the story of a girl, Pretty Pearl, who travels on a slave ship from Africa to the New World with her older brother, John de Conquer. She re-emerges during the Reconstruction, and finally with a group of blacks and Cherokees, who eventually set off for Ohio. There is both magic and history. The language is lush, difficult, exciting. This is rich and provocative fiction.

THE MOONLIGHT MAN   [1009]

Written by Paula Fox
Cloth: Bradbury
Paper: Dell
Published: 1986

Catherine spends part of her summer vacation with her father, the first time she has really been with him since her parents' divorce, when she was very young. Despite his charm and wit, he is, she realizes, an alcoholic. This is a beautifully written and haunting novel of self-discovery and maturation.

MOTOWN AND DIDI:
A LOVE STORY   [1010]

Written by Walter Dean Myers
Cloth: Viking
Paper: Dell
Published: 1984

A convincing novel about two teenagers in Harlem, coping with life and getting on with it. There is a strong, implicit antidrug message.

THE MOVES MAKE THE MAN   [1011]

Written by Bruce Brooks
Cloth: Harper & Row/HarperCollins
Paper: Harper Trophy
Published: 1984   Prizes: Newbery Honor

This fine novel about growing up and friendship is also a very good novel about basketball, as both a game and a metaphor. Jerome Foxworthy is the first black at his high school, and Bix is the best white athlete he's ever seen.

MY BROTHER STEALING SECOND   [1012]

Written by Jim Naughton
Cloth: Harper & Row/HarperCollins
Paper: Harper Trophy
Published: 1989

The title of this affecting novel of emotional recovery refers to Bobby's favorite memory of his older brother, Billy, who died in an accident before the story begins. The author, a sportswriter, uses baseball scenes deftly.

NIGHT KITES   [1013]

Written by M. E. Kerr
Cloth: Harper & Row/HarperCollins
Paper: Harper Trophy
Published: 1986

Erick Rudd has a difficult, provocative girlfriend, a rather pompous father, and a kind older brother, who, it turns out, has AIDS. The

novel deals with the problem of AIDS within a family, and acknowledging the sexual preference of an adult child with skill and tact as the background to Erick's own maturation.

ONE FAT SUMMER   [1014]

Written by Robert Lipsyte
Cloth: Harper & Row/HarperCollins
Paper: Harper Trophy
Published: 1977

The first of three books about Bobby Marks, who starts out, at fourteen, in the 1950s, fat and insecure. This one tells about his first job. He deals with first love in *Summer Rules* and, when he is eighteen, hazardous working conditions in a laundry where he works in *The Summerboy*.

THE OUTSIDERS   [1015]

Written by S. E. Hinton
Cloth: Viking
Paper: Dell
Published: 1967

A classic gang novel, filled with suspense and action. It is writ large and compelling in a story that details both the relationships of the city gang members to each other and their remove from social conventions. Successive generations of high school readers have been discovering it with stunned delight for more than twenty years. The companion tales are *Rumble Fish* and *That Was Then, This Is Now. Tex* has a rural setting.

PAGEANT   [1016]

Written by Kathryn Lasky
Cloth: Four Winds
Paper: Dell
Published: 1986

Attending a mostly Christian private school in Indianapolis, Indiana, a Jewish girl comes of age during the Kennedy years. Funny and touching at the same time. It doesn't feel like historical fiction.

THE RANDOM HOUSE BOOK
OF SPORTS STORIES   [1017]

Written by L. M. Schulman
Cloth: Random House
Published: 1990

Is there a young athlete in your house who complains about nothing to read? A collection of sporting stories that includes the work of Roger Angell, Ring Lardner, Jack London, William Saroyan, and William Faulkner, among others, is a guaranteed winner. It's a wonderful collection for couch potatoes or team captains.

THE RETURN   [1018]

Written by Sonia Levitan
Cloth: Atheneum
Published: 1987

This is a novel about the Falasha, the Ethiopian Jews, and the so-called Operation Moses, which took a small number of them to Israel via the Sudan. The heroine is a brave girl named Desta. Full of fascinating anthropological detail.

THE RUBY IN THE SMOKE   [1019]

Written by Philip Pullman
Cloth: Knopf
Paper: Knopf
Published: 1985

Sally Lockhart's search for clues to solve the puzzle of her father's death and to take revenge for it leads the young woman through the seamy byways of mid-Victorian London. It is 1872 and the fog is thick with menace. The sequel is *Shadow in the North*.

SATURNALIA [1020]

Written by Paul Fleischman
Cloth: Harper & Row/HarperCollins
Published: 1990

December 1681, Boston. Christmas looms—but first, Saturnalia, the Roman "pagan festivity in which masters and servants traded places." This slim, dense novel involves two sets of characters and events, one set in daylight and the other at night. There are masters and servants and one linking character, William, the printer's apprentice, a young Indian who has mastered the Bible better than others his age. Gripping.

SHABANU [1021]

Written by Suzanne Fisher Staples
Cloth: Knopf
Paper: Knopf
Published: 1989   Prizes: Newbery Honor

In a remote part of modern Pakistan, in a corner of the Cholistan desert, the idea of an arranged marriage for Shabanu, the twelve-year-old daughter in the household of a camel driver, is appropriate. But due to convulsive circumstances, her eventual betrothal to the brother of the hateful landowner (who already has three wives) presents a dilemma. Shabanu's bravery is memorable in this skillfully written and affecting first novel.

SODA JERK [1022]

Written by Cynthia Rylant
Illustrated by Peter Catalanotto
Cloth: Orchard Books
Published: 1990

The thoughts and dreams of a soda jerk at the drugstore in a small town somewhere form a poem cycle, punctuated at the middle of the book with a series of episodic illustrations. Inherently interesting but also provocative.

SOMEHOW TENDERNESS SURVIVES: STORIES OF SOUTHERN AFRICA [1023]

Written by Hazel Rochman
Cloth: Harper & Row/HarperCollins
Paper: Harper Trophy
Published: 1988

Here is a thoughtful collection of autobiographical stories and fiction by Southern African writers (who generally address adult audiences). It comes with useful notes on the contributors—among them Doris Lessing, Nadine Gordimer, Gcina Mhlope, and Mark Mathabane.

THE SUMMER OF MY GERMAN SOLDIER [1024]

Written by Bette Greene
Cloth: Dial
Paper: Bantam
Published: 1973

A Jewish storekeeper's young daughter living in Arkansas during World War II befriends an escaped German prisoner-of-war. It is a poignant coming-of-age story in which Patty confronts a number of subtle issues.

SWEET WHISPERS, BROTHER RUSH [1025]

Written by Virginia Hamilton
Cloth: Philomel
Paper: Avon
Published: 1982   Prizes: Newbery Honor

Tree, a fourteen-year-old girl, is alone most of the time and in charge of her older, retarded brother. In this well-written novel, Tree comes to terms with her family's tragic history, and with her memories and fantasies of a dead uncle. For older readers.

TIGER EYES   [1026]

Written by Judy Blume
Cloth: Bradbury
Paper: Laurel Leaf
Published: 1981

One of the most serious of the Blume novels, addressed to older readers, is about a girl called Davey. Her father was killed in a holdup of his store, and she must cope with grief and fear and learn to go on. Davey and her mother head west, to visit relatives in New Mexico, where Davey is befriended by a boy called Wolf.

TOUCH WOOD: A GIRLHOOD IN OCCUPIED FRANCE   [1027]

Written by Renée Roth-Hano
Cloth: Four Winds
Paper: Puffin
Published: 1988

This fictionalized account of growing up in a Jewish family in occupied France begins when Renée is nine years old. The Roths come to Paris from Alsace, but their freedoms are steadily curtailed. Eventually, the daughters are sent to Normandy, to a kind of dormitory run by Roman Catholic nuns. Although Renée is young, the powerful account is for older readers.

THE TRICKSTERS   [1028]

Written by Margaret Mahy
Cloth: McElderry
Paper: Scholastic
Published: 1987

Perhaps the most sophisticated of the imaginative New Zealand novelist's efforts yet, this is the story of a family Christmas holiday at the beach and the arrival of three handsome strangers. Harry, the seventeen-year-old who is secretly writing a novel, has a special sense of who they are and their powers.

THE TRUE CONFESSIONS OF
CHARLOTTE DOYLE   [1029]

Written by Avi
Cloth: Orchard Books
Paper: Avon (1992)
Published: 1990   Prizes: Newbery Honor

In 1832, Charlotte Doyle, then thirteen years old, was sent on a trans-
atlantic voyage by herself. No sooner was she on board than the cook
slipped her a knife. Before the trip was over, she was tried for murder.
A galloping thriller from the first page to the last, with a skillfully
controlled plot.

WEETZIE BAT   [1030]

Written by Francesca Lia Block
Cloth: Harper & Row/HarperCollins
Paper: Harper Trophy
Published: 1989

Postmodern, hip, chic, glittering, glitzy, but still just a kid, Weetzie Bat
is coming of age in eighties L.A. She's best friends with Dirk, finds a
Secret Agent Lover Man, and dreams of a little house and living happily ever after. Very stylish first novel.

THE WITCH OF
BLACKBIRD POND   [1031]

Written by Elizabeth George Speare
Cloth: Houghton Mifflin
Paper: Dell
Published: 1958   Prizes: Newbery Medal

The setting is Puritan New England and the subject is the coming of
age and to trial of an independent-minded young woman.

WOMEN WHO CHANGED THINGS [1032]

Written by Linda Peavy and Ursula Smith
Cloth: Scribner's
Published: 1983

This bouquet of biographical studies of unheralded but splendid women, including a reformer, an astronomer, an educator, and a psychologist, will intrigue readers trying to imagine adult careers.

THE YEAR WITHOUT MICHAEL [1033]

Written by Susan Beth Pfeffer
Cloth: Bantam
Published: 1987

What happens to a family when one child disappears? This novel gives episodic glimpses of the stresses and strains in Jody's family—on herself, her kid sister, and her parents—over the year after her brother, Michael, leaves the house and never gets to softball practice.

INDEXES

All the books listed in this guide are numbered consecutively, and their permanent record numbers remain consistent. Every reference to a title throughout this guide carries that record number, so you can go back to the main entries and check the description.

There is an index to the indexes. A legend in the upper left-hand corner of each double-page spread identifies the index category on those pages. The legend in the lower right-hand corner tells you, at a glance, the reading levels.

THE INDEXES

The indexes are the key to this guide, but you must use them to make it work.

Every title in the guide that has its own entry (there are 1033) has a permanent record number. Every reference to the title carries the record number, so you can go back from the indexes (or an illustration) to the entry and see the description, as well as the bibliographic information you need to borrow or buy the book.

I tried to anticipate dozens of ways you might want to look for a book. So, in addition to the indexes of titles, authors, and illustrators, all but the young-adult books have been regrouped under age-appropriate categories. Many books carry a publisher's age designation—say, for five- to eight-year-olds—yet because children can understand books they cannot read themselves and because children develop so differently, the same book can be enjoyed by lap-listening toddlers and preschoolers and read critically by a ten-year-old. In the age-appropriate categories, I am suggesting broader guidelines than the publisher might, but you know your children, what they have read or heard, and how strong their interests are and can make judgments accordingly.

There is a large, separate index of books that lend themselves to being read aloud—a special pleasure for both adult and child. Some titles are included for the sheer beauty of the language; all are enjoyable.

The fifty-one subject indexes cover a wide range of special interests and categories. But a word of warning. Bibliotherapy—looking to a book to solve a problem—is a little like an over-the-counter cold remedy: It may help, but it isn't likely to solve the problem alone. I have included some fine books about sibling rivalry, death, divorce, and health issues. Loving families working with children to address those problems integrate such stories into their lives. The books just help. It's the family attention that really counts.

There are familiar categories—adventure, fairy tales and folklore, ghosts and monsters, poetry and verse. There are also cats, dogs, boys, girls, holiday, and school stories, and some titles recur in many categories, the better to help you find them. I have sorted out anthologies, series, titles in which other editions are described, Spanish-language editions, and books included on *Reading Rainbow* through the fall of 1991. There are also books about religion, minorities, immigrants, and nature and a category I called information and science, which includes both fiction and nonfiction.

Please take some time to play with both the guide and the indexes. A reference book can be full of serendipitous surprises if you let it fall open to random pages. If you are working your way, book by book, through a special index, flip occasionally to another or scout around for a new book by a writer you admire.

INDEX TO INDEXES

INDEX TO ALL TITLES

WORDLESS BOOKS   [1–19]

PICTURE BOOKS   [20–274]

STORY BOOKS   [275–592]

EARLY READING BOOKS   [593–660]

MIDDLE READING BOOKS   [661–969]

YOUNG ADULT BOOKS   [970–1033]

[66]

WORDLESS BOOKS [1-19]

PICTURE BOOKS [20-274]

STORY BOOKS [275-592]

EARLY READING BOOKS [593-660]

MIDDLE READING BOOKS [661-969]

YOUNG ADULT BOOKS [970-1033]

WORDLESS BOOKS   [1-19]

PICTURE BOOKS   [20-274]

STORY BOOKS   [275-592]

EARLY READING BOOKS   [593-660]

MIDDLE READING BOOKS   [661-969]

YOUNG ADULT BOOKS   [970-1033]

WORDLESS BOOKS   [1-19]

PICTURE BOOKS   [20-274]

STORY BOOKS   [275-592]

EARLY READING BOOKS   [593-660]

MIDDLE READING BOOKS   [661-969]

YOUNG ADULT BOOKS   [970-1033]

[296]

[252]

WORDLESS BOOKS   [1-19]

PICTURE BOOKS   [20-274]

STORY BOOKS   [275-592]

EARLY READING BOOKS   [593-660]

MIDDLE READING BOOKS   [661-969]

YOUNG ADULT BOOKS   [970-1033]

WORDLESS BOOKS   [1-19]

PICTURE BOOKS   [20-274]

STORY BOOKS   [275-592]

EARLY READING BOOKS   [593-660]

MIDDLE READING BOOKS   [661-969]

YOUNG ADULT BOOKS   [970-1033]

[154]

WORDLESS BOOKS   [1-19]

PICTURE BOOKS   [20-274]

STORY BOOKS   [275-592]

EARLY READING BOOKS   [593-660]

MIDDLE READING BOOKS   [661-969]

YOUNG ADULT BOOKS   [970-1033]

INDEX OF AUTHORS

Collier, Christopher [862]
Collier, James Lincoln [862]
Collington, Peter [1, 13]
Collodi, Carlo [664]
Colum, Padraic [717]
Cone, Molly [853]
Conrad, Pam [244]
Cooney, Barbara [381, 408, 450]
Cooper, James Fenimore [835]
Cooper, Susan [514, 736]
Cormier, Robert [982, 1000]
Cowcher, Helen [34]
Craft, Ruth [270]
Craven, Carolyn [953]
Cresswell, Helen [680]
Crews, Donald [88]
d'Aulaire, Ingri and Edgar Parin [336, 337]
Dahl, Roald [348, 690, 713, 735, 813, 851, 976]
Daly, Nicki [177]
Daniel, Mark [323]
Danziger, Paula [978]
Davis, Jenny [995]
De Brunhoff, Jean [532]
de la Mare, Walter [644]
de Regniers, Beatrice Schenk [126, 155, 249, 427, 520]
De Trevino, Elizabeth Borton [803]
DeClements, Barthe [872]
Dee, Ruby [564]
DeJong, Meindert [954]
Delton, Judy [830]
dePaola, Tomie [172, 240, 331, 357, 536, 554]
Devlin, Wende and Harry [56]
Dickens, Charles [722]
Dickinson, Peter [407, 712]
Disch, Thomas M. [703]
Dragonwagon, Crescent [279]
Drescher, Henrik [19]
du Bois, William Pène [562]
Duke, Kate [102]
Duncan, Lois [1005]
Dunn, Judy [137]
Duvoisin, Roger [194]

Eager, Edward [779]
Eastman, P. D. [597]
Edelman, Elaine [119]
Ehlert, Lois [54, 79]
Eichenberg, Fritz [35, 59]
Elledge, Scott [960]
Elliott, Dan [618]
Emberley, Barbara [65]
Engvick, William [433]
Enright, Elizabeth [932]
Estes, Eleanor [802, 855]
Exum, J. Cheryl [857]
Farjeon, Eleanor [422, 816]
Farley, Walter [697, 848]
Feelings, Muriel [128]
Field, Rachel [789]
Fields, Julia [617]
Fisher, Leonard Everett [378]
Fitzgerald, John [776]
Fitzhugh, Louise [781, 869]
Flack, Marjorie [531]
Fleischman, Paul [996, 1020]
Fleischman, Sid [958]
Flournoy, Valerie [483]
Fonteyn, Margot [540]
Forbes, Esther [817]
Foreman, Michael [947]
Forest, Heather [294]
Fosburgh, Lisa [859]

WORDLESS BOOKS [1-19]

PICTURE BOOKS [20-274]

STORY BOOKS [275-592]

EARLY READING BOOKS [593-660]

MIDDLE READING BOOKS [661-969]

YOUNG ADULT BOOKS [970-1033]

[636]

Homes, A. M.   [1003]
Hooks, William H.   [453]
Hopkins, Lee Bennett   [216, 653]
Houston, Gloria   [590]
Houston, James   [654]
Howard, Elizabeth Fitzgerald   [325]
Howard, Katherine   [460]
Howe, Deborah and James   [706]
Howe, James   [793]
Howker, Janni   [679]
Huck, Charlotte   [497]
Hughes, Dean   [876]
Hughes, Shirley   [144, 278]
Hurd, Thacher   [148]
Hutchins, Pat   [8, 187, 208, 264]
Hutton, Warrick   [299, 414, 467]
Hyman, Trina Schart   [522]
Irwin, Hadley   [1006]
Isaacson, Philip M.   [903]
Jakes, John   [539]
Jarrell, Randall   [368, 671, 683]
Jeschke, Susan   [487]
Johnson, Angela   [231]
Johnson, Crockett   [104]
Johnston, Tony   [80, 273]
Jonas, Ann   [21, 110, 259, 558]
Jones, Malcolm   [821]
Joslin, Sesyle   [255]
Joyce, William   [91, 340]
Jukes, Mavis   [421, 639]
Juster, Norton   [885]
Kalman, Maira   [511]
Kassirer, Norma   [846]
Keats, Ezra Jack   [217]
Keller, Holly   [92]
Kellogg, Steven   [47, 302, 485, 493]
Kelly, Eric P.   [940]

Kennedy, Richard   [645, 668]
Kennedy, X. J.   [309]
Kerr, M. E.   [986, 1013]
Khalsa, Dayal Kaur   [394, 542]
Kimmel, Eric   [385]
Kimmelman, Leslie   [358]
King-Smith, Dick   [782]
Kipling, Rudyard   [822, 824]
Kisam, Ole   [116]
Kismaric, Carole   [507]
Kitamura, Satoshi   [256]
Kitchen, Bert   [2]
Kjelgaard, Jim   [691]
Klein, Norma   [856, 994]
Knight, Eric   [834]
Kohn, Bernice   [297]
Komaiko, Leah   [399]
Konigsburg, E. L.   [764, 891, 908, 943]
Korczak, Janusz   [828]
Kraus, Robert   [260]
Krauss, Ruth   [109]
Krementz, Jill   [657, 796, 797, 798, 799]
Krensky, Stephen   [344]
Krumgold, Joseph   [670, 879]
Kunhardt, Dorothy   [191]
Kurelek, William   [496]
Kuskin, Karla   [207, 413, 490, 649]
L'Engle, Madeleine   [966]
Lamorisse, Albert   [503]

[504]

400

Maris, Ron [167]
Mark, Jan [780]
Marshall, Edward [527, 613]
Marshall, James [129, 364]
Martin, Bill, Jr. [584]
Martin, Charles [409]
Martin, Rafe [18, 83]
Maruki, Toshi [788]
Matthews, Louise [46]
Mayer, Mercer [7]
Mayne, William [771]
McCleery, William [964]
McCloskey, Robert [43, 147]
McCord, David [25]
McCully, Emily Arnold [16]
McDermott, Gerald [60, 222, 275]
McDonald, Amy [201]
McDonald, Megan [125]
McKinley, Robin [686, 787, 880]
McKissack, Patricia C. [355, 448]
McLeod, Emile Warren [40]
McNulty, Faith [133, 882]
McPhail, David [77, 82]
Meltzer, Milton [970]
Menotti, Gian Carlo [281]
Merriam, Eve [274]
Merrill, Jean [892]
Mikolaycak, Charles [293]
Miles, Miska [286]
Miller, Mary Beth [379]
Milne, A. A. [581, 963]
Minarik, Else Holmelund [627]
Montaufier, Poupa [474]
Montgomery, L. M. [673]
Moore, Clement C. [175]
Mordvinoff, Will and Nicholas [75]
Morey, Walt [709, 769]
Morozumi, Atsuko [185]
Mosel, Arlene [239]
Most, Bernard [579]
Mowat, Farley [744]
Muller, Jorg [320]
Munro, Roxie [124]

Murphy, Jill [81]
Musgrove, Margaret [290]
Myers, Walter Dean [907, 1010]
Nash, Ogden [733]
Naughton, Jim [1012]
Nesbitt, E. [756]
Neville, Emily Cheney [811]
Newton, Laura P. [269]
Newton, Suzanne [1001]
Nhuong, Quang Nhuong [832]
Nic Leodhas, Sorche [280]
Nilsson, Lennart [801]
Noble, Trinka Hakes [63]
Nones, Eric Jon [578]
Norton, Mary [702]
Numeroff, Laura Joffe [122]
O'Brien, Robert C. [860]
O'Connor, Jane [632]
O'Dell, Scott [696, 810, 829, 914]
O'Donnell, Elizabeth Lee [436]
O'Kelley, Mattie Lou [361]
Oakley, Graham [329]
Olson, Arielle North [115]
Oneal, Zibby [1002]
Oram, Hiawyn [31, 463]
Orgel, Doris [738]
Ormerod, Jan [12, 186]
Owens, Mary Beth [49]
Parker, Nancy Winslow [313]

[253]

WORDLESS BOOKS   [1-19]

PICTURE BOOKS   [20-274]

STORY BOOKS   [275-592]

EARLY READING BOOKS   [593-660]

MIDDLE READING BOOKS   [661-969]

YOUNG ADULT BOOKS   [970-1033]

[637]

INDEX OF ILLUSTRATORS

[805]

408

Lofting, Hugh [663]
Lorenz, Lee [577]
Low, Joseph [156]
Macaulay, David [711, 724, 942, 949]
MacDonald, Suse [26]
Madden, Don [806]
Mai, Vo-Dinh [832]
Marcellino, Fred [499]
Maris, Ron [167]
Marrella, Maria Pia [912]
Marshall, James [129, 364, 449, 527, 613]
Marstall, Bob [133]
Martin, Charles [409]
Maruki, Toshi [788] .
Mathers, Petra [358]
Mathieu, Joe [572, 573]
Mayer, Mercer [7, 351, 776]
McCarthy, Patricia [212]
McCloskey, Robert [43, 147]
McCully, Emily [800]
McCully, Emily Arnold [16, 632]
McDermott, Gerald [60, 222, 275]
McElderry, N. M. [127]
McPhail, David [40, 77, 82, 904]
Meddaugh, Susan [176, 564]
Mikolaycak, Charles [293, 321, 434, 438, 507]
Montaufier, Poupa [474]
Montresor, Beni [155]
Mordvinoff, Will and Nicholas [75]
Morozumi, Atsuko [185]
Moser, Barry [676, 804, 821]
Most, Bernard [579]
Muller, Jorg [488]
Munoz, Rie [419]
Munro, Roxie [124]
Munsinger, Lynn [197, 620]
Murphy, Jill [81]
Mussino, Attilo [664]
Narahashi, Keiko [266]
Natti, Susanna [553]
Nicholson, William [569]
Nones, Eric Jon [578]
O'Kelley, Mattie Lou [361]

Oakley, Graham [329]
Ohtomo, Yasuo [113]
Ormerod, Jan [12, 186, 884]
Owens, Gail [397, 819]
Owens, Mary Beth [49]
Oxenbury, Helen [252]
Palladini, David [773]
Parker, Nancy Winslow [170, 180, 313]
Parnall, Peter [286, 341, 350, 383, 402, 576]
Pearson, Tracey Campbell [20]
Peck, Beth [391]
Peek, Merle [153]
Peet, Bill [479, 692]
Peters, David [366]
Pincus, Harriet [253, 546]
Pinkney, Jerry [448, 483, 500, 544, 617, 655, 929]
Pinkwater, Daniel [619]
Pinto, Ralph [420]
Pogany, Willy [717]
Polacco, Patricia [132, 552]
Politi, Leo [219]
Potter, Beatrix [228]
Priceman, Marjorie [201]
Primavera, Elsie [327]
Provensen, Alice [311]
Provensen, Alice and Martin [271, 372, 486, 518, 574]
Pyle, Howard [923]
Raible, Alton [748, 784]

WORDLESS BOOKS [1-19]

PICTURE BOOKS [20-274]

STORY BOOKS [275-592]

EARLY READING BOOKS [593-660]

MIDDLE READING BOOKS [661-969]

YOUNG ADULT BOOKS [970-1033]

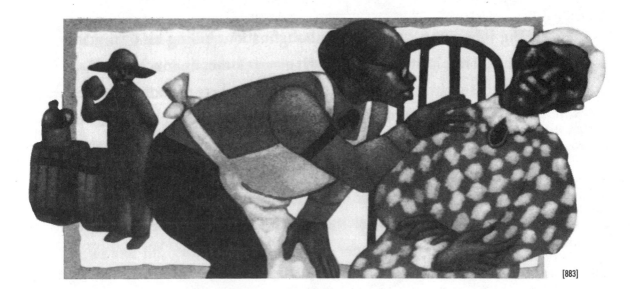

[883]

[547]

WORDLESS BOOKS [1-19]

PICTURE BOOKS [20-274]

STORY BOOKS [275-592]

EARLY READING BOOKS [593-660]

MIDDLE READING BOOKS [661-969]

YOUNG ADULT BOOKS [970-1033]

411

[223]

AGE-APPROPRIATE INDEXES

INFANTS

American Folk Songs for Children   [283]
The Baby's Bedtime Book   [39]
Finger Rhymes   [76]
Goodnight Moon   [98]
Green Eggs and Ham   [616]
Have You Seen My Duckling?   [107]
How Do I Put It On?   [113]
I Am a Bunny   [116]
The Little Duck   [137]
The Little Fur Family   [140]
Lullabies and Night Songs   [433]
The Lullaby Songbook   [434]
The Maggie B   [146]
Mary Had a Little Lamb   [152]
Mother Goose: A Collection of Classic
   Nursery Rhymes   [454]
My Red Umbrella   [171]
The Nativity   [174]
One Fish Two Fish Red Fish Blue Fish   [184]
The Orchard Book of Nursery Rhymes   [189]
Pat the Bunny   [191]
The Raffi Singable Songbook   [202]
The Random House Book of
   Mother Goose   [501]
Read-Aloud Rhymes for the
   Very Young   [203]

The Real Mother Goose   [204]
Richard Scarry's Best Word Book
   Ever   [206]
Roar and More   [207]
The Runaway Bunny   [210]
17 Kings and 42 Elephants   [212]
The Tale of Peter Rabbit   [228]
Ten, Nine, Eight   [232]
The Three Billy Goats Gruff   [234]
The Very Hungry Caterpillar   [248]
Where's Spot?   [262]
Where's the Bear?   [263]
Who Said Red?   [266]

WORDLESS BOOKS   [1-19]

PICTURE BOOKS   [20-274]

STORY BOOKS   [275-592]

EARLY READING BOOKS   [593-660]

MIDDLE READING BOOKS   [661-969]

YOUNG ADULT BOOKS   [970-1033]

[16]

[692]

[603]

WORDLESS BOOKS   [1-19]

PICTURE BOOKS   [20-274]

STORY BOOKS   [275-592]

EARLY READING BOOKS   [593-660]

MIDDLE READING BOOKS   [661-969]

YOUNG ADULT BOOKS   [970-1033]

423

[664]

WORDLESS BOOKS [1–19]

PICTURE BOOKS [20–274]

STORY BOOKS [275–592]

EARLY READING BOOKS [593–660]

MIDDLE READING BOOKS [661–969]

YOUNG ADULT BOOKS [970–1033]

[7]

WORDLESS BOOKS   [1–19]

PICTURE BOOKS   [20–274]

STORY BOOKS   [275–592]

EARLY READING BOOKS   [593–660]

MIDDLE READING BOOKS   [661–969]

YOUNG ADULT BOOKS   [970–1033]

[24]

[188]

WORDLESS BOOKS   [1–19]

PICTURE BOOKS   [20–274]

STORY BOOKS   [275–592]

EARLY READING BOOKS   [593–660]

MIDDLE READING BOOKS   [661–969]

YOUNG ADULT BOOKS   [970–1033]

MIDDLE GRADE READERS

[636]

READ-ALOUD BOOKS

A, My Name Is Alice   [593]
Aardvarks, Disembark!   [21]
Abel's Island   [661]
Abiyoyo   [22]
The Accident   [276]
The Adventures of Doctor
  Dolittle   [663]
The Adventures of Pinocchio   [664]
Alexander and the Terrible, Horrible, No
  Good, Very Bad Day   [277]
Alfie Gives a Hand   [278]
All God's Critters Got a Place in
  the Choir   [24]
All Small   [25]
All-Of-A-Kind Family   [667]
Alphabatics   [26]
Always Room for One More   [280]
Amahl and the Night Visitors   [281]
Amanda Pig and Her Big Brother
  Oliver   [594]
The Amazing Bone   [282]
Amelia Bedelia   [595]
Amos & Boris   [28]
Amy's Eyes   [668]
Angry Arthur   [31]
The Animal Family   [671]

Animals Should Definitely NOT
  Wear Clothing   [32]
Annie and the Old One   [286]
Annie and the Wild Animals   [287]
Anno's Counting Book   [3]
Ape in a Cape: An Alphabet of Odd
  Animals   [35]
Applebet   [36]
Are You My Mother?   [597]
Arnold of the Ducks   [288]
Around the World in Eighty Days   [676]
An Artist   [37]

> WORDLESS BOOKS   [1–19]
>
> PICTURE BOOKS   [20–274]
>
> STORY BOOKS   [275–592]
>
> EARLY READING BOOKS   [593–660]
>
> MIDDLE READING BOOKS   [661–969]
>
> YOUNG ADULT BOOKS   [970–1033]

[295]

WORDLESS BOOKS   [1–19]

PICTURE BOOKS   [20–274]

STORY BOOKS   [275–592]

EARLY READING BOOKS   [593–660]

MIDDLE READING BOOKS   [661–969]

YOUNG ADULT BOOKS   [970–1033]

[104]

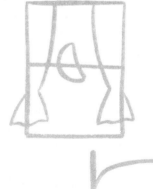

[351]

[165]

[861]

SPECIAL SUBJECT INDEXES

WORDLESS BOOKS   [1-19]

PICTURE BOOKS   [20-274]

STORY BOOKS   [275-592]

EARLY READING BOOKS   [593-660]

MIDDLE READING BOOKS   [661-969]

YOUNG ADULT BOOKS   [970-1033]

The Twenty-one Balloons   [562]
Up from Jericho Tel   [943]
Up North in Winter   [568]
Very Last First Time   [570]
Westmark   [951]
The Wheel on the School   [954]
Where the River Begins   [583]
Where the Wild Things Are   [261]
Where's the Bear?   [263]
The Whipping Boy   [958]
The Wild Swans   [586]
Will's Mammoth   [18]
The Witch of Blackbird Pond   [1031]

ALPHABET

A Apple Pie   [20]
Alphabatics   [26]
Alphabears: An ABC Book   [27]
Animal Alphabet   [2]
Anno's Alphabet: An Adventure in
   Imagination   [33]
Ape in a Cape: An Alphabet of Odd Animals
   [35]
Applebet   [36]
Ashanti to Zulu: African Traditions   [290]
A Caribou Alphabet   [49]
A Farmer's Alphabet   [72]
The Guinea Pig ABC   [102]
Handtalk: An ABC of Finger Spelling and
   Sign Language   [379]
Have You Ever Seen . . . ? An ABC
   Book.   [382]
Jambo Means Hello: Swahili
   Alphabet Book   [128]
On Market Street   [181]
A Peaceable Kingdom: The Shaker
   Abecedarius   [486]
Pigs from A to Z   [491]
What's Inside?   [256]

ANIMALS

A, My Name Is Alice   [593]
Aardvarks, Disembark!   [21]

Abel's Island   [661]
The Adventures of Doctor Dolittle   [663]
All God's Critters Got a Place in
   the Choir   [24]
Alphabatics   [26]
Alphabears: An ABC Book   [27]
The Amazing Bone   [282]
Amos & Boris   [28]
And My Mean Old Mother Will Be Sorry,
   Blackboard Bear   [29]
Angelina Ballerina   [30]
Animal Alphabet   [2]
Animals Should Definitely NOT
   Wear Clothing   [32]
Annie and the Wild Animals   [287]
Antarctica   [34]
Ape in a Cape: An Alphabet of
   Odd Animals   [35]
Are You My Mother?   [597]
Arthur's Honey Bear   [598]
Arthur's Nose   [289]
Aunt Nina and Her Nephews and
   Nieces   [291]
The Bat-Poet   [683]
A Bear Called Paddington   [600]
A Bear's Bicycle   [40]
The Big Green Book   [304]
Big Red   [691]
The Bionic Bunny Show   [305]

WORDLESS BOOKS	[1–19]
PICTURE BOOKS	[20–274]
STORY BOOKS	[275–592]
EARLY READING BOOKS	[593–660]
MIDDLE READING BOOKS	[661–969]
YOUNG ADULT BOOKS	[970–1033]

[130]

WORDLESS BOOKS   [1–19]

PICTURE BOOKS   [20–274]

STORY BOOKS   [275–592]

EARLY READING BOOKS   [593–660]

MIDDLE READING BOOKS   [661–969]

YOUNG ADULT BOOKS   [970–1033]

ANTHOLOGIES

[146]

WORDLESS BOOKS   [1-19]

PICTURE BOOKS   [20-274]

STORY BOOKS   [275-592]

EARLY READING BOOKS   [593-660]

MIDDLE READING BOOKS   [661-969]

YOUNG ADULT BOOKS   [970-1033]

[24]

[413]

DINOSAURS

DIVORCE

DOGS

FAMILY LIFE AND PROBLEMS

WORDLESS BOOKS   [1–19]

PICTURE BOOKS   [20–274]

STORY BOOKS   [275–592]

EARLY READING BOOKS   [593–660]

MIDDLE READING BOOKS   [661–969]

YOUNG ADULT BOOKS   [970–1033]

FANTASY

[154]

WORDLESS BOOKS   [1–19]

PICTURE BOOKS   [20–274]

STORY BOOKS   [275–592]

EARLY READING BOOKS   [593–660]

MIDDLE READING BOOKS   [661–969]

YOUNG ADULT BOOKS   [970–1033]

GRANDPARENTS

Come a Tide   [332]
The Crack-of-Dawn Walkers   [334]
Dawn   [62]
The Eyes of the Amaryllis   [754]
Five Little Foxes and the Snow   [80]
Georgia Music   [365]
Going Backwards   [994]
Higher on the Door   [387]
Hurry Home, Grandma!   [115]
I Know a Lady   [398]
I Like the Music   [399]
My Grandmother's Stories: A Collection of
    Jewish Folktales   [864]
My Grandson Lew   [168]
Nana Upstairs & Nana Downstairs   [172]
The Night Journey   [868]
One Summer at Grandmother's House   [474]
The Patchwork Quilt   [483]
The Purple Coat   [498]
Saying Goodbye to Grandma   [510]
Spinky Sulks   [528]
Tales of a Gambling Grandma   [542]
Through Grandpa's Eyes   [551]
Thunder Cake   [552]
The Two of Them   [563]
Up North in Winter   [568]

GROWING UP

Afternoon of the Elves   [665]
Anastasia Krupnik   [669]
. . . And Now Miguel   [670]
The Animal Family   [671]
Anna Banana and Me   [285]
Anne of Green Gables   [673]
Annie and the Old One   [286]
Are You My Mother?   [597]
Are You There, God? It's Me,
    Margaret.   [675]
Arnold of the Ducks   [288]
Arthur, for the Very First Time   [677]
Arthur's Nose   [289]
An Artist   [37]

"B" Is for Betsy   [599]
Badger on the Barge: And Other
    Stories   [679]
Ballet Shoes   [681]
Baseball in April   [682]
Bea and Mr. Jones   [296]
The Bears' House   [685]
Bedtime for Frances   [300]
Behind the Attic Wall   [687]
The Berenstain Bears' Trouble with
    Money   [301]
Betsy-Tacy   [602]
Bill Peet: An Autobiography   [692]
Blowfish Live in the Sea   [698]
Caddie Woodlawn   [707]
The Cat Ate My Gymsuit   [978]
The Chalk Box Kid   [605]
The Chocolate War   [982]
Come Sing, Jimmy Jo   [727]
Cousins   [729]
Daddy's Girl   [984]
A Day No Pigs Would Die   [985]
Did You Carry the Flag Today,
    Charley?   [608]
Dinky Hocker Shoots Smack!   [986]
Dinosaurs Divorce: A Guide for Changing
    Families   [343]
The Doll's House   [745]
Feelings   [74]

WORDLESS BOOKS   [1-19]

PICTURE BOOKS   [20-274]

STORY BOOKS   [275-592]

EARLY READING BOOKS   [593-660]

MIDDLE READING BOOKS   [661-969]

YOUNG ADULT BOOKS   [970-1033]

[506]

WORDLESS BOOKS   [1-19]

PICTURE BOOKS   [20-274]

STORY BOOKS   [275-592]

EARLY READING BOOKS   [593-660]

MIDDLE READING BOOKS   [661-969]

YOUNG ADULT BOOKS   [970-1033]

[332]

WORDLESS BOOKS [1–19]

PICTURE BOOKS [20–274]

STORY BOOKS [275–592]

EARLY READING BOOKS [593–660]

MIDDLE READING BOOKS [661–969]

YOUNG ADULT BOOKS [970–1033]

WORDLESS BOOKS   [1-19]

PICTURE BOOKS   [20-274]

STORY BOOKS   [275-592]

EARLY READING BOOKS   [593-660]

MIDDLE READING BOOKS   [661-969]

YOUNG ADULT BOOKS   [970-1033]

WORDLESS BOOKS   [1-19]

PICTURE BOOKS   [20-274]

STORY BOOKS   [275-592]

EARLY READING BOOKS   [593-660]

MIDDLE READING BOOKS   [661-969]

YOUNG ADULT BOOKS   [970-1033]

IMMIGRANTS

SWORDFISH [366]

The Old Synagogue [472]
Onion John [879]
The Pilgrims of Plimoth [492]
The Rainbow People [896]
Tales of a Gambling Grandma [542]
Through Moon and Stars and
Night Sky [237]
Tortillitas Para Mamma: And Other Spanish
Nursery Rhymes [241]
Turkeys, Pilgrims and Indian Corn: The
Story of the Thanksgiving Symbols [560]
Upon the Head of a Goat: A Childhood in
Hungary, 1939–1944 [944]

INFORMATION AND SCIENCE

Aardvarks, Disembark! [21]
Animal Fact, Animal Fable [284]
Anno's Counting House [674]
Antarctica [34]
The Beachcomber's Book [297]
The Bionic Bunny Show [305]
Bones, Bones, Dinosaur Bones [44]
The Buck Stops Here: The Presidents of the
United States [311]
Bugs [313]
Cat's Cradle, Owl's Eyes: A Book of String
Games [604]
Cathedral: The Story of Its
Construction [711]
The Changing City [320]
Chimney Sweeps: Yesterday and Today [719]
City: A Story of Roman Planning and
Construction [724]
Commodore Perry in the Land of the
Shogun [728]

The Desert Is Theirs [341]
Digging up Dinosaurs [609]
Dinosaurs Are Different [611]
Dinosaurs, Beware! [344]
Dinosaurs Walked Here: And Other Stories
Fossils Tell [740]
Einstein Anderson, Science Sleuth [750]
The Emergency Room [68]
Everybody Needs a Rock [350]
Evolution [352]
Fireflies [354]
From Path to Highway: The Story of the
Boston Post Road [360]
Giants of Land, Sea & Air: Past and
Present [366]
The Glorious Flight: Across the Channel with
Louis Blériot [372]
The Great Wall of China [378]
Handtalk: An ABC of Finger Spelling and
Sign Language [379]
How Much Is a Million? [392]

WORDLESS BOOKS [1–19]

PICTURE BOOKS [20–274]

STORY BOOKS [275–592]

EARLY READING BOOKS [593–660]

MIDDLE READING BOOKS [661–969]

YOUNG ADULT BOOKS [970–1033]

485

MANNERS

[4]

MICE

MINORITIES

WORDLESS BOOKS   [1–19]

PICTURE BOOKS   [20–274]

STORY BOOKS   [275–592]

EARLY READING BOOKS   [593–660]

MIDDLE READING BOOKS   [661–969]

YOUNG ADULT BOOKS   [970–1033]

WORDLESS BOOKS   [1-19]

PICTURE BOOKS   [20-274]

STORY BOOKS   [275-592]

EARLY READING BOOKS   [593-660]

MIDDLE READING BOOKS   [661-969]

YOUNG ADULT BOOKS   [970-1033]

It's Raining Said John Twaining: Danish
  Nursery Rhymes [127]
James Marshall's Mother Goose [129]
Jelly Belly [412]
A Light in the Attic [838]
Madeline [145]
The Man Whose Mother Was a Pirate [439]
Marguerite, Go Wash Your Feet! [441]
Mother Goose: A Collection of Classic
  Nursery Rhymes [454]
The Night Before Christmas [175]
One Fish Two Fish Red Fish Blue Fish [184]
The Orchard Book of Nursery Rhymes [189]
The Oxford Book of Poetry for
  Children [881]
Piping down the Valleys Wild [888]
The Random House Book of
  Mother Goose [501]
The Random House Book of Poetry for
  Children [502]
Read-Aloud Rhymes for the
  Very Young [203]
The Real Mother Goose [204]
Rhymes and Verses: Collected Poems for
  Young People [644]
Secrets of a Small Brother [512]
17 Kings and 42 Elephants [212]
Sing a Song of People [215]
Sing a Song of Popcorn: Every Child's Book
  of Poems [520]
The Sky Is Full of Song [216]
Small Poems [917]
Soda Jerk [1022]
Something on My Mind [525]
Something Sleeping in the Hall [649]
Surprises [653]
Tomie dePaola's Mother Goose [240]
Tortillitas Para Mamma: And Other Spanish
  Nursery Rhymes [241]
Turtle in July [655]
Under the Sunday Tree [567]
A Visit to William Blake's Inn: Poems for
  Innocent and Experienced Travelers [574]

Wendy Watson's Mother Goose [254]
When the Dark Comes Dancing: A Bedtime
  Poetry Book [580]
When We Were Very Young [581]
Where the Sidewalk Ends: Poems and
  Drawings [957]
Whiskers & Rhymes [265]
Wider Than the Sky: Poems to Grow up
  With [960]
Yertle the Turtle and Other Stories [591]
You Be Good and I'll Be Night [274]
You Read to Me, I'll Read to You [592]

PROBLEMS
Always, Always [279]
Are You There, God? It's Me,
  Margaret. [675]
The Balancing Girl [295]
The Berenstain Bears' Trouble with
  Money [301]
Brats [309]
The Chocolate War [982]
Cracker Jackson [731]
Dear Mr. Henshaw [737]
Dinosaurs, Beware! [344]
Dinosaurs Divorce: A Guide for Changing
  Families [343]
First Flight [77]
Fix-It [82]

WORDLESS BOOKS [1-19]

PICTURE BOOKS [20-274]

STORY BOOKS [275-592]

EARLY READING BOOKS [593-660]

MIDDLE READING BOOKS [661-969]

YOUNG ADULT BOOKS [970-1033]

RABBITS

READING RAINBOW TITLES

[468]

RELIGION

WORDLESS BOOKS [1-19]

PICTURE BOOKS [20-274]

STORY BOOKS [275-592]

EARLY READING BOOKS [593-660]

MIDDLE READING BOOKS [661-969]

YOUNG ADULT BOOKS [970-1033]

SCHOOL

SERIES TITLES

WORDLESS BOOKS   [1-19]

PICTURE BOOKS   [20-274]

STORY BOOKS   [275-592]

EARLY READING BOOKS   [593-660]

MIDDLE READING BOOKS   [661-969]

YOUNG ADULT BOOKS   [970-1033]

[588]

BIBLIOGRAPHY

There are a great many books about children's books and reading as they relate to child development. This core list will lead you to other titles.

Choosing Books for Children: A Commonsense Guide. Revised, Expanded and Updated. By Betsy Hearne. New York: Delacorte Press/Delta, 1990.

Choosing Books for Kids: Choosing the Right Book for the Right Child at the Right Time. By Joanne F. Oppenheim, Barbara Brenner, Betty D. Boegehold. New York: Ballantine Books, 1986.

For Reading Out Loud!: A Guide to Sharing Books with Children. Revised and Expanded Edition. By Margaret Mary Kimmel and Elizabeth Segel. New York: Dell Trade Paperback, 1991.

Mother Goose Comes First: An Annotated Guide to the Best Books and Recordings for Your Preschool Child. By Lois Winkel and Sue Kimmel. New York: Holt, 1990.

The New Read Aloud Handbook, revised edition. By Jim Trelease. New York: Penguin 1989.

Reading for the Love of It: Best Books for Young Readers. By Michele Landsberg. New York: Prentice-Hall, 1987.

The RIF Guide to Encouraging Young Readers. Edited by Ruth Graves. New York: Doubleday, 1987.

The Uses of Enchantment. By Bruno Bettelheim. New York: Alfred A. Knopf, 1976.

PERMISSIONS ACKNOWLEDGMENTS

IN THE TEXT: